www.routledgesw.com

Alice A. Lieberman, The University of Kansas, Series Editor

An authentic breakthrough in social work education . . .

New Directions in Social Work is an innovative, integrated series of texts, website, and interactive case studies for generalist courses in the Social Work curriculum at both undergraduate and graduate levels. Instructors will find everything they need to build a comprehensive course that allows students to meet course outcomes, with these unique features:

- All texts, interactive cases, and test materials are **linked to the 2015 CSWE Policy and Accreditation Standards (EPAS).**
- **One web portal with easy access** for instructors and students from any computer—no codes, no CDs, no restrictions. Go to www.routledgesw.com and discover.
- **The series is flexible and can be easily adapted for use in online distance-learning courses as well as hybrid and bricks-and-mortar courses.**
- Each text and the website can be used **individually** or as an **entire series** to meet the needs of any social work program.

TITLES IN THE SERIES

Social Work and Social Welfare: An Invitation, Third Edition by Marla Berg-Weger

Human Behavior in the Social Environment: Perspectives on Development, the Life Course, and Macro Contexts, Fourth Edition by Anissa Taun Rogers

Research for Effective Social Work Practice, Third Edition by Judy L. Krysik and Jerry Finn

Social Policy for Effective Practice: A Strengths Approach, Third Edition by Rosemary K. Chapin

The Practice of Generalist Social Work, Third Edition by Julie Birkenmaier, Marla Berg-Weger, and Martha P. Dewees

Human Behavior in the Social Environment

by Anissa Taun Rogers, University of Portland

In these supplemental chapters and companion custom website you will find:

- Four new chapters that cover theoretical foundations and issues surrounding spirituality, families and groups, organizations, and communities. These chapters offer in-depth information and discussions on mezzo and macro content that supplement information provided in the core HBSE text.

- A focus, similar to that of the core HBSE text, that encourages students to use conceptual lenses to inform their mezzo and macro practice.

- Particular emphasis on the ways in which poverty, diversity, and strengths affect human development and behavior.

- The opportunity to see how the concepts fit into social work practice using case examples that open each chapter and are referred to throughout the chapter.

- Interactive case studies at www.routledgesw.com/cases: six easy-to-access fictional cases with dynamic characters and situations that students can easily reach from any computer and that provide a "learning by doing" format unavailable with any other text. Your students will have an advantage unlike any other they will experience in their social work training.

- A wealth of instructor-only resources at www.routledgesw.com/hbse that provide full-text readings that link to the concepts presented in each of the chapters; a complete bank of objective and essay-type test items, all linked to current CSWE EPAS (Council on Social Work Education Educational Policy and Accreditation Standards) PowerPoint presentations to help students master key concepts; annotated links to a treasure trove of social work assets on the Internet; and a forum inviting all instructors using books in the series to communicate with each other and share ideas to improve teaching and learning.

- Ideal for use in *online* as well as *hybrid* course instruction—in addition to traditional bricks-and-mortar classes.

Human Behavior in the Social Environment

These new supplemental chapters provide instructors with an opportunity to choose the chapters that best fit the layout of the course: Instructors can use all four new chapters with the core HBSE text; or they may choose one or several to augment the core HBSE text, allowing the text to be customized to the way in which the course is taught. Along with the bestselling core HBSE text, these supplemental chapters are ideal for use in either one-semester or year-long generalist human behavior courses. Why? Because the combined texts are concise and easily used in a one-semester course. But the combined texts also come with a companion set of readings and six unique cases that encourage your students to "learn by doing" and to apply their knowledge of human behavior to best practices. Go to www.routledgesw.com/ hbse to learn more. These additional resources easily allow you to use the text (and its related resources) in a two-semester sequence.

Anissa Taun Rogers, PhD, MSW, MA, LCSW, is Professor of Social Work at the University of Portland in Portland, Oregon, where she serves as the Director of the Social Work Program and Co-Director of the Gender and Women's Studies Minor. She teaches courses across the social work curriculum as well as courses on the body, gender, human sexuality, international social work, and suffering and death. She is also registered, with her dog, Sookie, as a pet therapy team, working primarily with older adults and hospice patients.

Human Behavior in the Social Environment

Mezzo and Macro Contexts

Anissa Taun Rogers

Routledge
Taylor & Francis Group

NEW YORK AND LONDON

First published 2016
by Routledge
711 Third Avenue, New York, NY 10017

and by Routledge
2 Park Square, Milton Park, Abingdon, Oxon OX14 4RN

Routledge is an imprint of the Taylor & Francis Group, an informa business

©2016 Taylor & Francis

British Library Cataloguing in Publication Data
A catalogue record for this book is available from the British Library

Library of Congress Cataloging-in-Publication Data
A catalog record for this book has been requested

ISBN: 978-1-138-63850-1 (hbk)
ISBN: 978-1-138-63851-8 (pbk)
ISBN: 978-1-315-62927-8 (ebk)

Typeset in StoneSerif
by Servis Filmsetting Ltd, Stockport, Cheshire

Printed and bound in the United States of America
By Edwards Brothers Malloy on sustainably sourced paper.

To all social workers, both students and those in the field, who helped to shape my ideas and inspired me personally and professionally.

BRIEF CONTENTS

DETAILED CONTENTS

PREFACE

The supplemental chapters that make up *Human Behavior in the Social Environment: Mezzo and Macro Contexts* provide students with an overview of the issues related to mezzo and macro social work. This information offers students an in-depth look at the theoretical underpinnings of work with spirituality, families and groups, organizations, and communities as well as the various and complex issues that often are involved in mezzo and macro social work.

For the new editions of all five books in the New Directions in Social Work series, each addressing a foundational course in the social work curriculum, the publisher offers a uniquely distinctive teaching strategy that revolves around the print book but offers much more than the traditional text experience. The series website www.routledgesw.com leads to custom websites coordinated with each text and offering a variety of features to support instructors as you integrate the many facets of an education in social work.

At www.routledgesw.com/hbse, you will find a wealth of resources to help you create a dynamic, experiential introduction to social work for your students. The website houses companion readings linked to key concepts in each chapter, along with questions to encourage further thought and discussion; six interactive fictional cases with accompanying exercises that bring to life the concepts covered in the book, readings, and classroom discussions; a bank of exam questions (both objective and open-ended) and PowerPoint presentations; annotated links to a treasure trove of articles, videos, and Internet sites; and an online forum inviting all instructors using texts in the series to share ideas to improve teaching and learning.

You may find most useful a set of sample syllabi showing how *Human Behavior in the Social Environment,* fourth edition, along with these supplemental chapters, can be used in a variety of course structures. A master syllabus demonstrates how the text and website used together through the course satisfy the 2015 CSWE EPAS.

The interactive cases offer students rich and detailed examples of complex situations they will face in their work as well as additional opportunities to apply theory and concepts to real-world situations. Other cases provide students opportunities to apply concepts to mezzo- and macro-level situations and to better understand how individual issues are interconnected to and impacted by larger, more macro issues.

The organization and content of this book and companion website are such that students at the bachelor's and master's levels of their social work education can utilize the knowledge gained from studying the material; specifically, this knowledge can be applied to both generalist and specialized practice. The fourth edition, along with the new supplemental chapters, can be used throughout a two-semester sequence as well as a one-semester course, and the integrated supplements and resources on the Web make the text especially amenable for online distance-learning and hybrid courses.

ORGANIZATION OF THE BOOK

Each supplemental chapter in *Human Behavior in the Social Environment: Mezzo and Macro Contexts* can be used separately or combined with other chapters and the core HBSE text to customize material in ways that best fit the way the course is taught.

The following paragraphs briefly introduce each of the chapters included in this book, with emphasis on the updated content.

Chapter 14

Spirituality and Human Behavior offers an in-depth discussion about the definitions of spirituality, religion, and faith as well as ways in which these constructs are conceptualized in social work. Information on how spirituality can intersect with individuals, families, the workplace, and the larger social environment is presented along with information on how social workers might interact with aspects of spirituality through politics and ecological and spiritual movements. The next few chapters give students an overview of the theoretical concepts often used by social workers to help them make sense of the interactions between human behavior and the social environment.

Chapter 15

Families and Groups presents definitions and conceptualizations of families along with contemporary issues facing families. This chapter offers a discussion on the diversity of families and their functioning as well as ethical issues in family work. Content on groups offers a discussion on definitions, types, and purposes of groups to give students foundational knowledge on how and why groups are formed. The chapter also presents conceptualizations and processes of group work.

Chapter 16

Social Organizations and the Social Environment provides an overview of what social organizations are and a brief history of social organizations in the United States. Theoretical underpinnings of social organizations are offered in this chapter, as are the types and functions of organizations. Students are introduced to social workers' roles in organizations and issues around organizational diversity and ethics in organizational social work.

Chapter 17

Communities and the Social Environment takes a look at the different ways in which communities can be defined and the functions they can serve. Conceptualizations of communities are discussed as well as ways in which social workers conduct community assessments and interventions. A discussion is provided on the diversity of communities, and specific examples are offered on unique communities that bring various characteristics and issues that affect community members. The chapter also discusses how ethical issues can affect communities and how communities can be empowered to improve the well-being of their members.

INTERACTIVE CASES

The website www.routledgesw.com/cases presents six unique, in-depth, interactive, fictional cases with dynamic characters and real-life situations that students can easily access from any computer. They provide a "learning by doing" format unavailable with any other text. Your students will have an advantage unlike any other they will experience in their social work training. Each of the interactive cases uses text, graphics, and video to help students learn about engagement, assessment, intervention, and evaluation and termination at multiple levels of social work practice. The "My Notebook" feature allows students to take and save notes, type in written responses to tasks, and share their work with classmates and instructors by email. These interactive cases allow you to integrate the readings and classroom discussions:

The Sanchez Family: Systems, Strengths, and Stressors The 10 individuals in this extended Latino family have numerous strengths but are faced with a variety of challenges. Students will have the opportunity to experience the phases of the social work intervention, grapple with ethical dilemmas, and identify strategies for addressing issues of diversity.

Riverton: A Community Conundrum Riverton is a small Midwest city in which the social worker lives and works. The social worker identifies an issue that presents her community with a challenge. Students and instructors can work together to develop strategies for engaging, assessing, and intervening with the citizens of the social worker's neighborhood.

Carla Washburn: Loss, Aging, and Social Support Students will get to know Carla Washburn, an older African–American woman who finds herself living alone after the loss of her grandson and in considerable pain from a recent accident. In this case, less complex than the Sanchez family, students will apply their growing knowledge of gerontology and exercise the skills of culturally competent practice.

RAINN: Rape Abuse and Incest National Network The RAINN Online Hotline links callers to local Rape Crisis Centers and hospitals, as well as other services. In addition, rape crisis telephone hotlines have played an important role in extending services to those in communities in which services are not available. Students will learn how and why this national hotline was developed; they will evaluate both qualitative and quantitative data to assess how the program can better achieve its goals.

Hudson City: An Urban Community Affected by Disaster Hudson City has just been devastated by Hurricane Diane, a category-four hurricane with wind speeds of 140 miles per hour. Students will take up the role of a social worker who also resides in the community, who has been tasked with finding workable solutions to a variety of problems with diverse clients systems. Students will learn about disaster response and how to focus on many clients at once.

Brickville: Families and Communities Consider Transitions Brickville is a low-income community faced with a development proposal that would dramatically change the community. Students will take the role of a social worker who lives in the community and works for a community development corporation. Students will learn about community development and approaches that can be used to empower community members.

This book takes full advantage of the interactive element as a unique learning opportunity by including exercises that require students to go to the Web and use the cases. To maximize the learning experience, you may want to start the course by asking your students to explore each case by activating each button. The more the students are familiar with the presentation of information and the locations of the individual case files, the Case Study Tools, and the questions and tasks contained within each phase of the case, the better they will be able to integrate the text with the online practice component.

IN SUM

Human Behavior in the Social Environment: Mezzo and Macro Contexts provides material that will offer breadth and depth to students' understanding of mezzo and macro social work. Concepts in each chapter are set in a framework that will help students to think about the types of problems their clients might be likely to face in a wide range of settings. Students will also learn that organizing their knowledge about these areas into a theoretical context that "makes sense" to them will help them to manage the seemingly endless stream of information at their disposal. Ultimately, then, students will become more and more proficient at applying concepts to client problems. Meanwhile, students can enjoy the process of learning about them.

Being an effective social worker means being able to understand the complexities of human behavior, the societies and cultures in which we live, and the interplay between them. Being an effective social worker also means having a solid grounding in various disciplines, such as psychology, sociology, and human biology. It means possessing a well-rounded education and an ability to apply this knowledge to the myriad client problems and situations that students will face in the profession. This edition is intended to help students understand this complexity in the field and to help them gain the knowledge and critical thinking skills they will need to practice social work.

ACKNOWLEDGMENTS

I owe my gratitude to all the social work students I have known since the beginning of my career, for their questions, musings, and insights, and for pushing me to think about what it means to be a social worker. They are the inspiration for this book. I would like to extend my thanks to Tara Benavente and Patricia Stein, graduates of the Social Work Program at the University of Portland, who gave a great deal of their time and energy to help me with revisions of this book. Similarly, Rayne Funk, administrative assistant to the Social Work Program, was extremely helpful in the production of this book. Without her, most of my work would be impossible. I would also like to give a heartfelt thank you to Dr. Joseph Gallegos, my former colleague at the University of Portland, for all his support and mentorship. And for his support, I would like to thank Michael Andrews, Dean of the College of Arts and Sciences.

A big thank you goes to Samantha Barbaro and Elsa Peterson for their time, energy, and insights as well as their editorial and writing assistance. The project coordinator, Alice Lieberman, and the other authors of the book series, Rosemary Chapin, Marla Berg-Weger, Jerry Finn, and Judy Krysik have been great sources of inspiration and motivation. I have appreciated their feedback and insights throughout the process of writing this book. I am grateful to the editors and staff at Routledge, whose input was invaluable in helping me to move the book forward in a meaningful way.

Finally, I want to thank Tammy Rogers for her unwavering show of enthusiasm and encouragement for my work, and my family, Jim Koch, Olivia, and Grady, for their support, patience, and tolerance for my endeavors.

ABOUT THE AUTHOR

Anissa Taun Rogers, PhD, LCSW, MA, is Professor of Social Work at the University of Portland in Portland, Oregon. She also serves as the Director of the Social Work Program and Co-Director of the Gender and Women's Studies Minor. She teaches courses across the social work curriculum as well as courses on the body, human sexuality, and suffering and death. She is also registered, with her dog, Sookie, as a pet therapy team, working primarily with older adults and hospice patients.

Before finding her way to social work, Dr. Rogers studied psychology, in which she earned undergraduate and graduate degrees. After receiving her MSW and PhD in social work, Dr. Rogers began her career in undergraduate social work education and clinical practice. In addition to teaching, her main clinical and research interests are sexuality, gerontology, mental health, and end-of-life care.

CHAPTER 14

Spirituality and Human Behavior

Imani is a 16-year-old African–American teen living in a rural town in Texas. She lives with her deeply conservative and religious family of six; the family is very emotionally close and supportive of one another. Imani's town is located in a remote area with few health care and other resources. The closest town is about 60 miles away. Imani is very popular and is doing well in school. Recently, she became sexually active with her boyfriend of one year. She also has been experiencing painful periods and was recently diagnosed with endometriosis; her physician prescribed oral contraceptives to help manage the pain. Imani is considering taking them for pain and to prevent pregnancy, but Imani's family is vehemently against the use of contraceptives for any reason. Because of her situation with her health and relationship, Imani is beginning to question her beliefs, but she doesn't want to upset her family. She decided to fill her prescription, but the pharmacist at the only drugstore in town refuses to fill it, citing religious beliefs. Imani doesn't have the resources to drive to the next town to another drugstore, and she's not sure where she can go to get her prescription filled. Imani's situation has caused her a lot of distress as she reconsiders her spirituality, religious practices, and relationship with her family and community. Imani's friend has convinced her to talk with the school social worker about her situation.

SPIRITUALITY, RELIGIOSITY, FAITH—THESE ARE CONCEPTS with which we all are familiar. But as the case study brings to light, they can be complex aspects of our lives, influencing every realm of our lives. Given social work's orientation to the person in environment, we must be cognizant of and knowledgeable about religiosity and spirituality and how these realms impact our and our clients' everyday lives on micro, mezzo, and macro levels.

This chapter explores issues related to spirituality, religion, and faith and how they affect our work with clients. We will discuss definitions of spirituality and related concepts and take a look at how these concepts intersect with the lives of our clients, the functioning of our institutions and communities, and ultimately, our collective well-being.

WHAT IS SPIRITUALITY?

What does it mean to be spiritual, religious, faithful, or believing? What is the difference between a spiritual practice and a religious one? Many different terms are used to refer to spirituality, religiosity, and faith, and often they get used interchangeably, but they can mean many different things to different people and in different contexts. And, some definitions are more inclusive than others. Here we will explore the definitions of some of these concepts and take a look at the differences between them as well as the ways they can be applied in social work.

Definitions of Spirituality, Religiosity, and Faith

The realm of spirituality is an area that social workers assess and often work with, whether the work is with individuals or larger institutions or communities. For example, using biopsychosocial or ecosystems frameworks, a social worker might include spirituality in the assessment of a client's psychological realm or engagement with a religious organization in the client's microsystem. Or, while assessing a community for strengths, a social worker might notice the accessibility of a variety of spiritual practices for community members. But, what do we mean by spirituality or religiosity? How do we define these concepts so they capture the variety of experiences people have; can be studied to build our knowledge about them; and are amenable to assessment, intervention, and evaluation of our interventions?

Within the social work literature, there are many definitions of spirituality, many of them are limited in their inclusivity of different perspectives and experiences or ability to be assessed for research or clinical purposes. However, many are also broad enough to include concepts of faith and religiosity. **Religiosity** can be defined as belief in institutional doctrines (Vaughan, 1991) or a divine being with superhuman powers and the worship and rituals that accompany those beliefs (Argyle & Beit-Hallahmi, 1975). It can also be defined as the experience of reflecting upon and aligning with the divine, however a person defines it (James, 1961). Religiosity is often associated with the word religion. **Religion** refers to the social institutions that help us organize systems of beliefs and practices that are usually associated with the supernatural and that include a community of believers. These institutions normally provide rules and norms for behavior (Durkheim, 1965). **Faith** can be viewed as devotion or commitment to or belief or trust in a divine entity, without having actual proof that this entity exists (Canda & Furman, 2010).

Spirituality, on the other hand, is often defined in more nebulous terms. Various definitions of spirituality include subjective experiences of love, purpose, meaning, compassion, and human potential (La Cour & Götke, 2012; Tart, 1983; Vaughan, 1991), but many definitions tend to either lack inclusiveness that acknowledges diverse belief systems, or to lack enough specificity to lend themselves to assessment and measurement (Canda & Furman, 1999). For example, one definition of spirituality used in social work includes a relationship with God or an ultimate force that gives one a sense of purpose and meaning in life (Hodge, 2001); however, this definition is not suitable for those who may not believe in a God or other entity. Other definitions refer to spirituality as the human experience of finding meaning, morality, connection, and purpose in life (Derezotes, 2006; Zastrow, 2013). While these definitions are inclusive, they are broad, vague, and can be difficult to use in practice or research.

In an attempt to address the shortcomings of existing definitions of spirituality, Senreich (2013) offers the following definition, which is more inclusive than some other definitions and articulates constructs in a way that social workers can use them in clinical work and research:

> **Spirituality** refers to a human being's subjective relationship (cognitive, emotional, and intuitive) to what is unknowable about existence, and how a person integrates that relationship into a perspective about the universe, the world, others, self, moral values, and one's sense of meaning.
>
> (p. 553)

Let us take a look at how these definitions might apply when working with Imani's situation. Since Imani and her family belong to an organized religion, it would be important to explore her views on the teachings and practices of this community. The social worker might want to discuss the role her religious community plays in her life and how she sees herself fitting into this community. Similarly, since Imani is questioning her faith and her place in her religious community, it would be important for the social worker to spend time discussing these issues with Imani and getting a better understanding of how her spirituality might be changing in light of the questions and doubts she has around her organized religion. It is likely that aspects of spirituality, religiosity, and faith are changing and developing for Imani, particularly given that she is moving into adulthood and she is in a relationship that challenges her traditional beliefs.

Regardless of the definitions used to assess and work with spirituality, religiosity, and related concepts, it is important that social workers keep these concepts in mind when working with people, organizations, and communities. The social work profession has a long history of work with concepts related to spirituality and religiosity, and they have been important factors in this work. However, there have been shifts in and debates about the nature and importance of spirituality in social work, how these concepts should be incorporated into social work, and how the profession should move forward with these ideas in research and practice. In the next section, we will take a look at some of these trends and debates.

Historic and Current Trends around Spirituality and Religion in Social Work

The social work profession was founded on Judeo-Christian principles and other religious movements of the late 1800s. The profession's development included religious beliefs and philosophical teachings of many groups (Cnaan, 1999; Leighninger, 2000). However, in the early 20th century, as the medical model, scientific inquiry, and theoretical perspectives like Freud's psychoanalytic theory began to guide and define the work of many professions such as medicine and psychology, social work began to organize itself in a way that aligned with these perspectives. The emphasis on evidence-based science and biopsychosocial models in practice meant that any focus on spiritual aspects of human behavior began to be viewed as biased, unscientific, and immeasurable (Land, 2015; Seinfeld, 2012). Consequently, the focus on aspects of spirituality and religion was diminished. Social work education began to focus more on areas of human behavior, social welfare policy, and specific practice methods, leaving out an emphasis on religion and spirituality within its educational foundation (Austin, 1986). Indeed, in the educational policies and standards of the Council on Social Work Education (CSWE) in the 1970s and 1980s, no specific attention was given to content on spirituality and how it should be incorporated into social work programs.

This changed in 1992, when content on spirituality was incorporated into CSWE's policies and standards, guiding the development of programs and their curricula that was more inclusive of diverse spiritual and religious experiences (Sheridan & Amato-von Hemert, 1999). This shift was in line with cultural changes that saw an increased emphasis on spirituality. Since then, CSWE has continued to include aspects of religiosity and spirituality in its policy statements. The most recent version of these educational policies includes attention to religion and spirituality under the section on student competency to engage in diversity and difference (Council on Social Work Education, 2015). Further, the Code of Ethics of the National Association of Social Workers provides a statement on professionals' obligations to be knowledgeable about and respectful of diversity among clients and colleagues, which includes aspects of religion, and to practice in a non-discriminatory manner based on many cultural factors, including religion (National Association of Social Workers, 2008).

In line with professional and social shifts in the past several decades toward attention to the role spirituality plays in human behavior, the concept of spirituality has been of increasing interest in the social work profession as well as other fields like nursing, psychology, and medicine (Canda & Furman, 1999; Weaver, Pargament, Flannelly, & Oppenheimer, 2006). With these changes have come research, clinical, and educational efforts to better understand how spirituality impacts human well-being using theoretical and evidence-based knowledge, and how to better define and operationalize it so constructs can be used more consistently and effectively in the field. This shift has also called attention to the need to better prepare social work professionals to work with clients in a competent manner around issues of spirituality (Canda, 1988; Derezotes & Evans, 1995). At the same time, we have seen a separation of the meanings behind religion on the one hand and spirituality on the other, so that these two terms can mean very different things to different people. Much of this has to do with a concurrent rise in secularism and mistrust

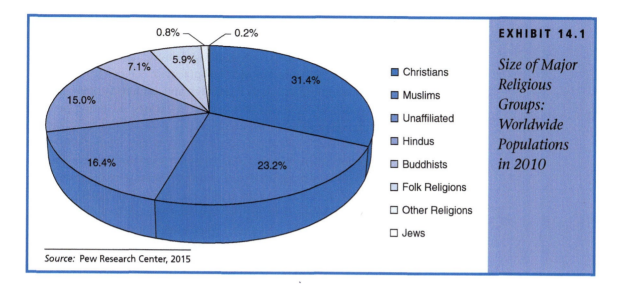

EXHIBIT 14.1

Size of Major Religious Groups: Worldwide Populations in 2010

0.8% — — 0.2%

5.9%

7.1%

31.4%

15.0%

16.4%   23.2%

■ Christians
■ Muslims
■ Unaffiliated
■ Hindus
■ Buddhists
□ Folk Religions
□ Other Religions
□ Jews

Source: Pew Research Center, 2015

of organized religious institutions. Consequently, many people have sought alternative routes to spirituality and spiritual development outside of organized religion (Turner, Lukoff, Barnhouse, & Lu, 1985; Roof, 1993). Further, membership in organized religious groups is changing. While Christianity is currently the largest religious group worldwide, Muslims are the fastest growing religious group. Between the years 2010 and 2050, the Muslim population is projected to grow by 73 percent compared to the Christian population at 35 percent. Exhibit 14.1 displays the percentages of religious group membership worldwide (Pew Research Center, 2015).

In addition to the increased interest in spirituality in the field, social workers often encounter issues related to spirituality, religion, and faith in different professional contexts, such as providing services to clients who belong to different religious groups or encountering the intersection of religion in situations where one might not expect it (e.g., in work with people in the workplace). Thus, social workers need to have a good understanding of the ramifications these realms bring to their work.

One way that religiosity and spirituality impact social work has to do with religious differences that intersect many facets of life, from the personal to the political. For example, differences in religious philosophy, which can be viewed on a continuum from conservative or fundamentalist to liberal or interpretationist, often affect our personal lives as well as the environmental contexts in which we engage. On the conservative end of the religious continuum, religious traditions tend to accept the literal meaning of scripture and sacred texts and reject religious pluralism or flexibility in interpretation of texts or traditions. Some examples include fundamentalist congregations of larger denominations like Baptists and many Pentecostal churches. On the liberal end of the religious continuum, sacred texts tend to be interpreted through historical and cultural lenses, and there is flexibility in how religious texts and traditions are expressed and practiced. Some examples include

Unitarian, Reform Judaism, and congregations in the Episcopalian church. While there are many other examples, it is important to note that there is a great deal of complexity and nuance to the beliefs and teachings between and within different denominations of all world religions and spiritual practices.

Different interpretations of religious teachings and traditions often provide the lenses through which we view our and others' behaviors, including personal choices and actions as well as the development of laws, policies, and social institutions that govern the behavior and expectations of society as a whole. While religious and spiritual beliefs often influence our views on social and political issues, this relationship is not always straightforward or simple. Because of the complexity of beliefs and experiences, it is important that social workers not make assumptions about people's motivations or behaviors based on religious or spiritual beliefs and teachings. This is particularly relevant in the United States where, because of our Constitutional freedom of religion and our doctrine of separation of church and state, the lines between the secular and religious in public life can be blurred. On one hand, it behooves social workers to understand how religious and spiritual perspectives can have an impact on areas like human behavior, social policy, and service delivery. On the other hand, social workers need to avoid reacting in their work based on stereotypes and biases from their own religious or spiritual perspectives or expectations about others' behaviors based on religious affiliation. We will explore this more later in the chapter. First, let us look at ways in which spirituality and faith development can be conceptualized in the field.

CONCEPTUALIZATIONS OF FAITH, RELIGIOSITY, AND SPIRITUALITY

As we discussed earlier, there has been a great deal of attention paid to spirituality and religiosity as they impact human behavior. Social workers and other helping professionals want to know what role these constructs play in supporting the health and well-being of individuals, organizations, and communities and how they can be applied in our work. Here, we will explore ways of conceptualizing spirituality, faith, and religiosity and how they impact the individual across the lifespan.

Conceptualizations of Spiritual Development and Their Applications

In the past several decades, efforts have increased to conceptualize work with individuals and issues around spirituality, beyond the philosophies and teachings of established religious traditions. These conceptualizations help us to think about how spirituality and related concepts develop and how to assess and incorporate facets of spirituality, faith, and religiosity in practice.

Even with the increased interest in spirituality in social work, the development of cohesive, empirical theories and models around spirituality and faith development has been lagging. Much of what exists to guide our work is broad, atheoretical, and based in experiences and theories from different realms of practice and disciplines such as hospice, theology, psychology, sociology, anthropology, and clerical counseling (Glicken, 2007; Liechty, 2013). While interdisciplinary contributions to ideas around spirituality are useful, the models that do exist do not necessarily lend themselves well to research that can help validate and clarify constructs that can be applied in our work. Still, practitioners and researchers have been moving forward in developing effective models for work with spirituality to overcome some of the shortcomings of what exists now. Some of this work has utilized existing theories in which spirituality concepts can be incorporated into practice, while other work has resulted in models that attempt to address spirituality more comprehensively.

Viewing Spirituality through Developmental Stage Theories and Conventional Frameworks One approach to conceptualizing, assessing, and working with spirituality and religiosity is to incorporate these constructs into existing theoretical approaches and frameworks. For example, spirituality can be conceptualized through a cultural lens or as a facet of ecosystems, biopsychosocial, and similar frameworks (Banks, 2001). A common approach is to incorporate aspects of spirituality or religiosity through the biopsychosocial framework. In this sense, spirituality becomes a component of the social or psychological realm, or it becomes its own realm that can be assessed in work with a client. Similarly, with Ecosystems Theory (Bronfenbrenner, 1979), religion, faith, belief, and spirituality can be assessed and addressed in any of the realms, depending on the issues with which a client may be grappling. For example, a social worker may want to learn more about a client's personal religious and spiritual beliefs in the client's microsystem or how predominant religious beliefs in society are affecting the client's macrosystem. Similarly, a social worker might want to explore how a person's religious and spiritual beliefs interact with those of others in the client's community, so spirituality might be assessed in the mesosystem.

Another approach to understanding spirituality can be to incorporate it into constructs of existing stage theories. In Erikson's Stages of Psychosocial Development (Erikson, 1950) for instance, spirituality can be woven into the major life stages and tasks for development. Religiosity, spirituality, and related concepts can be viewed as part of the processes involved in identity formation, development of intimate interpersonal relationships, a sense of social fit and solidarity with a social group, an ability to care for and contribute to the well-being of others and the community, and a sense of wisdom and fulfillment in life.

Similarly, spirituality could be incorporated into Piaget's theory of cognitive development (Piaget, 1952). Social workers can conceptualize how constructs related to religiosity and spirituality are developed based on children's ability to think critically about these constructs and relate them to concrete and abstract thinking. For example, children may think about and relate to ideas around spirituality very differently when in the preoperational stage than when they enter the formal operations stage. Further, Piaget's ideas around schemas, accommodation, and assimilation can help us to think about how we incorporate spiritual or religious beliefs, rituals, traditions, and philosophies into our ways of thinking about the world.

Another avenue of conceptualizing spirituality is through the use of models and theories that directly address faith, moral, and spiritual development, of which there are many. For example, as an outgrowth of conventional developmental stage theories, James Fowler (1981), a developmental psychologist, proposed a theory of faith development. This theory posits that individual faith develops in seven stages from childhood to midlife and describes how we develop faith through our interactions with others, experiences in our environment, and critical thinking about these interactions and experiences. Fowler's theory can help explain the progression of faith development, particularly in relation to cognitive development and increased interactions with our environment as we age, but it stops short of describing faith development and experiences as we move into old age.

Kohlberg (1976) and Gilligan (1982) proposed stage theories of moral development that also could be helpful in work with clients; these describe the developmental processes of moral reasoning. Constructs regarding pre-conventional, conventional, and post-conventional moral reasoning as well as orientation to survival, self-sacrifice, and nonviolent responsibility could offer frameworks from which to address beliefs about moral behavior and offer insights into issues around spirituality for clients. More specific descriptions and critiques of Fowler's, Kohlberg's, Gilligan's, and other developmental theories and their stages can be found in the core HBSE text.

Helminiak's (1987) **stages of spiritual development** is yet another theory that can help guide our thinking around spiritual development. Organized according to the model of stage theory, this theory views spiritual development as a process not separate from other realms of development (e.g., cognitive, emotional) but rather occurring in relation to them. Spiritual development is characterized by increasing presence of wholeness, openness, self-responsibility, and authentic self-transcendence in oneself, and includes an ongoing integration of spirituality into the personality until the person achieves true authenticity. Exhibit 14.2 displays the stages and characteristics of spiritual development articulated in this theory.

Viewing Spirituality through Broad Perspectives Several approaches to spirituality development utilize broad conceptualizations of spirituality, religiosity, and faith. These can be useful for us and our clients in thinking about spirituality and religiosity in new ways and in finding ways to move forward in development and problem solving. Specifically, these frameworks can be used to think about issues as well as to provide language for clients to explore and articulate spirituality, faith, belief, religiosity, and other concerns with which they might be grappling.

One model that focuses specifically on the spiritual realm is the **transpersonal perspective** that emanates from transpersonal psychology and theorists such as Carl Jung and Ken Wilber. This perspective draws from Eastern and Western spiritual

STAGE	DESCRIPTION	
Conformist	The beginning of spiritual development in which an individual holds an extensive, rationalized, and deeply felt world view based on external authority and approval of significant others.	**EXHIBIT 14.2** *Helminiak's Stages of Spiritual Development*
Conscientious Conformist	Characterized by an increasing separation from an inherited worldview and responsibility for one's life and direction.	
Conscientious	First true stage of spiritual development characterized by living life according to one's own understanding of the world and accepted responsibility for one's life, community, and commitment to principles.	
Compassionate	Characterized by surrender of self-constructed worldview replaced by more realistic and nuanced commitment to principles and compassion toward self and others.	
Cosmic	Characterized by a fuller, responsive, more authentic and flexible approach to life and an enduring sense of harmony with and integration between self, spirit, others, and all that is.	

Source: Based on Helminiak, 1987

traditions as well as scientific knowledge to explain aspects of consciousness, mystical experiences, and questions regarding the value and meaning of life and existence. It provides a perspective on how humans develop and experience love, meaning, existence, creativity, spirituality, and self-actualization (Canda, 1991; Cortright, 1997).

From this standpoint, psychological and spiritual development take place through complex processes that often interact with one another but that are still distinctly different from one another. Indeed, many transpersonal clinicians believe that we are essentially spiritual beings, and spiritual development takes place through the process of psychological work. Thus, many people find spiritual fulfillment and realization through work like psychotherapy, but it is not a requirement for this realization to happen. For example, from a transpersonal point of view, many clients seeking therapy are "stuck" in their development and are struggling to achieve full consciousness. They may suffer from defenses or blocked awareness that result in symptoms or maladaptive behavioral problems. Therapy can help clients gain insight into their development to reach a higher level of consciousness and spiritual wholeness (Cortright, 1997).

Another approach to conceptualizing religiosity and spirituality is Streng's (1985) **ways of being religious**. This perspective brings attention to spiritual and religious experiences as well as to patterns in which humans suffer, creating categories of religious and spiritual orientation and commitment. The categories assist in explaining a person's worldview and way of making sense of worldly experiences. Exhibit 14.3 describes these categories.

EXHIBIT 14.3 *Streng's Ways of Being Religious*	CATEGORY	DESCRIPTION
	Personal Experience of the Holy	Pride, incompetence, imperfection, and separation from a higher being lead to increased trust, faith, feeling, obedience, and submission. The result is trust in a higher order and divine being and existence beyond the worldly experience.
	Creation of Community through Myth and Ritual	Chaos, ignorance, and alienation lead to connection with healers, rituals, and other practices that create connection. The result is transcendence, creative activity, and connection to a higher being.
	Daily Living that Expresses the Cosmic Law	Immaturity, inauthenticity, and disharmony with self, others, and a higher being lead to cultivating wisdom, social relations, and a connection with a higher order. The result is creating harmony with all and a higher social order.
	Spiritual Freedom through Discipline	Lack of insight, self-realization, and connection to a higher being lead to discipline, self-reflection, and personal work to connect to a higher self. The result is transcendence and a higher level of consciousness.
	Achieving an Integrated Self through Creative Interaction	Loneliness, alienation, depersonalization, and identity loss lead to acceptance of self, deeper human interaction and relationships, and attention to problems of life for self and others. The result is love, trust, concern, integrity, and interconnectedness.
	Social and Economic Justice as an Ultimate Concern	Injustice and inequality in social institutions and violation of human rights leads to inclusion, commitment to create a just world, and social action to reform social institutions. The result is social reform, social and economic justice, and respect for human rights.

		EXHIBIT 14.3
New Life through Technocracy	Chaos and confusion caused by the inability to control the environment and our ultimate deaths leads to a quest for scientific objectivity, suppression of intuition, and a social commitment to a worldly utopia and institutionalization of technology that can solve problems. The result is order, comfort, security, and the promise of extended life.	*Continued*
Full Life through Sensuous/Artistic Experience	Sterility, lifelessness, and lack of creativity and sensuality lead to increased perception, spontaneity, attention to sensuous experience and rejection of social convention. The result is creativity, aesthetic reality, and power in sensual experience.	

Sources: Based on Streng, 1985

Applying Conceptualizations of Spirituality

How might these developmental conceptualizations of spirituality and religiosity be applied in Imani's case? Any one of the theories and models discussed above could be used in work with her situation. Much depends on what seems to fit and be beneficial for Imani. For instance, the social worker could utilize Ecosystems Theory and explore with Imani how her religious community interfaces with other systems in her life like her family, school, and health care. This exploration may reveal beneficial information about how these systems are interacting with one another and how problem solving might happen to help the systems work together more harmoniously. Or the social worker could look at her situation through Erikson's stages of psychosocial development, in which Imani would be transitioning from adolescence into the young adult stage. Imani's developmental tasks are to establish intimacy in relationships without giving up her self-identity. The social worker might want to explore how spirituality and religiosity might be supporting her or creating barriers for her as she works on these tasks. Similarly, the social worker could look at Imani's situation from the stages of spiritual development where, through further discussion, she might place Imani in the conscientious conformist stage. It appears that Imani is beginning to separate from her inherited worldview as developmental, relational, and health care needs become important and begin to conflict with her inherited views. The social worker could also utilize several theories and models simultaneously to help explore with Imani some of the issues she is facing around spirituality and religiosity.

Of course, more work is needed to develop empirical and cohesive models and theories around religiosity and spirituality development and experiences, but much of the work that has been accomplished toward this goal has been helpful in moving the profession forward with regard to incorporating spirituality into its frameworks more fully and effectively. Conceptual models around spirituality and faith are not only useful to help the profession organize constructs and guide assessment and work in this realm, but they are in line with the values and principles on which the profession was founded, particularly around promoting human dignity and social and economic justice (Brenner & Homonoff, 2004; Payne, 1997). Next we will examine ways in which spirituality and religiosity interface with our individual lives.

THE INDIVIDUAL AND SPIRITUALITY

Research largely supports the idea that incorporating spirituality into practice, when appropriate for clients, allows them to achieve more profound and lasting change. Evidence suggests a strong positive correlation between spirituality and individual and community well-being and empowerment (Canda & Furman, 1999; Hodge, 2005a). For example, among other benefits, research indicates that higher levels of spirituality are associated with better mental and physical health (Chapple, 2003; Seeman, Dubin, & Seeman, 2003); higher levels of life satisfaction; fewer consequences of traumatic life events (Ellison, 1991); and improved coping, adjustment, and quality of life (Koenig, MuCullough, & Larson, 2001).

Spirituality Across the Lifespan and Demographic Contexts

Across the lifespan, benefits of spirituality and religiosity have been well documented. Among children and adolescents, spiritual development has been associated with resiliency, improved life satisfaction (Marques, Lopez, & Mitchell, 2013), enhanced ability to handle grief and loss (Muselman & Wiggins, 2012), improved adjustment to and outcomes for health problems (Benore, Pargament, & Pendleton, 2008; Renani, Hajinejad, Idani, & Ravanipour, 2014), and ability to cope with trauma and adversity (Noguera, 2013). One study of more than 800 adolescents found that personal spirituality or a connection with a higher, sacred power was associated with positive adjustment, parental relationships, and academic performance. Involvement in religious organizations was associated with lower current and future substance use (Good & Willoughby, 2014).

Spirituality and religiosity among young adults appears to help protect against mental health issues, violent behavior, and risky health behaviors, with the exception of unprotected sex. Specifically, higher religious affiliation and stronger spiritual beliefs have been associated with inconsistent contraceptive use (Burris, Smith, & Carlson, 2009; Ganga & Kutty, 2013; O'Brien et al., 2013; Rida & Iram, 2014). Spirituality also is associated with increased generativity activities such as contributing to one's community and finding meaning in life and actions (Brady & Hapenny, 2010).

Once we reach middle and older adulthood, greater spirituality and religiosity are associated with wisdom, creativity, personal growth, and generativity activities such as involvement with others and in the community (Wink & Dillon, 2003). As we age, religiosity, spirituality, and church membership have been associated with longevity; positive adjustment to aging; psychological well-being; and lower risk of cognitive decline and health and mental health problems (Dillon & Wink, 2007; Lawler-Row & Elliott, 2009; Von Humboldt, Leal, & Pimenta, 2014).

Findings on the effects of spirituality for our well-being tend to suggest that the benefits of spirituality are similar for people regardless of gender, ethnicity, socio-economic status, and other demographic variables. However, the experiences surrounding religiosity, participation in institutionalized forms of religion, and how spirituality is expressed because of formal religion may differ for people depending on different demographic and cultural contexts. For example, some researchers argue that women's experiences of spirituality are different from men's (Briggs & Dixon, 2013). Women's orientation toward spirituality (as opposed to any religious beliefs or practices they might follow) is often embedded in justice and equity; this may be because of women's experiences of unjust treatment in patriarchal systems as well as dominant attitudes in society and many religions that women are subservient, dependent, second-class citizens. Women often find they are not represented in many religious symbols and rituals, and when they are, they are represented as weak (Kidd, 1995), even with efforts to increase inclusivity in religious language and references. Further, women's spirituality may develop in circular, relational patterns, where development ebbs and flows over time based on experiences and interactions with others. Conversely, men's spiritual development may take a more linear, goal-directed pattern over the lifespan (Borysenko, 1999). Consequently, some researchers and practitioners argue that women's spirituality is not well represented in existing theories and measures of religiosity or spirituality (Houtman & Aupers, 2008; McGuire, 2008).

Spirituality and religiosity experiences are also unique to individuals among the GLBT community, but in general, research has suggested that spirituality is more prominent than religiosity for GLBT individuals (Halkitis *et al.*, 2009; Heermann, Wiggins, & Rutter, 2007). With regard to the GLBT community, there are many issues that can impede as well as support spiritual development for its members. Many studies have suggested that institutionalized religions can be problematic for their GLBT members (Sherry, Adelman, Whilde, & Quick, 2010). Specifically, many religions' philosophies and teachings tend to support traditional gender and sexual identities and roles, viewing deviance as a sin. Consequently, many GLBT members find themselves either being ostracized by their religious communities or leaving them altogether to find more accepting, supportive spiritual communities (Fallon *et al.*, 2013; Wilcox, 2012). The rejection of homosexuality and non-traditional gender roles by many religions can complicate the spiritual development of their GLBT members, making the journey more difficult and painful in many ways. For example, conservative faiths have been associated with higher levels of shame and internalized homophobia, often leading to a high incidence of posttraumatic stress and recovery for GLBT individuals from religious-based homophobia (Bowers, Minichiello, & Plummer, 2010; Sherry *et al.*, 2010). Transgender individuals may experience conflicts between their perceived selves and socialized gender and find themselves defying gender norms of their religious community (Levy & Lo, 2013).

Conversely, affirming faith communities can be a source of support for spiritual development and are associated with positive psychological health and self-acceptance for members of the GLBT community (Lease, Horne, & Noffsinger-Frazier, 2005). Many people find support and affirmation in their religious and spiritual community. For example, transgender individuals may find a communal space where they can explore gender and religious identities and reconcile social norms with personal experiences and gender expression (Levy & Lo, 2013). Many denominations welcome GLBT individuals; some examples include the Alliance of Baptists; Baptists Peace Fellowship; Christ Catholic Church; Covenant Network of Presbyterians; and Evangelical Anglican Church in America. GLBT individuals may have a variety of responses to religious institutions and practices, including adopting different expressions of spirituality that better fit their experiences, seeking to minimize the impact of anti-gay teachings of their chosen religion, leaving organized religion altogether, or rejecting their own sexual identity (Dworkin, 1997; Rodriguez & Ouellette, 2000).

Ethnicity also has an impact on spirituality and religiosity, but the nature of this relationship is complex. Research has offered mixed and sometimes contradictory results regarding the role ethnicity plays in religious and spiritual beliefs and practices and health and mental health outcomes. Some research suggests that participation in religious activities is beneficial for the health and mental health of ethnic minority group members. This may be because of the catharsis, social integration, social identity, and values affirmation church attendance can offer (Idler, 1987; Taylor, Chatters, & Levin, 2004). And, religious participation among ethnic minority groups can offer social, emotional, and instrumental support (Idler, 1987). However, other studies have not been able to support these findings. For example, one study suggested that there were no mental health benefits for certain groups like African–Americans and Hispanics who attended church regularly (Sternthal, Williams, Musick, & Buck, 2012). A clear understanding of the relationship between ethnicity, spirituality and religiosity, and health outcomes may be further complicated by socioeconomic factors as well as ethnic differences in the use of spiritual rituals and traditions for health and other purposes that are difficult to parse out (Gillum & Griffith, 2010).

Studies also have reported contradictory results on the effects ethnicity has for women and religious participation. Some studies indicate that women of color report little or no involvement with religious organizations, while significantly more Caucasian women report involvement. Other studies suggest that church attendance patterns for women vary greatly within and between ethnic groups (Wilcox, 2012). Yet other research suggests that women from all ethnic groups score higher than men on measures of religiosity and spirituality (Maselko & Kubzansky, 2006). And, regardless of the diverse characteristics and behaviors that describe people and groups, religious identification can affect how one experiences spiritual and religious constructs such as guilt, moral values, and social responsibility. For example, people participating in Catholic traditions may experience more guilt than those in non-Catholic traditions (Albertsen, O'Connor, & Berry, 2006; Braam, Sonnenberg, Beekman, Deeg, & Van-Tilburg, 2000).

Even with evidence that supports the benefits of spirituality and religiosity for general well-being, it is also important to consider that conflicts people may have in their experiences with spirituality and religiosity can often cause mental, emotional, relationship, and other distress. Indeed, these conflicts can result in violence and prolonged personal, interpersonal, and community discord (Mahoney & Cano, 2014). We will look at how some of these negative consequences can play out on the mezzo and macro levels later in the chapter.

Given the diversity and complexity we see in the development of spirituality and religiosity, it is not surprising that there has been a great deal of criticism of existing models that attempt to describe spirituality development. Indeed, some theories, like Kohlberg's (1976) theory of moral development, mentioned earlier, have been criticized for being far too individualistic, disregarding developmental processes that value interconnectedness and relationships, which often apply to women and people from different cultural contexts.

Spiritual Assessment and Applications

We have discussed some of the theoretical and other frameworks that can be used to conceptualize and work with spirituality and religiosity. Often, social workers and other professionals can explore clients' spirituality using these perspectives to guide assessment and interventions. In addition, there are other ways to work with spirituality that involve more specific assessment and conceptualization processes. We will look at some of these in this section.

Some therapeutic avenues target spiritual work that involves concepts around gratitude, forgiveness, and expressive methods that utilize the mind, body, and brain to explore clients' spirituality and issues associated with it. For example, gratitude and forgiveness often are associated with spirituality because they evoke images of giving power over to or thanking a higher power. This is particularly true in situations where a wrong has been done that is difficult to forgive. Examples include macro-level events like the Holocaust, the former Yugoslavia's "ethnic cleansing," and the Rwandan genocide; as well as individual situations like the death of a loved one at the hands of a stranger in a robbery or shooting. Work on forgiveness and gratitude often requires an exploration of clients' worldview and the meaning they place on the purpose of life and things that happen, both positive and negative. Sometimes this involves working through emotions of joy, anger, unknowing, uncertainty, and perhaps letting go of the need and conception of control over events in life. It may involve building empathy and moving beyond selfishness and isolation to embracing sacrifice, interconnectedness with others, and identifying the good in one's life as a source of gratitude (Watts, Dutton, & Gulliford, 2006). Forgiveness and gratitude work can be associated with specific teachings of established religions, but it can also be conducted within a broader framework of spirituality.

Expressive therapeutic methods use all the senses to help clients explore spiritual issues by asking clients to recall the images, sounds, tastes, smells, and thoughts associated with spirituality. For instance, a client may recall the smell of incense, the sound of bells or music, or the taste of wine associated with certain religious practices. We make meaning from these experiences, which can be explored to help resolve issues, draw on strengths, reconstruct meaning around our experiences, and enhance our interpersonal and transpersonal relationships (Land, 2015).

Sacred-sensitive expressive methods move beyond traditional talk therapy by allowing clients to engage and express emotions, thoughts, and feelings through modalities like art, music, writing, dance, meditation, psychodrama, mindfulness, and guided imagery. Many of these techniques have been studied over the years using a variety of research methods. This research suggests that these modalities are effective in improving well-being and life satisfaction for a variety of presenting issues related to spirituality, including trauma, major life transitions, and existential suffering. Further, they can be used with any client population (Land, 2015; Vianna *et al.*, 2013; Walton, 2012).

Many spirituality and religiosity assessments are available to work with clients around these issues. Assessment can be accomplished through using theoretical and other perspectives, like the biopsychosocial framework, to guide open-ended questions in this realm, but sometimes social workers and clients wish to use more structured, standardized instruments that can get at constructs more specifically. These instruments use a wide variety of definitions of spirituality and religiosity and measure a wide range of constructs in these realms, so it is important to understand the goals and purposes of different instruments before utilizing them.

Some of the structured, standardized instruments include the Duke Religion Index (Koenig, Meador, & Parkerson, 1997) that asks questions around spirituality, spiritual coping, and private and public religious practices. Another is the full and Brief RCOPE (Pargament *et al.*, 2000) that looks at religious coping. The Multidimensional Measure of Religiousness and Spirituality (Fetzer Insititute, 1999) assesses different realms of institutional and personal spirituality and religiosity. Still others are linked with specific issues like the Functional Assessment of Chronic Illness Therapy – Spirituality – Expanded (FACIT, 2007) that assess constructs like hope, peace, meaning, gratitude, and appreciation. Comprehensive measures can help social workers explore broader spirituality issues with clients. Some of these measures include spiritual histories (Hodge, 2001), lifemaps (Hodge, 2005a), genograms (Hodge & Williams, 2002), and ecograms (Hodge, 2005b).

We mentioned Jung earlier in this chapter with regard to how spirituality can be conceptualized. Jung's work provides the foundation for the Myers-Briggs-Type

Indicator (MBTI) (Briggs-Myers & Briggs, 1985) and ideas around psychological or personality type to describe people's preferences with regard to how they express themselves and interact with the world. Research has suggested that certain personality types predict religiosity. For example, regardless of culture and religious denomination, research indicates that people high in religiosity tend to be agreeable and conscientious (Saroglou, 2002). Building on these findings, the MBTI has been used extensively by religious institutions and others to assess spirituality development (Lloyd, 2007). For example, using constructs from the MBTI, four dominant psychological types emerge describing spirituality development, which can be used for assessment and exploration with clients. These are described in Exhibit 14.4.

Sometimes, the language used in spirituality assessment does not resonate with clients' worldviews or experiences, necessitating the use of more comprehensive assessment methods. In this case, social workers can ask broad questions that are sensitive to differences in meaning making such as how clients coped with challenges in the past; when clients feel most alive; what clients are grateful for; what nourishes clients' souls; how challenges have changed clients; what helps clients

PSYCHOLOGICAL TYPE	DESCRIPTION	
Sensing Spirituality	Sensing types are sure about their beliefs, draw a distinct line between the religious and secular, enjoy order and rules, and likely will be concerned with following the roles, rituals, and routine of specific beliefs and practices of religious institutions.	**EXHIBIT 14.4** *Four Dominant Psychological Types for Spirituality*
Intuitive Spirituality	Intuitive types find meaning in life through inspiration and motivation and do not make a strong distinction between the secular and spiritual. They value the complexity of spirituality and are open to interpretation of symbols, rituals, and different ways of thinking about spirituality.	
Thinking Spirituality	Thinking types value social justice and righteousness, using wisdom, fairness, objectivity, and intellectual questioning to create change. Often a connection between logic and emotions of spirituality needs to be made for thinking types to have faith without evidence for it.	
Feeling Spirituality	Feeling types find spirituality in relationship to others, particularly those who share similar values. Morality that promotes compassion and harmonious relations is valued.	

Source: Based on Hall, 2012

get through difficult situations; what clients are striving for in life; and what legacy clients would like to leave in the world (Hodge, 2013). Or, it may be that existing assessment methods are not appropriate for use with certain populations whose cultural or other demographic contexts may not fit with dominant spiritual world-views or language found in some assessments. Some assessment methods have been validated for use with different populations (e.g., Hodge & Limb, 2011), and social workers need to research assessment tools before working with different populations around spirituality and related issues.

Applying Individual Perspectives to Spirituality

In Imani's case, her strong spirituality and religiosity may prove to be a source of support and resiliency for her as well as provide some protection from stress and health and mental health problems as she develops. Conversely, her religiosity could be a source of stress and conflict, particularly with regard to her sexuality and health issues. This could cause personal and familial conflict as well as conflict with members of her religious community. And, being female may mean that her spiritual develop-mental process differs from what is expected from her religious community. The social worker may want to explore which assessment and intervention modalities resonate for Imani given her particular cultural background and interests.

We have looked at some of the ways spirituality and religiosity affect individuals. Next, we will turn our attention to how these concepts can play out in the family and other mezzo-level environments.

SPIRITUALITY'S ROLE IN THE FAMILY AND IMMEDIATE ENVIRONMENT

There are many ways to conceptualize spirituality and religiosity on the mezzo level and how they impact and function in different contexts. We will first take a look at broad theoretical lenses that can be used to view spirituality and religiosity on this level and then explore specific issues related to these constructs for families and the workplace.

Sociological Perspectives

Various sociological theories offer insights into how spirituality and religiosity impact mezzo-level environments. Two that are particularly helpful are functionalist (Durkheim, 1933; Merton, 1968) and symbolic interaction (Blumer, 1969) theories. Chapter 4 in the core HBSE text describes these theories and their concepts in some detail. Here we will explore these concepts as they apply to spirituality and religiosity.

Functionalist theory describes how aspects of our lives help us to function and maintain stability. From the standpoint of spirituality and religiosity, functionalist theory views aspects such as rituals, beliefs, traditions, and behaviors related to spirituality and religiosity as functional and often beneficial to our well-being. These aspects are considered necessary to help us maintain homeostasis in our lives and community (a concept related to systems theory), and they help us to organize into groups and communities to get our social, spiritual, and other needs met. Merton (1968) described the ways in which constructs function in our lives; these are the manifest and latent functions and dysfunctions. Manifest functions are the overt or readily identifiable functions of a construct, so spirituality and religiosity could be described as providing order, support, meaning, guidelines, community, and structure for people's lives. The latent functions, or covert purposes of a construct, of spirituality and religiosity might be to make money from the congregations' donations; gain political or other power; or persuade or socialize people to believe or behave in certain ways. The dysfunctions of spirituality and religiosity could be aspects that generate problems such as fighting and violence over beliefs and control; corruption and manipulation by religious leaders; destructive feelings and behaviors fostered by not "living up to" certain values and beliefs; or members judging, shunning, or ostracizing other members based on perceived transgressions that go against dominant beliefs.

From the functionalist theory, aspects of spirituality and religiosity could be viewed as growth-promoting values, beliefs, and behaviors that help people and communities maintain support and connectedness. But the theory also provides a lens through which to view and describe the ways in which spirituality and religiosity can be destructive or undermine the well-being of individuals and communities.

Symbolic interaction theory describes the ways in which people and systems interact and communicate with one another that, in turn, help us to create meaning in our lives. As we interact with our environment, we create narratives about these interactions and what they mean, thus building the foundation for our understanding of the world. We act on the world based on the ways we interpret our interactions with others and our constructed understanding of the world. From this viewpoint, our experiences and interactions with others and various systems contribute to the meaning we place on spirituality and religiosity and our attitudes and behaviors related to these realms. It may be that a person was reared in a supportive, spiritual environment that included various rituals and practices in the home and in the community. This person may consequently have developed a deep, rich connection with these aspects of spirituality, which in turn affects her or his behaviors and further interactions with others that reinforce these beliefs and views. Conversely, another person may have been exposed to no particular spiritual or religious belief, and when she or he interacts with others who hold very specific or rigid beliefs, she or he may struggle to make meaning out of these seemingly strange beliefs. This could cause the individual to react negatively, perhaps dismissing the beliefs as odd or nonsensical.

This perspective also helps to explain how people's views on spirituality and religion can develop or change over time. For example, a young person who was reared in a conservative religion may find that the beliefs of this religion are at odds with her or his experience and must find ways to reconcile the discrepancies. This reconciliation could happen through interactions with others outside her or his organized religion or through reconstructing the meaning attached to certain values and beliefs. It may be that a person who decides to marry someone from a different religion, for example, finds himself rejected by his religious community. Symbolic interaction theory would posit that beliefs about the separateness of one's and other religions have been constructed through interactions with the person's religious community. This meaning is at odds with the person's felt experience, and new meaning must be constructed for the person to continue to grow. It could also be that the person finds a way to reconcile his experience with his partner choice and his religious beliefs, perhaps even to the point of choosing not to continue a relationship with his partner. From this perspective then, there are many ways that reality and meaning about spirituality and religiosity are constructed and reconstructed as we interact with others and our environment.

Applying Sociological Perspectives on Spirituality

For Imani, religion and spirituality provide many functions for her and her family. It seems that their religion offers support and a sense of community that is comforting and connects them to others. It provides a sense of purpose and meaning to their lives. However, it could prove to be dysfunctional if the roles and rules of the religion require that Imani does not get appropriate health care for her needs or tend to her sexual relationship in ways that she feels is appropriate. Insofar as her religion causes Imani distress, it would be considered dysfunctional in those aspects. It does appear that Imani is beginning to recreate meaning around religion and spirituality and becoming aware of new narratives around these aspects. Symbolic interaction theory would help to explain how Imani made sense of religion through her interactions with her family and religious community when she was younger but is now changing her ideas and perspectives as she gains new and different experiences and interacts with others outside of her faith.

Spirituality and the Family

Aspects of many theories can be used to conceptualize spirituality and religiosity in the family context. Going back to the previous discussion, social workers could think about how spirituality and religiosity provide functionality (or dysfunction) for families and how members of families construct meaning around spirituality and religiosity through interactions with other family members and members of their spiritual and religious communities. Further, more individualistic theories and frameworks could be utilized to explore spirituality and religiosity among individual family members.

Another approach to looking at spirituality and religiosity for the family as a whole is systems theory (Bertalanffy, 1972). Through this lens, we can see how aspects of spirituality and religiosity affect the family as a dynamic system. In Chapter 2 of the core HBSE text, we discuss systems theory in detail. Here we will explore how spirituality and religiosity can be viewed and applied using systems theory.

Recall from systems theory that a family, like other systems, can be viewed as an entity that is made up of smaller, interdependent parts that together function as an organized whole. When we bring in concepts related to spirituality and religiosity, we can see how these concepts can help keep the family operating as an organized whole—that is, to maintain homeostasis—or to pull the family apart—that is, move it toward entropy. To maintain homeostasis and keep the family functioning smoothly, families may create rules, roles, and boundaries around the family's values and beliefs; how spirituality and religiosity are discussed and practiced; how family members should behave and interact with others in and outside religious institutions; and expectations for family members with regard to fulfilling religious or spiritual obligations both currently and in the future.

Family members receive feedback and input about their beliefs and behaviors from other family members, and when a family member does not follow rules or adhere to roles related to spirituality, it disrupts homeostasis for the family as a whole. The family also receives feedback and input from outside the system, such as from the interactions family members have with others outside the family (e.g., people from different faiths, experiences at spiritual or religious workshops or retreats) and from their own religious institutions. This feedback gives the family system information about how it is functioning with regard to its rules and roles and those of their religious or spiritual community. The family system may receive a great deal of positive input through its spiritual practices and interconnectedness with others in a religious community, creating a sense of purpose, meaning, and connection to one another and the larger community. This positive input may strengthen faith among family members and compel them to contribute to their spiritual practices and community. Similarly, a family system may receive negative feedback and input from others about their faith, which could further disrupt homeostasis of the family system and create contention and a sense of disconnect with their spiritual community. Ultimately, if a family system cannot adapt to and change with members' evolving ideas and practices around spirituality, the family system could experience entropy, for example in the form of conflict, disharmony, or estrangement. Conversely, if the family is able to adapt, it could lead to negative entropy or a new level of homeostasis that is more functional and supportive of all members than it had been previously.

Using systems theory when working with a family around spirituality and religiosity issues, a social worker might want to explore with family members their perspectives on personal spirituality and religiosity as well as how they see aspects of these unfold in the family. This type of exploration could help resolve misunder-standings between family members; reveal unspoken rules, roles, and boundaries that persist in a family to cause problems; and promote better understanding among and support for family members as their experiences of spirituality and religiosity change over time (Brelsford, 2013).

Spirituality and Its Effects on Family Members and Dynamics   As was discussed earlier, research suggests that spirituality and religiosity can have protective effects for people across the lifespan. Fewer studies have examined how spirituality and religiosity interact within family systems to impact the well-being of the family as a whole and its members. Here we will explore some of the research on spirituality, religiosity, and family dynamics.

As is the case with individual well-being, research suggests that greater spiritual-ity and religiosity is associated with better family outcomes. For example, religious service attendance has been linked to parental well-being, including—among other benefits—positive parenting attitudes, child health, and engagement in school (Wen, 2013). And, greater religiosity tends to be associated with greater parent–child closeness and relationship satisfaction (Regnerus & Burdette, 2006), particu-larly when beliefs are similar, children internalize parental beliefs, and constructive conversations around beliefs are facilitated (Dollahite & Thatcher, 2008). Research also suggests that spirituality and religiosity are strongly associated with reduced parental stress and negative parent–child interactions, even when families live in neighborhoods with high rates of crime, poverty, and dysfunction (Lamis, Wilson, Tarantino, Lansford, & Kaslow, 2014).

Religiosity and spirituality can be helpful during stressful events such as divorce and illness (Krumrei, Mahoney, & Pargament, 2009), particularly for people with limited resources like low-income, single women (Mahoney, 2010). For instance, religiosity and spirituality have been shown to play a role in families' abilities to cope with and adjust to illness. Studies have examined families dealing with issues like childhood asthma, prostate cancer, and other health-related issues. Results suggest that religiosity and spirituality help families find peace, strength, support, positive communication, and reduced stress and burden associated with particular disease and treatment processes (Greeff & Thiel, 2012; Renani, Hajinejad, Idani, & Ravanipour, 2014). However, death, end-of-life issues, or negative life events can also lead to spiritual or existential crises of sorts like spiritual distress, anger at God, or questioning faith, beliefs, and purpose and meaning of life. These crises can result in mental health issues like depression or severance of ties with a faith or organized religion; conversely, in other cases such events can lead to strengthening of faith and spirituality (Exline, Prince-Paul, Root, & Peereboom, 2013; Warner, Mahoney, & Krumrei, 2009).

Other research has suggested that spirituality and religiosity in families play a role with regard to desiring children, marriage and cohabitation, and children's overall well-being. Women who report being religious tend to have higher fertility and adoption rates than women who do not report high religiosity (Hollingsworth, 2000; Zhang, 2008). Higher fertility rates for these women could be tied to religious and spiritual beliefs about family. A pattern of cohabitation and marriage has been found to extend to adolescents who demonstrate strong religious commitment and participation, particularly those affiliated with conservative Protestant groups (Eggebeen & Dew, 2009). Petts (2014) found that children's attendance at religious services with parents was associated with children's well-being and with positive parent–child relationships. Further, religion may play a protective role in helping adolescents deal with harsh parenting and dysfunctional family systems (Kim-Spoon, Farley, Holmes, & Longo, 2014), particularly if their mothers model positive relationships with God (Goeke-Morey, Taylor, Merrilees, Shirlow, & Cummings, 2014).

Research has been conducted on the impact religiosity and spirituality have on incidence of divorce, and in general, these constructs are associated with lower divorce rates (Brown, Orbuch, & Bauermeister, 2008). However, this association is complicated by myriad factors beyond religiosity and spirituality that affect marital relationships (Mahoney, 2010). Moreover, the results of studies on religiosity and marital satisfaction have been mixed. Marital satisfaction is affected by multiple factors, such as partners' mental health, vocational choices, religious engagement, and spiritual and political views (Sullivan, 2001; Wilcox & Wolfinger, 2008). While greater religiosity is associated with less marital conflict, partners who differ in religious beliefs tend to experience more marital conflict (Curtis & Ellison, 2002). People who are affiliated with religious groups and who attend services regularly are more likely than those who are not affiliated with a religious group to remarry after divorce, though there are differences in remarriage rates by specific religious group (Brown & Porter, 2013).

Research indicates that greater religiosity is associated with attitudes that support child obedience, and more conservative beliefs predict support for the use of corporal punishment (Gershoff, Miller, & Holden, 1999). Research also suggests, however, that strong religious beliefs may foster calm, thoughtful approaches to childrearing (Mahoney, 2010), and higher religiosity tends to be associated with fewer incidents of child abuse (Brown, Cohen, Johnson, & Salzinger, 1998). Research has not found a clear association between religiosity and domestic labor and decision making in the family (Mahoney, 2010); conflict with gender roles and decision making can sometimes lead to conflict and domestic violence. However, all of these associations are complicated by many socioeconomic factors, and much more work is needed in this area to better understand how beliefs affect conflict in gender roles and abusive behavior.

It is important to be aware that religious and spiritual beliefs can be used to justify and perpetuate emotional and physical abuse on family members. A parent, for example, may justify abuse based on theological teachings, arguing that the Bible or some other teaching supports physical punishment of a partner or child. The victim of abuse might feel fear, shame, or guilt in relation to theological teachings, assuming she or he deserves the abuse. Victims of abuse can feel isolated, worthless, and helpless to change their situation because of the family dynamics entrenched in particular religious beliefs that are used to justify the abuse (Bottoms, Nielsen, Murray, & Filipas, 2003; Capps, 1995; Walsh, 1999). Children are especially vulnerable to this type of abuse as they may be too young and isolated to think critically about and challenge dogma or misapplied teachings to argue against the abuse (Simonic, Mandelj, & Novsak, 2013).

An extreme example of what some consider abuse is "faith healing" by groups like the Church of Christ, Scientist (Christian Science), the Followers of Christ Church, and the General Assembly Church of the First Born. Members of these religious groups may argue that their faith, through means like prayer, gives them the ability to cure and heal. Followers may refuse medical treatment for potentially deadly illnesses, arguing that the strength of their faith is a legitimate treatment and to seek medical treatment is a sign of weakness (American Cancer Society, 2013). Exemptions to laws and religious-defense statutes in many states protect this prac-tice, calling it freedom of religion. Others argue it is a form of abuse being justified by extreme religious beliefs that have resulted in many needless deaths. In 1974, the U.S. Department of Health and Human Services required states that received funds for child abuse programs to enact exemptions for families practicing faith health. By the time this regulation was repealed in 1983, all states had some exemption in place, and most still use them. These exemptions vary widely from state to state. States like Arkansas and West Virginia provide immunity for parents whose children die from faith healing. Most states provide exemptions to parents from prosecution only when children are not seriously harmed, but they still often require parents to seek medical care in more serious cases. Some states like Oregon have begun to completely repeal religious-defense statutes, and members of these groups have been prosecuted for child abuse, child neglect, and murder, among other crimes (Pew Research Center, 2014).

Spirituality and Family Diversity   Much of the research that has been conducted on spirituality and family has explored relationships among traditional, white, hetero-sexual marriages and family constellations. However, much diversity exists among families, and even with how family is defined. Here we will take a look at some of the ways in which spirituality and religiosity may play out in diverse contexts.

For many families of color, religion and spirituality play an important role and are viewed as sources of strength. Institutionalized religion can provide a source of comfort, support, and community for families, particularly those struggling with issues around poverty, violence, displacement, discrimination, and oppression. For many African–American families, for example, religion can be a protective factor for teens, helping them avoid mental, emotional, physical, academic, and other prob-lems associated with discriminatory environmental contexts that come with many barriers to success and well-being (McBride, 2013). As is the case for many families, among other benefits, religion for many African–American families provides a sense of community; reduces risky behaviors; promotes self-esteem, self-regulation, and academic achievement among youth; increases social support, life satisfaction, family satisfaction, and mental and physical health; and buffers families from the effects of racism and discrimination (Abar, Cater, & Winsler, 2009; Goldston *et al.*, 2008; King, Burgess, Akinyela, Counts-Spriggs, & Parker, 2006; Pearce & Hayne, 2004).

For Latino families, religiosity and spirituality may play similar roles as well as provide support, comfort, and community for immigrating families who may find themselves with few resources as they move to new locations (Caplan *et al.*, 2013). Conversely, religion may prove to be a barrier to some, like female-headed Hispanic families, who may be faced with patriarchal beliefs and practices that keep women in oppressive, gender-stereotyped roles that afford few economic and other opportunities to support their families (Carneiro, 2013).

Religiosity and spirituality also play different roles for the many different family forms that have become increasingly prevalent over the past several decades. Today more than ever, we see diverse definitions of family and diverse family structures. For example, we have seen increases in blended families; cohabiting couples with and without children; single-parent and grandparent-headed families; gay, lesbian, bisexual, and transgender families, with and without children; and extended, chosen, and kinship families (Child Trends, 2013). Other alternative families include polyamorous, polygamous, and other family arrangements that might be considered deviant in mainstream society. People's values, beliefs, rituals, practices, and traditions all impact the functioning and well-being of these different family forms and dynamics. In some ways, religiosity and spirituality can be supports for families who may face discrimination, persecution, or lack of resources and community. In other ways, religiosity and spirituality may create barriers for people who want to form alternative families. These families may face intolerance or persecution from their communities, or individuals may experience spiritual or existential crises as they form families that deviate from socially acceptable family structures and traditions. Given the changing landscape around families and definition of family, it is important for social workers to explore with clients their definitions of family, their religious and spiritual experiences and values, and how these can either support or hinder their efforts to develop and maintain a family they feel is best for them.

Applying Family Perspectives on Spirituality

For Imani's family, religion seems to have provided many rules and roles for the system, which has maintained their homeostasis as a family. Imani is beginning to challenge many of these rules and roles, and the family is receiving input from Imani's physician about health care issues and treatments that go against the family's beliefs, which are disrupting the family's homeostasis. The family must either adapt to these changes and find a new level of functioning that incorporates new ideas and perspectives, or the family will be threatened with entropy, perhaps resulting in Imani being estranged or disowned by the family or her choosing to leave the family and religion.

The social worker could help Imani and possibly even her family to explore some of these dynamics and adapt to the changes that are occurring so that the family does not disintegrate.

Spirituality in the Workplace

Until recently, religiosity and spirituality have been kept separate from the workplace. However, this separation increasingly is being called into question given research suggesting that incorporating workers' spirituality into their work can help increase integrity, motivation, creativity, productivity, commitment, job satisfaction, and ethical practices (Alford & Naughton, 2001; Garcia-Zamor, 2003; Milliman, Czaplewski, & Ferguson, 2003; Mitroff & Denton, 1999). This is particularly relevant in contexts such as human service organizations, where high job turnover rates, low salaries, large caseloads, and resulting stress and declines in job satisfaction are often problematic (Hong, 2011).

What does spirituality in the workplace mean? Mitroff and Denton (1999) surveyed close to 200 U.S. executives in different businesses and organizations to explore how they defined spirituality in this context. Common descriptions from respondents indicated that spirituality was something experienced both within and outside of formal religions, and that included a personal experience of the sacred and connectedness to others inside and outside of the workplace. To the respondents, spirituality encompassed feelings of meaning and purpose in life that are universal, inclusive, and not formally organized. In the workplace, then, spirituality could be applied loosely to focus on employees' well-being, work-life balance, and opportunities to reflect on the meaning of one's work as well as to recharge and reconnect with others. It provides an opportunity to help employees grow and attend to the whole person: the mental, physical, emotional, and social aspects of employees' lives (Milliman, Ferguson, Trickett, & Condemi, 1999).

Some scholars and professionals are calling for new management models that move from the traditional hierarchical, scientific, bureaucratic models that emphasize rational, logical, financially driven processes to models that are more sensitive and responsive to spiritual aspects of workers and the workplace. An increase in awareness of spirituality, separate from religion, has propelled this movement the past few decades (Hong, 2011). The **Spiritual Sensitive Organizational Practice Model** is one such model that recognizes spirituality as one facet of human behavior, and it emphasizes the purposeful and meaningful aspects that people derive from work and the work context. This model posits that finding meaning in their work can empower workers and help to increase motivation, commitment, and interconnectedness with the workplace and the people they serve. This model also gives us a way to view organizations and their clientele in more holistic ways, particularly with regard to how they are connected to the community and larger environment, which is akin to the person-in-environment stance valued by the social work profession. Thus, by including the spiritual dimension in management and organizational styles, organizations and workers are viewed as interconnected teams, and social relationships and the ties to larger social environments are valued, as is the diversity of the employees who make up the organizations and the clientele they serve (Ashmos & Duchon, 2000; Hicks, 2003).

Utilizing concepts from this model and from the general emerging thought around spirituality can help to transform organizations and their employees to create healthier, more sustainable workplaces. For instance, the inclusion of spiritually based concepts could transform organizational leadership, mission, and vision. Such inclusion could also empower organizations to more fully embrace compassion and emotional facets of employees and their work as well as promote mindfulness of everyday functions to help workers find meaning in even mundane tasks. And, situations involving conflict can be approached in such a way where there are no "losers." Rather, a supportive, team-based approach can be employed that is rooted in trust and collaboration so that the needs of all employees are met (Hong, 2011).

Increasingly, organizations are incorporating these ideas of spirituality into their practices. Some examples include Tom's of Maine, Ben and Jerry's, and The Body Shop (Bygrave & Macmillan, 2008). And, as was mentioned earlier, many are calling for transformations of human service organizations, especially because of the issues workers often face. Thus, more than ever, new models of management and operations are needed to help workers get in touch with the meaning of their work and ways to care for themselves in doing it. Because of the profession's values and focus on person-in-environment, social workers are well poised to be leaders in this type of organizational change.

SPIRITUALITY AND THE LARGER SOCIAL ENVIRONMENT

As we have discussed, the role of spirituality in society has been increasing. Since the 1990s the United States has seen a resurgence of the debate about separation of religion from secular society and the importance of religious pluralism in mainstream society and its institutions. With this has come a renewed focus on spirituality and tolerance for different worldviews and the ways they play out in everyday life (Wilcox, 2012). Globally, the trend seems to be moving toward religious and spiritual diversification from new forms of fundamentalism to spiritual movements that do not adhere to specific religious beliefs (Barker, 2008). We find more people who see themselves as landing in the middle of religious and secular—what has been referred to as "fuzzy fidelity" (Storm, 2009). In this section, we will examine how spirituality and religiosity play out in larger social contexts given the movement toward spiritual and religious diversification and how this interaction affects the social work profession.

Religious Patterns and Affiliations

Throughout the world, we see religion and spirituality organized and practiced in many different ways. Some countries have state religions—religions officially endorsed by the state; examples include Argentina (Roman Catholicism), Greece (Church of Greece, part of the Eastern Orthodox communion), Norway (Church of Norway, an Evangelical Lutheran denomination), Iran (Shi'a Islam), Saudi Arabia (Sunni Islam), and Cambodia (Buddhism). Although the United States does not have a state religion, it does have a civil religion, as do many other countries. **Civil religion**, a term proposed by the 18th-century French philosopher Jean-Jacques Rousseau, is defined as a society's moral and spiritual foundation that is expressed through collective beliefs, symbols, and rituals (Bellah, 1967). The language used in civil religion may differ from religious points of view, but it plays an integrative role for political order and gives the nation its identity. While civil religion plays out differently for different countries, Bellah (1967) argues that in the United States, civil religion is a self-understanding based in the country's unique history, achievements, symbols, imagery, and narratives. For example, civil religion is practiced every time we sing the national anthem or raise the flag.

The extent to which countries separate church and state differs, as does the extent to which religion plays a role in politics and other aspects of social life. The United States, for instance, embraces religious plurality and separation of church and state. However, we see religious language, symbols, and rituals, both civil and sacred, enter into many state functions. Local and federal governments support religion through tax and other policies, publicly supported chaplains, and prayer and other rituals at public functions such as inaugurations of elected officials. And, most Americans support the inclusion of religion in these ways and feel it would be unpatriotic to attack religion or disallow it in our national identity (Thio, 2000). Compared with other countries, the United States tends to be more religious, and religious views tend to permeate all aspects of public life (Macionis, 2014).

Globally, faith and religious affiliation differ by ethnicity and nationality. In the United States, we can see religious ethnic segregation, which is rooted in the culture of different groups. For example, Latinos are likely to be Catholic, African–Americans are likely to belong to black Baptist or African Methodist Episcopal churches, and many from Southeast Asia identify as Buddhist (Pew Forum on Religion & Public Life, 2013). Worldwide, church attendance has fallen over the past several decades while the number of people who identify as spiritual has grown. This is more of a shift away from experiences that are more organized and traditional to experiences that are more personal and individualized. And in the United States, there is a great deal of interface between the religious and the spiritual (Ammerman, 2013). Indeed, research suggests that for people in the United States, those who identify as strongly spiritual are also those who are most religiously active (Chaves, 2011; Marler & Hadaway, 2002).

Religious and Spiritual Social Movements and Conflict

Globalization and the changing ethnic and cultural landscape of the United States have meant shifts in spirituality and religiosity and the ways in which people define themselves in these realms. Through immigration and trends in changing demographics, the United States alone has seen increases in the numbers of different ethnic groups, including Asians and Latinos (Bhaskar, Arenas-Germosen, & Dick, 2010). Not only large cities such as Los Angeles, but also smaller communities around the country are home to diverse groups of people, with hundreds of different languages spoken. This demographic diversity includes religious and spiritual diversity. Millions of people identify as Catholic, Jewish, Buddhist, Hindu, Islamic, Sikh, Baptist, Lutheran, Episcopal, and Mormon, to name just a few. And within organized religions such as these, there are many sects and splinter groups that form in response to disagreements over church doctrine (ARDA, 2010).

The diversification of the United States has seen the rise of movements and organizations such as the megachurch, New Age spirituality, Eastern religions, individually defined spirituality, and new, single-ethnic churches. Many of these movements have infiltrated public and personal life (Land, 2015). Some of these movements are economically and politically powerful, impacting public policy and laws. As an example, Hobby Lobby, a crafts retail company owned by an Evangelical Christian family, won a court case (*Sebelius v. Hobby Lobby Stores Inc.*) against the Affordable Care Act's mandate that companies provide prescription drug coverage to their employees as part of the health insurance plan. Specifically, the owners of Hobby Lobby argued that providing contraceptives went against their religious beliefs (The American Prospect, 2014).

Sometimes, influential religious and spiritual movements can have far-reaching, sometimes devastating consequences in the form of large-scale collective violence. Take, for example, the "Jonestown massacre" of 1978 in which more than 900 members of the Peoples Temple, led by a self-styled faith healer named Jim Jones, committed suicide under his direction. This event, a culmination of a social movement from the 1950s to the 1980s, took place in a settlement in Guyana, South America, after Jones moved over 1,000 of his followers to the area in response to increasing U.S. government scrutiny (J. R. Hall, 2004). Another example is the Bhagwan Shree Rajneesh (later known as Osho) cult whose followers poisoned salad bars in public restaurants in Oregon in 1984, sickening more than 750. This group also bussed hundreds of homeless individuals into their Oregon community in an unsuccessful attempt to alter county elections (Goldman, 2009).

Changing religious and spiritual realms also can bring with it tension and conflict, particularly when they interface with human rights. Areas such as Israel, Ireland, and the Middle East experience a particularly complex dynamic interplay of religion, culture, and politics, which have implications for human rights and well-being. Often there are tensions between the values of religion and human rights, particularly in areas where religion plays a central role. The emergence of spirituality in the public sphere serves to complicate this relationship for communities where religion is prominent, creating the need to redefine political identity and human rights where conflict is widespread (Zembylas, 2014).

In these religious settings in particular, there are at least two ways of viewing human rights. One is the incompatibility between human rights and religious beliefs. From this point of view, the rights of vulnerable and oppressed groups such as women and GLBT individuals are violated by religious teachings; thus, religion and human rights need to be viewed and treated separately to keep the influence of religion from human rights issues (Bowie, 2011; Ghanea-Hercock, 2010). Conversely, some religious groups contend that claims of human rights, like the Universal Declaration of Human Rights (United Nations, 1948), do not include any reference to religious doctrine and reflect Western imperialist values (Mills, 1998). And sometimes, diversity and inclusion are not welcome or seen as positive in certain religious communities (Zembylas, 2014). Regardless of the viewpoint, the interface of religious beliefs and human rights, along with the complex cultural, historical, and political contexts of areas where issues occur, have created conflicts that have cost millions of lives and continue to create ethical and other dilemmas that are seemingly unsolvable. Many social workers are involved in these situations worldwide, including professionals who work in the United States, either directly with immigrants from these areas, for example, or who work on global policy or other practice in attempt to impact injustices that occur due to these conflicts.

The Role of Spirituality in Macro Settings

Even as spirituality is increasingly permeating public spaces, some organizations and institutions are not embracing the movement or are slow to respond to the changing landscape of inclusion and diversity. For instance, while several large organizations in the United States like USAID and Catholic Relief Services have policies that address issues around gender, violence against women, and the environment, they do not have policies directly addressing issues around religiosity and spirituality. Nor are organizations like the World Bank and the United Nations providing any direction on such policies for other organizations. A lack of policy on such issues in a world where the landscape is changing can cause problems for workers and communities. Many of these organizations are becoming increasingly aware of the importance of providing policies and guidance on the interface of religion and spirituality in the workforce and global development, but changes are slow (Lunn, 2009).

The interplay of religion and spirituality can be seen in non-governmental organizations (NGOs) and religious organizations (ROs), also known as faith-based organizations. Aspects of spirituality have increasingly been incorporated in NGOs, and for decades, NGOs have been addressing some of the world's most pressing problems, like poverty. ROs increasingly have filled in gaps for social and health services where governmental and NGOs have fallen short, particularly in areas where communities are in significant need, whether as a result of natural disasters, war and civil unrest, or endemic poverty. ROs provide significant domestic and international relief and development efforts through the use of social capital, exposing members to the needs of others and recruiting members to contribute financially and provide resources and labor. Religious groups also have the power to inspire and motivate large numbers of people to act (Mylek & Nel, 2010). ROs are able to provide community support, but their operations are not without criticism. Some view ROs as having hidden religious or proselytizing agendas, from which they attempt to manipulate or oppress others, which can undermine their legitimacy. For example, the history of many faith-based charities is viewed with skepticism, as Christians felt it was their duty to civilize seemingly "uncivilized" individuals (Lunn, 2009; Mylek & Nel, 2010).

Spirituality and Politics   Earlier we discussed state religion, civil religion, and the plurality of religion as they help shape national identity and promote political order. Much attention has been given to how religion affects political processes and the relationship between law and religion, particularly with the growth of religious plurality in nations like the United States and as other nations—like Iraq, Afghanistan, Cambodia, Nepal, and Timor-Leste (East Timor)—attempt to develop new constitutions (Berger, 2011). We see debates continue about whether or not religious symbols like the Ten Commandments can be displayed in public spaces; how strongly individual religious beliefs impact legislators' political behavior; and whether religious beliefs can be trumped by law. Questions such as these have led to numerous court cases in the United States and other countries.

In the United States, there is no constitutional requirement that any person should adhere to particular religious beliefs to hold a political office. However, as late as 1961, eight Southern states had provisions in their state constitutions that required political candidates to believe in God. The Supreme Court subsequently struck down these provisions (Boston, 2010). Since then, we have seen leaders like John F. Kennedy, the country's first Roman Catholic president, be challenged on religious beliefs (Garnett, 2008). In the 2008 and 2012 presidential elections, debates included questions on candidates' religious beliefs. Indeed, many Americans believed that Barack Obama was Muslim, and many wondered about Mitt Romney's Mormon background.

Particularly in the United States, it is evident that religion and spirituality impact the political sphere and, subsequently, our policies and laws. It is in this interface between religion and politics that many social workers find themselves becoming involved to protect the rights of individuals and communities and to ensure access to social and health care services. Social workers play a role on the macro level by influencing policy and lawmakers to ensure that individual beliefs do not impede the rights of others. For example, we discussed earlier the situation of Hobby Lobby and the company's argument that given the owners' beliefs, they should not have to provide health care coverage for contraceptives. Many other companies worldwide make the same argument, and this stance affects the lives and well-being of millions of women who must pay out of pocket for contraceptives and other services. Another realm this intersection of religion and politics has impacted is access to abortion and other reproductive health care services. Many states have enacted extremely restrictive laws that make it all but impossible for women to access safe abortions. Women in these states must adhere to long waiting periods or travel hundreds of miles, often to neighboring states, to access abortion. These laws can be prohibitive for many women, particularly poor women, disenfranchising them from receiving quality health care. Indeed, access to quality reproductive health care is a serious issue for women worldwide, where almost half of the 42 million abortions are performed by unskilled practitioners because of restrictive laws, putting women at risk for health problems and death (IPAS, 2009). We see religious views impact other social policy areas like physician-assisted suicide and even liquor laws.

Social workers, like the nation in general, have diverse religious beliefs that impact their views on issues like these. While the profession's Code of Ethics and policy statements like Social Work Speaks (National Association of Social Workers, 2012) guide social workers' practice in areas such as these, many social workers still struggle with their own values and how to proceed with clients in situations where values may clash. This is one reason why it is so important for social workers to explore their own values and beliefs before they encounter situations like these so they can be aware of their own biases and how these biases may affect the clients and communities with which they work. Regardless of individual beliefs and views on difficult social issues, social workers can be prepared to be leaders in social and policy change, to ensure the rights of all individuals.

Ecological Consciousness A new field of thought is related to religious environmentalism, brought about by culturally diverse environmental ethics and questions about environmental degradation. Religiosity and spirituality viewed from a connection to the natural environment is yet another way different groups have been responding to ecological issues and climate change. Christianity, Confucianism, indigenous traditions, and Hinduism, for instance, all have long histories of connection to the natural world and a sense of oneness with nature and the world. It may be that religion's roots in nature may be a response to the consumeristic "religion" that has developed over time, replacing respect and stewardship of the earth. Some have argued that religion plays a role in discouraging our drive toward satisfying material needs that are depleting our natural resources. Indeed, faced with environmental crises, many people are revisiting the meaning and purpose of life as well as the earth we live on and our human–Earth relationship. Many argue that spirituality and religiosity may facilitate ethical decision making and contemplation about our interrelationship with and responsibility to nature (Grim, 2011).

Our world is turning to ecological consciousness, requiring commitment and cooperation by all to take responsibility of the environment (Edwards, 2010). This stance is emerging in light of technological and other developments that challenge old, widely held beliefs that God will always provide and "save us from ourselves" as we continue on the path of climate change and depletion of our resources. As we begin to realize the reality of what is happening with climate change, it is becoming increasingly evident that humans must take responsibility for our environment, which begs for a re-visioning of our spiritual relationship with the earth, our purpose on it, and the meaning we construct from our roles (Kaufman, 2001).

Many social workers are employing theories and frameworks such as eco-systems, ecofeminism, ecopsychology, relational cultural theory, and person-in-environment to call attention to climate change, our role in it, and how to be better stewards of the environment. The profession's value base provides a foundation on which to build interventions around environmental and social sustainability and foster the interconnectivity humans have with their environment. This work helps create conditions in which individuals and communities can heal from environmental and social degradation and thrive, becoming self-sufficient and self-sustaining. Social workers can bring in concepts to help empower and promote a deeper awareness of our connection to the earth and each other (Norton, 2012). Much of this is tied to concepts of spirituality and our larger purpose and work on the planet.

Applying Macro Concepts to Spirituality

Imani lives in a rural area where religious beliefs are strong and resources scarce. She is experiencing the interface of religion and politics in her lack of access to contraceptives. The pharmacist in her small town refuses to fill the prescription on the grounds of religious beliefs, yet she is unable to find or access other resources for this medication. Without it, she is left dealing with pain from her endometriosis, and is at risk for a possible pregnancy. How do social workers deal with situations like these, where ethical dilemmas posed by opposing rights, beliefs, and views create problems for individuals and communities? Often, these situations must be viewed from both an individual perspective (e.g., helping Imani find the resources she needs and has a right to, while simultaneously respecting and upholding the beliefs and rights of others who might create barriers to accessing those resources) and a macro perspective (e.g., working toward education, legislation, and policy that would prevent these types of dilemmas from occurring in the first place).

Use of Spirituality in Social Work and Other Professions

What happens when the spiritual and secular realms clash within the organizations where we work? What if this clash impairs the well-being of clients? The increased use of spirituality and similar concepts has raised ethical issues for social workers, law and policy makers, and many people in other professions.

Earlier, we discussed the emergence of spirituality in the National Association of Social Workers' Code of Ethics (National Association of Social Workers, 2008) and the Council on Social Work Education's Educational Policy and Accreditation Standards (Council on Social Work Education, 2015); they both specifically state that social workers need to attend to spiritual and religious diversity and practice competently in these areas. Research on how spirituality is used in the profession indicates that many social workers employ methods to help clients explore their religious and spiritual beliefs, practices, and support systems to determine which may be helpful and which may be harmful, creating barriers to growth and causing conflict in their relationships. However, many social workers feel they do not receive enough instruction on theory and methods of spirituality in their social work programs (Sheridan, 2009; Williams & Smolak, 2007). Further, research indicates that the spiritual and religious beliefs of social workers affect their use of these methods. However, as with general education on such practices, there is insufficient content on ethical dilemmas spirituality practice may bring, such as when values between the social worker and client or organization clash or when the social worker feels underprepared to work with clients on spiritual matters (Canda & Furman, 2010). While the social work profession embraces diversity and client self-determination, many argue that more attention is needed in social work programs on improving students' tolerance and empathy for others' worldviews; exploring students' own beliefs and biases; and building new skills to become effective practitioners in areas of spirituality and religiosity (Hodge & Bushfield, 2006). Journals such as the *Journal of Religion and Spirituality in Social Work* offer research in the field to help guide and educate practitioners, but many argue this content needs more prominence in social work education.

The lack of attention to spirituality in social work education can lead to practitioners feeling disenfranchised from incorporating components of religion and spirituality and unable to competently utilize the theory and tools that do exist in their practice. Further, it can lead to ethical dilemmas in practice that are difficult to manage. These issues extend past the social work profession, where we see ethical issues and conflicts appearing in different contexts. For example, increasingly we have seen situations in the news where pharmacists refuse to dispense contraceptives to customers, even when the medicine is intended for purposes other than birth control, as in Imani's case that opened this chapter. While the situation may seem easily remedied by advising the customer to visit another pharmacy, some people do not have this option. For instance, people living in rural areas or interacting with a pharmacist who refuses to transfer the prescription may not have viable options to access medication. Some people believe pharmacists and other professionals have a right to practice according to their beliefs. Others argue their actions are discriminatory and based on personal beliefs rather than medical or professional advice and should be kept out of the professional realm because they can harm people. And, what happens if social workers support these actions when the Code of Ethics states social workers should support client self-determination? Or when social workers' beliefs conflict with the profession's support of clients' rights to abortion and physician-assisted suicide? What is the role of faith-based organizations in light of human rights? These are all questions and situations that are still playing out in the profession and beyond.

While many professions, like social work, have a Code of Ethics to help guide practice and decision making, decisions made based on personal beliefs is a gray area. State laws regulate many professions, like social work, but these laws can exempt practices based on personal religious beliefs. State laws can be challenged in courts, decisions that further help to shape policy and laws guiding these behaviors (National Women's Law Center, 2012). Further, state licensing boards can regulate behaviors, revoking licenses of practitioners who are found to practice unethically or illegally. Even though these situations can be difficult and complex, it is imperative for social workers to be leaders in the debate to help shape policy and law, and to help guide practitioners' practices in ways that are ethical and inclusive for all parties involved while supporting clients' rights.

CONCLUSION

Many changes are occurring globally, nationally, and even within the social work profession around how we view spirituality and religiosity. These changes affect our personal lives as well as larger environmental contexts with which we interact. With these changes come new opportunities to redefine our personal and social lives in ways that benefit us individually as well as our relationships with others and our natural environment. These changes also create new challenges around conflict, violence, ethical dilemmas, and human rights that can be difficult to solve. The social work profession, with its person-in-environment perspective, is well poised to incorporate concepts of spirituality and religiosity in its work to help support and sustain individuals and communities. Further, social workers can be leaders and change agents when spirituality and religiosity create tension and conflict for people on micro, mezzo, and macro levels.

MAIN POINTS

- Spirituality, religion, religiosity, and faith are all terms that are used to describe our experiences and beliefs around a higher power and how we make meaning from our lives. While these terms are often used interchangeably, they are separate constructs meaning different things to different people.

- The social work profession was founded on Judeo-Christian principles, but it was not until the past several decades that it began to fully incorporate aspects of spirituality into education and practice.

- Many theories and frameworks exist that help us to conceptualize how spirituality develops. Some of these are stage theories, while others offer broader conceptualizations of spirituality development. These can be helpful tools for social workers for assessment and intervention, but they all have limitations that need to be considered.

- Research suggests that spirituality has positive effects on individual health, mental health, and well-being. This is particularly true for diverse and marginalized groups, who may find support and community through spirituality and religiosity. Conversely, religious communities may be a source of stress and conflict for people who do not follow religious norms.

- Functionalist and symbolic interaction theories can help explain how spirituality and religiosity provide structure for our lives as well as how we construct ideas around spirituality and religiosity through our experiences and interactions with others.

- Research suggests that spirituality and religiosity can provide support and other benefits to families, reducing risks for many negative outcomes including conflict, health and mental health issues, parental–child discord, and behavioral problems for children.

- Increasing aspects of spirituality in the workplace includes incorporation of models like the spiritually sensitive organizational model that focuses on workers in a holistic fashion, helping them achieve work–life balance, find meaning in work, and foster a nurturing work environment.

- Globally, we see many different expressions of spirituality and religiosity, from state and civil religions to religious plurality. The extent to which religion impacts public life varies a great deal from one region to another depending on culture, history, politics, and other factors.

- Increased diversification of the world's population has brought many changes to the characteristics of spirituality and religion and the ways in which they are expressed and practiced. While these changes can be positive in many ways, they can also bring tension, conflict, and violence, creating problems and distress for individuals and communities.

- Incorporation of spirituality in the vision and mission of non-government and religious organizations has both helped to support the human service work of these entities as well as brought about debate regarding their roles and religious agendas in working with communities.

- Even in nations like the United States, which value separation of church and state, spirituality and religiosity affect politics, laws, and public policy. The implications of this influence can be far-reaching for individuals and communities, particularly for vulnerable and marginalized populations.

- In response to climate change, social workers and other professionals are incorporating ecological consciousness principles into social work to help emphasize the spiritual connection humans have with each other and the environment to help create sustainable change for communities and the planet.

- Even though the social work profession embraces the role spirituality and religiosity has in our work, many social workers feel underprepared to do this work competently.

EXERCISES

1. *Sanchez family interactive case at* www.routledgesw.com/cases. Review information for each family member and the ways in which family members interact with one another. Using the information in the chapter, answer the following questions:

   a. What information do you have about the spirituality, religiosity, and faith of individual family members? Pick two family members and develop a few open questions for each that could help you explore these areas in more depth.

   b. In what ways might spirituality, religiosity, and faith be creating conflict or barriers for individual family members and their interactions with others as well as providing support and strength? Use systems theory language to help give context to your answers.

   c. Pick a theory or lens to describe spirituality development and apply it to a family member or the family system as a whole. Why might you want to use this particular theory or lens? Why might it be helpful? What might some of the limitations be in applying it?

2. *Carla Washburn interactive case at* www.routledgesw.com/cases. Read about Carla's situation and the interactions she has with others and systems in her area. Then, answer the following questions:

   a. Thinking about how spirituality and religiosity generally affect well-being for African–Americans, how might Carla's well-being be affected, both positively and negatively, by participating in a spiritual or religious practice or community?

   b. What type of assessment might you want to conduct with Carla around spirituality and religiosity, and why? What benefits would be gained for both of you by engaging in this assessment process?

   c. What has been the historic role of spirituality and religiosity for African–Americans, and in what ways do you think this role could help support Carla?

3. *Brickville interactive case at* www.routledgesw.com/cases. Explore the history and current situation of the town and the interaction of its residents. Then, respond to the following questions:

    a. How might the history, culture, and demographic diversity of the town and its members affect the spirituality and religiosity of the residents and how groups interact with one another in the community?

    b. What might be some of the strengths and limitations as well as sources of support, conflict, and problems coming from religiosity given the current state of the community and future plans?

    c. How could you use the information from the last two questions as well as information from the chapter to help the community better utilize faith and religiosity to improve the community as a whole?

4. *Hudson City interactive case* at www.routledgesw.com/cases. Review the situation and issues for Hudson City and its residents. Using information from the chapter, respond to the following:

    a. How might you use concepts around ecological consciousness and its connections to spirituality and religiosity to help the residents find connection and investment in rebuilding their community and finding long-term solutions to its sustainability?

    b. Given the information you have about the city and the situation, in what ways might politics and spirituality interface and influence one another in the rebuilding of the city?

    c. How do you see spirituality and religiosity influencing NGOs and ROs in the city? How could this influence help and hinder the city and its residents?

CHAPTER 15

Families and Groups

The Alexander family lives in a small apartment in an inner-city neighborhood in a medium-sized city. The family consists of a divorced mother, Susan, age 46, and her two daughters, ages eight and 12. The children's father lives in the same city but has limited contact with the family and does not provide consistent financial support. Susan has several other children—three daughters and a son—who are now adults living independently. All of these children except the son live in the same city as Susan. Susan often relies on her older daughters to provide childcare for the younger daughters as well as intermittent financial support for things like food and rent. Susan relies on her brothers for support as well. Susan's neighbors in the apartment next to her often take the daughters out on excursions (e.g., to museums, movies, and the park) to give Susan a break and to give the girls respite from their stressful environment.

The relationship between Susan and her ex-husband, Rich, is very tumultuous. Rich is known for his violent outbursts and criminal behavior, which is often targeted toward Susan. For example, Rich slashed Susan's tires one morning shortly after she got a job as an office assistant at a local hospital. She almost lost that job after the incident because she was late. Susan also has had a long struggle with alcohol and substance use as well as depression, which has caused her to be hospitalized on many occasions, leaving the daughters to live temporarily with their older siblings or Susan's brothers. Susan has few marketable skills and has trouble maintaining even low-paying jobs because of Rich's hostile actions and her own mental health and substance use issues. Susan's 12-year-old daughter has been showing symptoms of depression, manifested in increasing withdrawal from others as well as academic problems. Susan's eight-year-old daughter often takes on the mother role when Susan is unable to parent or take care of household chores like cooking and cleaning. The youngest daughter also often cares for Susan, who spends a lot of time in bed sleeping. The two daughters also argue frequently and have many conflicts.

Susan has sought help from a social worker to apply for housing, food, and mental health assistance. She also is interested in getting help from the state to collect overdue child support payments from Rich. Susan is concerned, however, that Rich will become more violent if the social worker contacts him about these payments.

SOCIAL WORKERS HAVE A GREAT DEAL OF CONTACT WITH FAMILIES and groups in practice. Even when social workers consider themselves micro or individual practitioners, they are extremely likely to have interface with individuals who have families and who are involved in groups. Some social workers prefer to practice on the mezzo level, working only with family and group systems. In this chapter, we will explore conceptualizations, issues, and work with families and groups. In the first section, we will take a look at families and the many facets of family definitions, dynamics, diversity, and ways to conceptualize and work with them. In the second section, we will explore different conceptualizations and types of groups and ways in which group process and group work can be facilitated.

WHAT IS FAMILY?

Increasingly, in industrialized countries like the United States, the definition of family and what constitutes family is changing and becoming more diverse and fluid. And, the definition differs by culture and context (Coontz, 2008). Because of this, pinning down an exact, agreed-upon definition is difficult. Here we will explore the definition of family and then look at the changing structures of families.

Definition of Family

For some, like many in the Western world, family means a nuclear group of blood-related kin. For others, for example many African–Americans, family might include an extended, informal network of people. Still for other groups like Asian Americans, family might include all ancestors and descendants (Hines, Preto, McGoldrick, Almeida, & Weltman, 1999). The U.S. Census Bureau defines family as a group of two or more people who reside together and are related by birth, adoption, or marriage (United States Census Bureau, 2013). From a sociological perspective, family formations are a way to organize groups of individuals into larger systems and subsystems that have their own functional integrity and purpose (Grotevant, 1989). This last definition is close to a systems theory perspective on family, where the family could be considered an entity consisting of interdependent parts that make an organized whole (Bertalanffy, 1972). A related term, **kinship**, is defined as family units with two heteronormative biological parents (Stone, 2001). Indeed, the term *family* is historically a blending of the ideas of household and kin, where people share genetic links. Some argue that families are groups that include adults who care for the young. According to this definition, a cohabiting couple without children, or an adult child caring for an older parent, would not be considered a family (Archard, 2012). However, this last definition, like many, is imprecise and open to interpretation.

Views on family and related definitions of family are important because they have moral, legal, economic, and social consequences (McGoldrick, Carter,

& Garcia-Preto, 2011). For instance, definitions of family dictate who can marry; who can adopt; and who gets custody of children in cases of death, divorce, or even through artificial reproductive procedures. Within Western culture and thinking, family and kinship are traditionally associated with biological ties that include marriage and a bond between biological parents and children, a tradition reflected in some of the definitions given above (Strathern, 1992). Changing family structures, which we will discuss below, as well as court cases deciding on reproductive, child custody, and other familial issues, are challenging traditional views and definitions of family (Holtzman, 2006) and paving the way for increased acknowledgment of family pluralism. Further, research in kinship has begun to reflect the changing nature of families (Stone, 2001). Feminism, gay and lesbian studies, and advances in reproductive technologies are driving this new direction of research (Butler, 2002). We are seeing more discussion and focus on the complexity of family and kinship relationships with others not included in traditional definitions of family. Rather, there is growing attention to biological and social kinship, parenting, and construction of family (Hicks, 2011; Smart, 2009).

Diversity of Family Formations

Over the past several decades, family structures have experienced dramatic changes due to processes such as industrialization, urbanization, and globalization. Shifts and changes in fertility patterns, delayed marriage, acceptance of divorce, legal sanction of same-sex and other family arrangements, and marriage for the purpose of companionship rather than to transfer property or have children have all affected how we view families (Thornton, 2010). Consequently, we see a great deal of diversity in the way family is conceptualized and formed.

Social workers increasingly interact and work with individuals who are members of families with diverse characteristics. Though many of these families can enjoy support and strengths that come from the family system, often members of these families face unique barriers and struggles due to the nature of the family system and how it interfaces with social systems and larger culture. Social workers need to be aware of these strengths and barriers to help families gain access to resources, support, and social and legal acceptance that can support and maintain family systems. Families form in many different ways; some of the ones more commonly encountered by social workers include single-parent families, by choice or through separation or divorce; two-parent families with heterosexual or GLBT parent couples; cohabiting couples with or without children; blended and adoptive families; grandparent- or sibling-headed families; extended and multigenerational families; chosen families including friendship networks and communal living; and polyamorous and polygamous families. We will take a look at some of the specific issues these families face later in the chapter.

With increasing diversity of family definitions and formations, where is the traditional family headed? What is its fate? One likely path is the continued diversification of families, with the separation of biological and social roles and how these shape different family configurations. It will become more important than ever for social workers to become leaders in ensuring the legal and social acceptance of this diversity to secure rights, resources, and support for their members.

How social workers understand diverse families and approach work with them depends on the theoretical and conceptual lenses through which social workers view families, the unique circumstances and experiences of family members and the families as systems, and the environmental context in which families live. We will explore theoretical and other perspectives that help us understand families in the next section as well as unique issues that diverse families face, but first let us take a look at ways in which the Alexander family formation differs from the traditional definition of family.

Applying Definitions of Family

How might we define the Alexander family? Susan is a divorced mother, with two children living with her, and she has frequent contact with her adult children. In many ways, Susan and her two children rely on other family members as well as neighbors for financial and other support. So, Susan has created networks outside of her nuclear family to help her meet her needs. Certainly, Susan's adult children would be considered family, but her connection with and reliance on her brothers and neighbors might warrant viewing these people as also being part of Susan's close family.

CONCEPTUALIZATIONS OF FAMILY

Many theories and models can be employed to help conceptualize families, the concerns they might bring to social workers, and approaches to work with issues. The approach you use to conceptualize families will guide the type of assessment and therapeutic intervention you use to work with families.

Family therapy is perhaps the most common route through which social workers interface with families. Family therapy gained increased attention by researchers and practitioners after World War II when families were reunited and significant familial discord emerged. Further, more than at any other time, people had unprecedented access to therapy. Professionals from different fields like Psychiatry, Psychology, and Social Work began to specialize in family therapy, and various theories and models to conceptualize family problems and work with families burgeoned (Goldenberg & Goldenberg, 2013). As a result, it was important for the social work field to grapple with issues of conceptualizing family.

Exhibit 15.1 displays several broad theoretical frameworks for family work along with some examples of the specific models and therapeutic approaches that flow from these frameworks. A few of these theories and models are discussed in

Psychodynamic Perspectives	Object relations theory	**EXHIBIT 15.1**
	Self-psychology	*Theoretical*
	Adlerian family therapy	*Perspectives*
	Relational psychoanalytic theory	*and Models to*
	Attachment and Neurobiology	*Conceptualize*
Transgenerational Perspectives	Bowen's family systems theory	*Families*
	Contextual therapy	
	Family life cycle stage model	
Experiential Perspectives	Symbolic experiential family therapy	
	Gestalt family therapy	
	Human validation process model	
	Emotionally focused therapy	
Structural Perspectives	Structural family therapy	
Strategic Perspectives	Mental Research Institute (MRI) interactional and brief family therapy	
	Strategic and systemic family therapy	
Behavioral and Cognitive Perspectives	Cognitive Behavioral therapy	
	Functional family therapy	
	Integrative couples therapy	
Constructionist Perspectives	Postmodern therapies	
	Social constructionist therapies	
	Solution-focused brief therapy	
	Collaborative and narrative therapies	
	Feminist therapies	

more detail in the core HBSE text in Chapters 3, 4, and 12. Below, we will examine more thoroughly several of the well-known theories used in family work.

Psychodynamic Perspectives on Family

Freud's psychodynamic theory (Freud, 1909) is discussed in Chapter 3 of the core HBSE text, and it has had some influence on family work. Concepts of transference, countertransference, defense mechanisms, and unconscious drives can be used to think about individual members and how they impact the family system (Scharff & Schraff, 1991). Freud's work, as well as work of other psychodynamic-oriented therapists, influenced the development of other theories like object relations theory (Klein, 1932) and Adlerian Theory (Adler, 1925), which are both utilized in family work. Object relations theory views infants' relationships with primary caregivers as the main determinant of personality development, and considers the attachments infants develop with caregivers to be of prime importance to the development of a sense of self (more on attachment theory is discussed below) (Scharff & Scharff, 1992). According to objection relations theory, the way we relate to others as adults is based in our attachment experiences as children (Nichols, 1987). In marital or family therapy, these ideas are used to assess how individual family members or couples bring personal histories of attachment into their relationships. This is particularly relevant for couples, who, according to this theory, recreate their parent–child relationships with significant others (Meissner, 1978) and pass along dysfunction to their children and other family members.

Alfred Adler, who helped develop psychoanalytic theory, deviated from some of Freud's initial ideas on sexual nature and its effect on development, instead emphasizing social relationships and their importance in human motivation. In Adler's view, children look to family relationships for feelings of significance, belonging, and competence. When we feel encouraged and capable, we will feel connected and behave in ways that facilitate positive relationships. When we feel discouraged, we may behave in negative ways by withdrawing, competing, or giving up. In Adlerian family therapy, a main goal is to understand children's motivations for belonging and significance and focus on repetitive, negative patterns that families display (Bitter, 2014). Many parenting books use Adlerian theory to help parents better understand children's motivation for disruptive behavior (e.g., when children feel discouraged or incompetent, they often act out) and to use methods that increase children's sense of belonging and competence.

In Chapter 7 of the original HBSE text, we look at attachment theory and how attachment can affect infant development and parent–child interactions. Concepts around attachment are also used to help conceptualize families and relationships among members. Recall that attachment refers to the bond or relationship between infants and their caregivers, particularly the mother (Bowlby, 1969), and Mary Ainsworth's research led to a description of attachment styles (Ainsworth, 1979). According to attachment theory and subsequent research, there are multidirectional interactions such that (a) caregivers' attachment styles affect infants' attachment styles, (b) infants' attachment styles and attachment to caregivers affect infants' future behavior and relationships, and (c) attachment styles are passed on from caregiver to infant (Main, Goldwyn, & Hesse, 2003; McElwain, Booth-LaForce, Lansford, Wu, & Dyer, 2008). Attachment theory and research can be used to help social workers and families think about how attachment styles impact relationships among members (e.g., between partners or caregiver and child), which can be used in couples and family therapy.

Similarly, in Chapter 3 of the core HBSE text, we describe advances in behavioral neuroscience. Research in neurological aspects of human behavior augments theories like attachment and object relations by showing how hyperactivation of the hypothalamic-pituitary adrenal axis can lead to hyperaroused states, negatively impacting interactions and relationships between family members. This research indicates that hyperaroused neurological conditions account for stressful family dynamics and negative social-emotional cuing in relationships (Schore, 2003). Therapeutic intervention can help family members attend to states of arousal and verbal and nonverbal communication to help improve interactions with family members (Goldstein & Thau, 2004).

Transgenerational Perspectives on Family

In Chapter 2 of the core HBSE text, we discussed systems theory in some detail and showed how concepts from this theory could be used to look at families using tools like genograms and ecomaps. Here, we will take a look at Bowen's family systems theory (1976), which shares broad concepts with systems theory. With his work on family systems, Murray Bowen is credited with providing the foundation on which subsequent theoretical and therapeutic concepts in family work are built.

Bowen's Family Systems Theory   Bowen's family systems theory considers family as an emotional unit with a network of relationships that are viewed from a multigenerational perspective. The nature of parent–child and sibling relationships is important in this theory, as they are considered to contribute to family problems. Family members often form alliances, creating what is known as triangulation, which can impact communication and the nature of relationships between family members. For example, if two parents fight, one parent might bring in an adult child with whom to complain or confide. Or, the third member can become the person who is projected upon to help stabilize the dyad. For example, a mother and son may unite in a perspective on an issue, and the daughter in the triad may be viewed by the other two members as rigid, immature, or irresponsible because she doesn't share that view. This helps strengthen the dyad between the mother and son as they unite against the daughter. It also serves to thwart the son's efforts to differentiate from his mother. Also important is the idea that problems can occur when family members become enmeshed or have a difficult time differentiating themselves from one other. These ideas are among the eight concepts or "forces" central to Bowen's theory that are thought to shape family functioning. These forces, along with their descriptions, are summarized in Exhibit 15.2.

According to Bowen's theory, family functioning lies on a continuum, and optimal family functioning occurs when members can successfully differentiate, regulate emotions, and maintain supportive relationships with one another. Optimal family functioning has characteristics including:

- balanced time spent together,
- allowance for both emotional closeness and separateness and for both individual and familial ownership of emotions,
- connectedness across generations,

EXHIBIT 15.2

The Eight Forces that Shape Family Functioning

FORCE	DESCRIPTION
Differentiation of self	This refers to the ability of family members to separate feelings from thoughts. When family members have successfully done this, they are able to define themselves separately from the family's process. They have opinions and values of their own while still remaining connected to the family. Otherwise, family members may have difficulty separating their own feelings from those of the family and look to the family to define how they think and feel.
Triangles	These are the basic units of systems in the family. Dyads in systems (e.g., two parents) are often unstable units as they vacillate between closeness and distance. Often a third party is brought in to help temper intense emotions. Members who are undifferentiated often triangulate to cope with difficult emotions or situations.
Nuclear family emotional system	These systems are the emotional patterns or processes of families that persist over generations. Often families pass on emotional views of the world and behavioral patterns from one generation to the next.
Family projection process	This is an extension of the family emotional system and refers to family members who serve as "screens" onto which the family projects the family's narrative or the family's problems. Often, it is a third member of a triangulated unit that becomes the screen to strengthen the bond between members of the original dyad.
Emotional cutoff	This is an extreme response to the projection process and refers to a member who has complete or almost complete separation from the family. While the person who is cut off may seem completely independent from the family, she or he will be more likely to repeat the family emotional system in her or his life and relationships.
Multigenerational transmission process	This refers to the way the family emotional system is transferred, maintained, and reinforced over generations.
Sibling position	Each child in a family has a place in the hierarchy and fits certain family projections and established roles (e.g., the oldest may be the "responsible" one). These projections help to draw people into dyads and triads to reinforce projected behaviors (e.g., the youngest sibling might be attracted to a partner who was also a youngest sibling).
Societal regression	This refers to the social expectations about SES, race, gender, sexual orientation, and other characteristics, the behaviors associated with them, and their impact on family functioning. Depending on a family's situation, they pass on behaviors that help them cope or succeed in society. For example, a family that dealt with discrimination may pass on coping behaviors to their children and future generations.

- little to no triangulation,

- supportiveness of differentiation,

- awareness of influences and pressure from society, and

- allowance of individual growth through experiences of pain and joy.

Families who are "disordered" or dysfunctional often experience emotional fusion and high anxiety. There is little differentiation of individual family members, and usually one member is targeted as the person who absorbs the tension and anxiety of the family. Problems may be passed down vertically, that is from parent to child, or horizontally, meaning that problems are caused by environmental factors or stressors such as trauma, discrimination, or problematic situations outside of a family's control. Therapeutic intervention is utilized to help families move from dysfunctional patterns to more functional ones by focusing on relationships, behaviors, and societal pressures that contribute to problematic individual and generational interactions.

Family Life Cycle Stage Model   Though families operate through interactive processes that are not necessarily linear, we can still view many of these processes as occurring in linear dimensions of time. From a life cycle stage model, families go through transitions of change as well as periods of stability that are affected by intergenerational transactions. These transitions occur in stages that, in concert with outside influences, often define and reorganize family systems and functioning. For example, families have boundaries, members have roles, and there are expectations for life events to occur at certain times. Parents may have to cope with children leaving the home or caring for aging parents. As these expected events occur, family members must change and adapt to new roles and bring the family to a new state of functioning. This is very similar to concepts discussed in Chapter 2 of the core HBSE text on systems theory. From a family life cycle stage model, though, we view families from the perspective of the milestones and events that happen, the issues and tasks that must be tackled when these occur, and the ways in which these can affect a family, both positively and negatively (Carter & McGoldrick, 2005).

The family life cycle stage model stresses the positive aspects of families' abilities to pass through stages with resilience, using resources, strengths, and interpersonal relationships to weather familial changes and events that might otherwise throw families into chaos and disarray. Thus, most families, most of the time, are able to deal capably with changes in a way that enables them to grow and become stronger. While this model does not suggest that these stages are easily handled or stress- or conflict-free, it does suggest that most families handle normally expected events in a successfully intact and healthy manner. Sometimes families become stuck between life stages, causing individual, interpersonal, or familial stress and conflict. Social workers and other professionals can help families successfully transition during times of change, especially when families may be struggling with tasks or when extraordinary or unexpected events occur.

The focus of the life cycle stage model is on developmental tasks families must negotiate. **Developmental tasks** are the activities families must undergo to facilitate movement to the next developmental stage. These tasks help to define the roles, norms, and behaviors of families and family members, which change as families move into different stages. Some of these tasks are universal, such as the tasks involved with parenting (e.g., development of the mother–child bond), while some are more culturally or geographically relevant (e.g., development of an independent vs. a communal identity). Let us take a look at some of the common developmental tasks families and individual members often face. During infancy, a child must attach to caregivers and learn skills like language and locomotion to adjust to the environment. New parents often must adjust to a new relationship with the child and partner and to life as caregivers. Sometimes these tasks can cause problems for family members—such as when a child cannot learn skills because of a disability, or when parents cannot agree on parenting approaches or find a new way of relating in their new roles. Other examples would be when adolescents struggle to develop identity and relationships outside of the family unit, or when parents have difficulty adjusting to their child's newly found independence. Still another example might be a family who immigrates to a new country and must deal with not only new cultural expectations about roles, norms, values, and behaviors, but also issues of oppression and discrimination that affect the family and its members.

According to this model, all families go through somewhat predictable (and often unpredictable) stages set within a cultural context. Death, birth, marriage, illness, graduation, leaving home, and other milestones are common events that families experience. Sometimes changes occur because of external forces, like when the family experiences a natural disaster or is displaced by political conflict. Regardless of the cause, the family must deal with and adapt to changes. The ways in which families deal with tasks then get carried over into future tasks, creating patterns of responses and behaviors that tend to get perpetuated throughout the family's life cycle and its subsequent generations (Zilbach, 1989).

Throughout this chapter, we discuss changing definitions of family, external forces that affect family functioning, and the diversity of family formations. All of these influence family life cycle stages and developmental tasks for families. Social workers can utilize this model to help conceptualize the unique developmental tasks of diverse families. Indeed, many theorists have built on this model to be more inclusive of shifting multicultural and multidimensional factors that can impact families (Carter & McGoldrick, 2005).

Experiential Views on the Family

Experiential approaches to family conceptualization and therapy are built upon experiential, humanistic, and existential foundations such as the Satir growth model

(Satir, 1967), Gestalt therapy (Perls, Hefferline, & Goodman, 1973), and person-centered therapy (Rogers, 1951), which is discussed in Chapter 3 of the core HBSE text. These approaches focus on the emotional aspects of family interactions (Johnson, 2004) and treat individual and family problems as separate. Of primary importance is the meaning that individuals and the family give to experiences. Therapists' use of self, warmth, and empathy are important in this realm of family work (Satir, Banmen, Gerber, & Gomori, 1991). In line with Carl Rogers's and systems work, these approaches assume that family members have an impact on one another, and that they tend toward and have the resources for positive growth. Experiential approaches will assess and work with the family system as well as individual functioning, family dynamics, roles, rules, communication, and life chronology.

Depending on the specific approach, the focus of family work might change slightly. For example, in symbolic experiential family therapy (Whitaker, 1975), the focus is on the emotional process and family structure. Emotionally focused therapy (Johnson & Greenberg, 1985), which is often used for couples, tends to focus on the emotional system of a couple with the goal of restructuring interactional patterns, increasing intimacy, and attending to attachment issues. Gestalt therapy, which is discussed in Chapter 3 of the core HBSE text, can be applied in family therapy to help family members become more authentic with one another and express feelings openly. This is done simultaneously with helping individual members separate and individuate from the family system (Kempler, 1974). Finally, the human validation model (Satir & Bitter, 2000) works to develop families' potential toward wellness by stressing clear, congruent communication; building family members' self-esteem; and fostering expression of honest emotion.

Structural Perspectives on Family

Structural family therapy is rooted in Salvador Minuchin's (1974) work on delinquent boys living in poverty. It focuses on the interaction of family members as a means by which to understand the structure or organization of a family. Attention is given to how family members relate to one another, which provides information about the structure of the family and the problems with which the family is struggling. Individual family members are viewed as living in a social context that is culturally diverse. The goal of therapy from this approach is to affect structural change for the family through active participation by the therapist.

Further work on this approach has contributed to ideas around structural aspects families use to help organize themselves. These structural aspects include **alignment**, which refers to how family members either join with or oppose other members. A second aspect is **force**, or power, which defines members' influence on outcomes. The final aspect is **boundaries**, which offers information about who is involved or not in the family and the roles members take in the family. By helping families modify interactional rules, roles, functions, and boundaries and by supporting the growth of individual family members, therapists can help families achieve structural change and better cope with stress and conflict. Further, this approach stresses the use of community systems like resources and services to help support families in their work (Aponte, 1994).

Strategic Perspectives on Family

Strategic perspectives on family work are based in communication principles and attempt to directly target problematic family behaviors and interrupt interactive patterns that contribute to problems. These approaches are less focused on the history and meaning of problems and more focused on strategies to alleviate them. Indeed, these models are very action-oriented, solution focused, and brief in nature.

Strategic and systemic models originate from the work of the Palo Alto research group and researchers and therapists like Jay Haley, Cloé Madanes, Gregory Bateson, Don Jackson, Paul Watzlawick, and John Weakland. Jay Haley (1963) coined the term *strategic therapy* to describe the work of Milton Erickson, on which much of this work was based. While there are a few main branches of strategic approaches, they share many of the same ideas and principles.

Because of the emphasis on communication in strategic models, attention to what is happening with the ongoing process among family members is important. This includes attending to how people interact; how they define relationships; how communication patterns play out with regard to style, clarity, and the type of information communicated; how family members resolve conflict; and how these interactions affect behavior. Importance is given to family dynamics and how these dynamics influence behavior. Strategic family therapists focus on ways to help families reframe issues to create cognitive shifts that alter perceptions of issues and situations. Therapists offer directives or instructions to family members for ways members can behave differently, sometimes offering a paradox or prescribing the symptom to families. This gives members permission to do something they are already doing to help lower resistance to other suggestions. Other techniques like exaggerating what family members are saying to shed light on problematic thinking, asking members to act out conflict, and helping families to give up troublesome symptoms are other therapeutic tools used in strategic approaches.

Behavioral and Cognitive Approaches to Family

In Chapter 3 of the core HBSE text, we discuss behavioral theories that help explain human behavior. These theories have been used in family work as well. Many behavioral and cognitive approaches are used in family therapy because they are brief and backed by empirical research to demonstrate their effectiveness. These approaches are built upon the work of people like Albert Ellis, B. F. Skinner, Aaron Beck, and Albert Bandura.

The same principles and concepts we see in behaviorism and cognitive approaches can be applied in family work. These include focusing on concepts like conditioning, reinforcers, rewards, punishment, irrational beliefs, cognitive distortions, cognitive schemas, automatic thoughts, mind reading, cognitive distortions, and many others found in these approaches. These models use ideas behind behavior and cognitive processes to assess and intervene with family members in ways that target maladaptive cognitive and behavioral patterns leading to family problems. One popular approach that uses these tools is cognitive behavioral therapy (CBT), where the goal is to assess many of these cognitive and behavioral processes as well as who in the family holds power and control, how parents function as a unit, and how boundaries are functioning in the family. For example, CBT works with family members on cognitive restructuring to identify distorted beliefs, attitudes, and expectations that may be maintaining problematic interactions between family members (Dattilio, 2005). Common cognitive distortions that can cause problems include *mind reading*, in which a family member assumes what another is thinking; and *minimization*, in which a situation is perceived as less important than it really is (Dattilio & Bevilacqua, 2000).

Integrative couples therapy uses behavioral strategies to promote collaborative attitudes among partners that lead to behavior change. This approach helps couples realize that differences in viewpoints are normal and that attempting to change others' behavior is not realistic. The therapeutic goal is to foster tolerance, understanding, and acceptance of perceived negative behavior and emotional states of partners. This helps reduce the amount of blaming partners engage in, and in turn can lead to partners feeling less defensive and more open to change (Jacobson & Christensen, 1996). Finally, functional family therapy is yet another approach that aims to bring about behavioral and cognitive change to family members and family functioning. In addition to incorporating behavioral and cognitive principles and techniques, functional family therapy utilizes learning theory to help families better understand the function their behavior plays in sustaining relationships. From this perspective, all behavior serves a function and should not be labeled as positive or negative. This helps decrease blaming and labeling of family members based on behavior and serves to increase understanding, cooperation, and new perspectives on behavioral patterns that can lead to behavior change (Alexander & Parsons, 1973).

Constructionist Perspectives on Family

Constructionist and postmodern theories and approaches have influenced family work for several decades. In Chapter 4 of the core HBSE textbook, we discuss many sociological theories that can be considered postmodernist or constructionist, including symbolic interactionist and feminist theories, all of which can be applied to conceptualizing families.

Constructionist and postmodernist philosophies, in contrast to modernist thinking, view reality as constructed through language and our interactions with others. According to these approaches, our beliefs about the world and reality are only social inventions—not observable, measurable, objective truth. All of our interactions with others in the world help to construct shared views of reality, and the development of knowledge is a shared, social phenomenon. Thus, constructionist and postmodernist approaches tend to challenge systems thinking (and other modernist approaches) in conceptualizing family.

Rather than looking for problems, dysfunction, and flawed family systems, constructionist and postmodernist theorists and therapists acknowledge that definitions of happy, functioning families stem from objective, socially constructed ideas. Rather, normality comes from those in the family and their perceptions. Thus, postmodernists may eschew existing theoretical perspectives that require family members to conform to particular constructs or DSM-5 diagnoses of family members. Further, a constructionist or postmodernist would look at diverse factors like age, gender, ethnicity, and socioeconomic status as well as interactions with social systems (e.g., school, workplace, social agencies) and the ways in which these factors and interactions affect personal experiences, viewpoints, and worldviews. How these factors affect the therapeutic relationship is also important from a constructionist or postmodern perspective. Therapists do not hold power over families in therapeutic relationships; they work with the family cooperatively to construct new meaning and understanding of the family and its struggles. Families are empowered to share their narratives, make their own choices, and reconstruct their own reality (Doherty, 1991; Parry, 1993).

Several theoretical perspectives and therapeutic approaches for family work have emerged from constructionist and postmodernist thinking. One of these is solution-focused brief therapy (SFBT)—and solution-oriented brief family therapy, an offshoot of SFBT)—which focuses on family change rather than causes of family problems. SFBT does not spend time examining family pathology or dysfunction. Instead, it encourages solution talk, asking family members what needs to happen to bring about change. This approach begins with the expectation that change will occur, families know what to do to create change, and families will be active participants in change (de Shazer, 1991; O'Hanlon, 1993). Motivational interviewing, discussed in Chapter 11 of the core HBSE textbook, is a method often used in solution-focused and solution-oriented approaches to individual and family work.

Other approaches, such as collaborative and narrative therapies, also stem from constructionist and postmodernist perspectives. The collaborative approach focuses on language and communication. It attempts to make family members' thoughts apparent so that members can engage in empathic conversations that will help them create new meaning and resolutions around problems (Gergen, 1985). In this approach, like others from postmodernist perspectives, the therapist and family members are partners in eliciting conversation and reconstructing the meaning behind people's thoughts and experiences. Narrative therapy, which is discussed in Chapter 12 of the core HBSE textbook, is yet another approach that focuses on the stories and narratives of families to help them make sense of their experiences (Kaslow, 2010). This approach uses family members' stories to gain insights into their actions and how they relate to one another; families make their reality through the stories they create about it (Freedman & Combs, 2000). For example, families often create negative, defeating explanations for things that happen in the family and members' behaviors. One goal of therapy using this approach is to help family members reconstruct these stories about their experiences to find alternative perspectives on what is happening in the family.

Feminist Perspectives

In Chapter 4 of the core HBSE textbook, we discuss feminist theory and different branches of feminism. Feminist theory is also used to conceptualize and work with families. While feminist perspectives, depending on their orientation, incorporate aspects of many other theories, feminism can be thought of as a broad perspective from which families can be approached. And, given the many branches of feminism, there is no one single unified feminist family therapy. Nevertheless, feminist approaches do share several assumptions, including:

1. Patriarchy is embedded in our sociopolitical structures.

2. A normal family system is defined from a heteronormative, patriarchal viewpoint.

3. Power structures that reinforce patriarchal views need to be challenged.

4. Families must be redefined in ways that empower women and other vulnerable groups.

5. Therapeutic approaches to family work must consider gender and other issues that call attention to how personal issues become political issues (Avis, 1986; Silverstein & Goodrich, 2003).

From a feminist perspective, current conceptualizations of family tend to pathologize women and keep them in subservient roles. This is done through family narratives and the ways society constructs families through hierarchical and patriarchal lenses. Feminists argue that many of the established theoretical models used for family work only ignore gender and power issues, further maintaining an oppressive narrative. Further, feminists posit that oppressive patriarchal patterns are pervasive and extend across cultures, nations, religions, and history, reinforcing families' narratives of their experiences (Luepnitz, 2002).

Family therapy from a feminist standpoint strives to acknowledge and honor the experiences and perspectives of women in the context of relationships and family life (Goldner, 1985). Important aspects of family work include consciousness-raising about sexism; gender roles and socialization; power imbalances in the family and society; and the devaluation of women's experiences. Pathologizing families is avoided; rather, the expression of psychological symptoms in response to years of oppression is viewed as normal and expected. Feminist family work involves helping families reframe issues in a social context and affirms women's experiences in this context to help empower all family members. As with other post-modernist and constructionist approaches, feminist family work includes helping families to reconstruct narratives about family from a stance free from stereotypes and rigid thinking about gender roles. Feminist theorists and therapists also believe that work must take place beyond the family. To truly change the way families function, societal structures must be transformed, which requires advocacy and education to alter societal values, norms, and narratives about family and patriarchy (Reynolds & Constantine, 2004). This includes exposing the inherent power imbalance that occurs with the patient–therapist relationship. Feminist therapies, therefore, work to provide an egalitarian therapeutic relationship with families that empower members. An egalitarian relationship with the therapist also helps model for family members different ways of structuring relationships.

Applying Conceptualizations of Family

Turning to the Alexander family, there are many ways the social worker could conceptualize the family and the problems they are experiencing. Let us take a look at three of these. One approach would be to look at Susan's nuclear family from a psychodynamic or medical model. In particular, how the family's problems are impacting the children both in terms of biological development and attachment are important factors to consider, as they can have consequences for the children in the future. For example, the environment in which the children are growing, which is marked by stress and poverty, can have lasting effects on the neurological development of the children's brains. Further, the seeming lack of affection and attention given by Susan to the children and the frequent moves the children make to other living arrangements can affect the quality of their attachments to others. This can, in turn, affect their relationships in the future.

Concepts from Bowen's family systems theory could also be applied to the Alexander family. Recall that Bowen's theory views family as an emotional unit with a network of relationships. Susan and her two children could be viewed as that unit, as could her older children, her brothers, and the family's neighbors. The relationship between Susan and her children and the relationship among the children would be important focal points in family work. The social worker could also apply Bowen's eight forces that shape family functioning. For instance, the social worker might want to explore how Susan and her children are able (or not) to differentiate in the context of their current family structure and functioning. It may be that the children especially are unable to form ideas and opinions of their own given the stressful environment or to express their needs. It is likely that the youngest child has been unable to separate her own feelings from her mother's, since this child has taken on so many of the caregiving roles for the family. The social worker may want to look at the nature of the relationships in the family to determine whether triangles have formed among members to help them cope with difficult emotions and situations. For example, an older sibling may be brought into a dyad to help temper conflicts or problems with communication. Given the 12-year-old daughter's withdrawal and academic problems, it could be that she has become the member onto which the family's troubles have been projected. Finally, in looking at societal regression, the social worker might want to attend to how societal expectations about family functioning are affecting the Alexanders. It could be the family has learned to cope in ways that align with the way society views poverty and mental health issues and is passing along these coping strategies to the children. For example, Susan is often ashamed of using her government-issued card to purchase groceries. She has taught her children how to hide its use at the checkout counter in the grocery store.

The social worker could also conceptualize the family through a feminist lens. Susan married at a young age, and she did not complete high school or maintain any kind of employment that would teach her marketable skills. She also never built up credit in her own name through buying a home or car or opening credit card accounts, so when she divorced, she had little to rely on to help support her family. These barriers could be viewed though feminist models to help explain how our patriarchal society sets up and maintains power that is beneficial to men and that oppresses women. Further, the violence that Susan is experiencing with her ex-husband has not resulted in his punishment, even though Susan has called the police on many occasions. She still must fight for custody and financial support, a fight that could put Susan in physical danger. A feminist lens would focus on how the system is creating patriarchal barriers for Susan to gain and maintain her independence and successfully support her family.

DIVERSITY AND FAMILY FUNCTIONING

Even with the many different theoretical perspectives on families, family systems are diverse and complex, and they are situated within broader, even more complex cultural, political, historical, and socioeconomic contexts. These contexts bring with them many diverse characteristics, situations, and issues that affect individual behavior and family systems. Indeed, many of the theories and approaches discussed in the last section have been criticized for their simplistic views on families. Here, we will explore some of the aspects of diversity that can affect the well-being of families and that need to be considered in family work. Many of these aspects, and more, are also discussed in the core HBSE text.

Low-Income Families

For low-income families and families living in poverty, there are many factors that can place added stressors on the family system. For example, poor families tend to disproportionately suffer from poor health (e.g., members with chronic illness or disability), mental health issues, and substance abuse (Jayakody & Stauffer, 2000;

Schiller, 1994). They are also more likely than non-poor families to have more children, lower education levels, little job flexibility, and unemployment or underemployment (e.g., being able to find only part-time work) (Kim, 2009). These aspects can negatively affect individual family members as well as the interactions and relationships between family members. Further, family members may be more prone to negative interactions and relationships with outside systems like school, the workplace, and social service agencies. For example, a low-income parent working at three jobs may have conflicts with her employer if she is late because of childcare issues or has to take time off from work because of family illness. This same parent may have issues with her child's school if she cannot get time off work to attend school functions or parent-teacher conferences. Families with more financial or social resources may be better equipped to deal with family needs that could interfere with work or other situations. Indeed, low-income working mothers are more likely than wealthier working mothers to be viewed as irresponsible by their employers if they take time off to care for family members (Dodson, 2013; Dodson & Luttrell, 2012). And, family dynamics can shift depending on how many wage-earners are in the family and who those wage-earners are (mother, father, single parent, etc.).

Ethnic and Sexual Diversity

Many historical, cultural, political, and structural issues affect ethnic and sexual minority families. Historical and persistent structural racism, for example, is an issue that many families must deal with on a daily basis and that can create chaotic and stressful living conditions for members (Tudge, Mokrova, Hatfield, & Karnik, 2009). Such racism can also lead to social, political, economic, educational, and other disadvantages and disparities for minority group members. These challenges can lead to higher adverse family outcomes such as conflict, divorce, and family dissolution (Cui, Fincham, & Pasely, 2008; Sweeney & Phillips, 2004). Further, cultural, political, and socioeconomic forces often create barriers for ethnic minorities who want to marry and begin and maintain families. For example, among African–Americans, two out of every three will marry, and as many as 70 percent of those who marry will later divorce (Cherlin, 2009).

Lesbian, gay, bisexual, and transgender individuals, couples, and parents can face many struggles in their own families of origin as well as when they desire to begin their own. Discrimination, oppression, rejection, and violence by families and religious and social communities can be devastating. For individuals and couples wanting to marry or begin a family, legal and social barriers can seem insurmountable and can be extremely stressful. Beginning in childhood, many GLBT individuals are faced with heteronormative expectations that affect developmental, interpersonal, and social realms. These experiences often affect individuals' views of families and relationships as they carry with them into their adult lives their interpersonal histories. Some GLBT individuals and couples have internalized messages that they are unworthy or incapable of becoming parents or raising a healthy family. Should an individual or couple choose to begin a family, other obstacles must be faced such as legal issues, societal attitudes, and logistics of having a child (e.g., if couples decide to use reproductive technology, cost and access can be an issue) (Glazer, 2014).

As GLBT individuals age, they often face further obstacles. Older adults who identify as GLBT are more likely than their non-GLBT counterparts to live alone and have no children for support in older age (Blane, 2006). Older adults who do not have adult children tend to have smaller social networks than older adults with children (Dykstra, 2006) and less contact with extended family networks. This situation can put older GLBT adults, especially women and people of color, at higher risk for health, social, financial, and other problems as well as culturally incompetent care if and when they should need it (Orel, 2004).

Divorce, Separation, and Remarriage

When two families join through remarriage, partnering, or other circumstances—forming a blended family—they can face challenges due to the dynamics they create. Blended families bring with them a whole host of unique issues with which social workers need to be familiar. And blended family formations are on the rise. For example, rates of remarriage are increasing, with approximately two-thirds of women and three-fourths of men remarrying, and around 65 percent of these remarriages involve creating blended families from prior marriages and relationships (Adler-Baeder & Higginbotham, 2004; Dupuis, 2007).

Reformation of families can bring issues around rules, roles, norms, subsystems, and boundaries as family members attempt to adjust to new members, ways of communication, and power differences. Adjusting to new relationships with siblings, step-parents, and ex-family members can be challenging, as can adapting to relationships with friends, schools, co-workers, and others outside of the family unit. Further, as families separate and reform, members may experience changes in schools, employment, financial status, and social networks.

These also can be issues for other types of family situations, such as when one parent remarries or re-partners or when both parents remain single after divorce. Each situation is unique to the family, bringing with it varied issues depending on the situation. Further, family members will perceive their situations in unique ways, warranting full exploration of how the issues and situations affect each member.

Cultural, religious, and other outside factors may also exert pressure on blended families. This includes factors like values; beliefs; worldviews; and personal and familial experiences in varied cultural, political, historical, economic, and spiritual contexts.

Other Diversity Considerations

Some of the theories presented earlier address other factors that can affect families: age and aging, ethnicity, communication patterns, gender and gender roles, birth order of siblings, and attachment styles of parent and children. Additional factors that could be important for families' functioning include spirituality, socioeconomic status, family violence, generational issues, and stability of residency (e.g., homelessness, instability in housing, or frequent moves because of military duty or employment). Another important facet to be explored is family resiliency, including the quality of nurturing relationships, established routines, shared expectations, adaptation to challenges, and connection to community (Roehlkepartian & Syvertsen, 2014).

One example of how family situations can create challenges as well as build resiliency is families that cope with illness and disability. Families with children with disabilities, for example, may experience impacts on finances, employment, relationships, parental health and mental health, and recreational and social activities. One in-depth study of 33 families who had members with disabilities suggested that parents felt they spent a great deal of extra time caring for the disabled family member, took on extra roles beyond parenting, and felt that their relationships with other family members and extended groups outside of the family were often compromised. For instance, some parents cited the loss of social and work opportunities and disruption to the household (Whiting, 2014). On the other hand, many families that cope with illness and disability are extremely resourceful and resilient, adapting to changing needs and roles and finding resources and support from within and outside the family system (Hall, Neely-Barnes, Graff, Krcek, & Roberts, 2012).

Other types of family formations can bring unique challenges. Some of these were mentioned earlier, including single, never married, or partnered parents; grandparent-headed families; couples who decide not to or cannot have children; families that add members through adoption or birth; families that have three generations living in one household; families with aging members who need care; and GLBT individuals who join together to form chosen families. What are some of the challenges and opportunities these situations can bring that might need to be considered in family work? How might these families be affected on micro, mezzo, and macro levels? All of the factors mentioned in the previous paragraph could apply to these types of family formations. Some may experience more pressure from culture or their religious or peer communities to conform to certain norms. Or some may find considerable support for their decisions.

Legal Issues and Social Policies

Larger social policies and laws also impact family functioning. Family leave policy; laws around breastfeeding at work and in public; and legal issues surrounding same-sex marriage, child custody, reproductive rights, and other matters involving families are important factors to consider when working with families. Further, emerging reproductive technologies not only impact individual family members, but legal issues surrounding their use are increasingly debated and brought into the courtroom. Technologies like egg freezing (which is now an employee benefit in some companies), sperm harvesting, in vitro fertilization, artificial insemination, and surrogacy all have benefits and drawbacks that can affect families.

ETHICAL CONSIDERATIONS IN FAMILY WORK

In addition to attending to the myriad issues a family may face, there also are many ethical concerns that may arise for social workers, particularly when working with families with children. Some of the most important ethical considerations are related to competence, consent, confidentiality, and competing interests (Koocher, 2008).

Competence

Competence refers to the practitioner's ability to work with families, especially given all of the diverse characteristics and situations that families can bring to the clinical setting. It is important that social workers and other professionals remain aware of the boundaries of their expertise so that when families come with issues outside of that expertise, they can be referred elsewhere. For example, a social worker might have experience working with couples and children, but if a family who seeks help has issues with an aging parent living in the home, the social worker may not be competent to provide services that involve knowledge about gerontology or issues related to aging and family dynamics. Koocher (2008) suggests we view competence on a continuum from beginner to intermediate, and expert, and judge our competence to work with families from that continuum depending on the issues involved.

Consent

When working with families, consent often becomes important because families may include children who are too young to consent to treatment. It is usually a parent, teacher, or some third party who thinks a child needs help. While more often than not caregivers and guardians want the best for children, sometimes there is conflict among caregivers and guardians about the goals of treatment, the desired outcomes, or whether treatment is warranted at all. And, these may conflict with the desires of the child. Children, by definition, are vulnerable, and their best interests must be held as a priority in family treatment. Whenever possible, children should be brought into the conversation in a fashion appropriate to their developmental level. Although children who may be old enough to comprehend the proposed treatment cannot give consent in the legal sense, they can be informed and give assent to enter into the therapeutic relationship.

Confidentiality

Along with consent, confidentiality can be tricky in family work, especially when children are involved. Confidentiality of what individual family members disclose can be complicated, as can the confidentiality of what children disclose when they are being seen by a social worker apart from other family members. This is particularly true if children's parents or guardians are adamant about being kept informed, even if disclosure would harm the therapeutic relationship with the child or her or his well-being. At what point are social workers and other professionals obligated to disclose information to other family members?

Discussions about confidentiality can begin at the start of the therapeutic relationship. These discussions can include clarification of and agreement about what will be disclosed and when, and the importance that confidentiality plays in trust and building the therapeutic relationship. Of course, social workers are mandated reporters when abuse and neglect are suspected, so a discussion about this with the family has to take place before work begins.

Competing Interests

In thinking about the complexity of family systems and the members involved, it is not difficult to imagine the many ways in which competing interests might emerge. Part of competing interests among family members has to do with different perspectives on problems, expectations about therapy outcomes, and goals for therapy. The therapeutic process might include exploring some of these differences, but it may be that conflict among members cannot be overcome and decisions need to be made about how to proceed with family work.

Applying Ethics in Family Work

What potential ethical issues do you see emerging in work with the Alexander family? Competence is something the social worker should consider given Susan's problems around substance use and mental health issues. It may be that the social worker is competent to work with housing and financial issues but not mental health problems. Because there are two young children included in the family, consent may become an issue if Susan were to decide she wants her children involved in counseling with the social worker. Further, confidentiality may be a consideration for Susan and the social worker if Rich is contacted for overdue child support. If he has the potential to demonstrate violent behavior, there is good reason Susan may not want Rich to know where she is or that she is receiving services. And, if the children are brought into the working relationship with the social worker, there may be competing interests to consider—those of Susan and those of each of her children. Making matters more complex, if Susan's older children or brothers were brought into the working relationship, then the social worker would need to consider all these areas to determine if any ethical dilemmas may present themselves, given all the parties involved in Susan's situation.

GROUPS

Several social work students at a small, urban, private university have met to talk about a recent incident that happened on campus. A student was harassed as he walked to his car parked in one of the campus parking lots. Three other students followed him to his car, threatening to kill him because he was a "fairy." The student reported the incident, but a week later, nothing had been done by the university nor had word about the incident been publicized. The student, a friend of several of the social work students, has been talking about leaving the university because of the incident.

In concern for social justice for everyone on campus and the safety and well-being of their friend, these students have decided to form a task group to address the issue. Specifically, they want to hold the university accountable for investigating the incident, bring awareness to the campus community about the problem of homophobia and violence against GLBT students, and obtain assurances from the university that it will invest in ongoing education on these issues and security for its students. The end goal of the students is to change the university culture to be safer and more welcoming to all students.

Group work has a long and important history in the social work profession. Since the time of settlement houses, groups were used to teach values and skills around citizenship and participation in the democratic process. Group work eventually was used with different populations such as children, teens, and immigrants, and to organize people geographically like those who worked together or lived in the same neighborhoods. Professionally, the American Association for the Study of Group Work was established in the 1930s (later to become the American Association of Group Workers), which eventually became the National Association of Social Workers in 1956 after it merged with other organizations (Ephross & Vassil, 2005).

Since then, a large body of knowledge has been developed about different types of groups and how they function, along with research on their effectiveness and the skills needed to develop and manage groups. A great deal of attention from professionals in many fields like business, psychology, and social work has been paid to aspects of groups such as group dynamics and group process, particularly as they play out for vulnerable and disempowered groups. Here, we will explore what groups are, different types of groups used in social work, theoretical perspectives on groups, and characteristics of groups.

Group Definitions, Types, and Purposes

Groups can be defined in many different ways. Incorporating several definitions and ideas of what groups are, a **group** could be defined as two or more people who identify and interact with one another in ways that are influenced by group norms and that influence behavior (Johnson & Johnson, 2000; Shaw, 1981; Toseland & Rivas, 2012). Some groups can be considered as **primary**, where members share close, enduring relationships, spend a lot of time together, and know each other well. Examples of primary groups are gangs, friends, families, roommates, or coworkers. **Secondary groups** are those that are formed, usually on a short-term basis, to achieve certain goals or pursue a specific activity. Members of secondary groups likely do not know each other well, spend much time together, or have a cohesive sense of identity as a group. Examples of secondary groups could be classmates for a semester, or a task group created to address a particular problem or issue. Groups can also be classified as informal or formal and natural or formed. Natural groups tend to be informal and primary. These could be groups of friendships that develop over time or classmates that become close and spend a lot of time together. Formed groups tend to be formal, secondary groups such as classmates assigned to a group project or parents appointed to a school board (Toseland & Rivas, 2012).

Groups differ in many ways, depending on their goals, composition, and purpose.

While there are numerous types of groups, generally we can think of groups as being in two distinct categories. One type of group is the **task group**, which is usually organized to accomplish specific tasks or activities that benefit a larger group, like a neighborhood, community, or organization. The other type of group is the **treatment group**, which is organized to meet people's emotional and social needs (Toseland & Rivas, 2012).

Task groups themselves vary a great deal, depending on their purpose and the context in which they occur. Examples of task groups include teams (e.g., teams convened for client service); committees and boards (e.g., for planning, directing, or implementing policy or activities); staff development and administrative groups; delegate councils (e.g., representatives from various agencies that make decisions on services for a community); and social action groups. Task groups take on a wide variety of activities like developing and reviewing policies and programs or planning to address client, community, organizational, or social needs.

There are many examples of treatment groups. Therapy groups usually target specific emotional, behavioral, or mental health problems and are led by trained professionals like psychologists or licensed clinical social workers. Psychoeducational groups often help people learn new skills like parenting, managing chronic pain, or caregiving for someone with Alzheimer's disease. These groups are often led by people who have knowledge on the topic and can guide lectures, workshops, or other activities on the topic (Reid, 1997). Self-help groups offer support and information for members dealing with particular issues, and they often do not have specific leaders with any particular expertise; rather, they are usually formed by members who want support with particular problems. Examples include Alcoholics Anonymous, Parents and Friend of Lesbians and Gays (PFLAG), and Parents without Partners. Mutual aid groups are similar to self-help groups, but they usually have trained, professional leaders. Members band together for support and sometimes advocate around a particular issue like victims of intimate partner violence or behavior problems in adolescence. Voluntary associations are groups made up of people who come together for a common purpose or interest like parent-teacher organizations, Boys and Girls Clubs, trade unions, or professional organizations. Finally, virtual communities, the newest type of group, includes groups of communities that form online using different technological platforms like discussion groups. These communities usually come together around common interests or issues (Menon, 2000).

Why are groups so important in social work? Probably the most obvious reason is that groups, regardless of their type, provide support, cohesiveness, resources, and commonalities that members share to help achieve tasks and goals. Groups also promote creativity and problem-solving because members benefit from hearing others' ideas and perspectives. Groups also are influential because individual members are held accountable for their actions (or inactions) and must participate if the group is to achieve its goals. Practically speaking, groups provide convenient venues by which to communicate and accomplish tasks (Garvin & Galinsky, 2008). Further, groups can be therapeutic by fostering trusting relationships, providing universality to problems (i.e., we're not alone with our struggles), instilling hope, and offering accepting, nonjudgmental environments where members can express themselves freely, test perceptions, and practice new behaviors in secure relationships. Groups also provide the building blocks for larger organizations and social action and change (Staub-Bernasconi, 1991).

Applying Types and Purposes of Groups

Looking at the social work students who met at the outset in our case scenario, we might label them as an informal, primary group just because the students likely have spent a lot of time together as a cohort for several years and have developed close friendships with one another. They seemingly share similar views on social justice issues, at least for GLBT populations. The group they are forming is a task group with the purpose of achieving social justice for GLBT students specifically and the campus community generally.

This particular group could just have easily formed as a formal, secondary group. Students from various departments in the university who are concerned about safety and inclusion of students could have formed to address the issues related to the incident. In this case, the students likely would not know each other before joining the group and might not interact with one another very often apart from group communications and meetings.

GROUP CONCEPTUALIZATIONS

Groups and the work we do with them have many ways of being conceptualized, like so many other entities and problems social workers encounter. In this section, we will look at a few of the more common conceptualizations used for groups.

Psychodynamic Approaches

Psychodynamic approaches are concerned with a universal pattern of group development, for both task and treatment groups. The focus of psychoanalytic approaches is on power, affiliation, and conscious and nonconscious processes in groups and how these aspects affect group performance. The assumptions of these approaches are that these processes exist for all groups; processes are often unconscious but they affect group performance nonetheless; and group effectiveness can be improved by bringing these processes into conscious awareness of group members (McLeod & Kettner-Polley, 2004).

Psychodynamic perspectives view groups from the medical model, including the idea that groups are biological entities that attempt to adapt to survive by working together with others. Through emotional processes of members, groups form the "group mind," or working together as if members were a single entity or organism (McLeod & Kettner-Polley, 2004). Further, groups create and cultivate group culture. In task groups, rational processes and a focus on the task to be completed may govern the culture. In treatment groups, the culture may be governed by emotional processes and relationships (Miller, 1998).

In many ways, group culture reflects concepts of Freud's id, ego, and superego. Emotions, drives, and needs are played out in group culture and influence the process of groups. For example, a parent-teacher organization may be formed to complete certain tasks for a school, but it also exists to care for and nurture the children. Thus, basic and complex emotions like survival, aggressiveness, and love can emerge in the group culture. These emotions can help or hinder group work, and members must learn to manage and channel emotions effectively for groups to be successful (Bion, 1961).

Kurt Lewin's (1951) field theory is a popular perspective used for group work that is couched in a psychodynamic lens. It also contains aspects similar to person-in-environment and systems approaches. Field theory views groups as entities that interact with and move through their environments to achieve their goals. Thus, the environmental context is important to groups (Toseland & Rivas, 2012). This approach focuses on the positive and negative forces from the environment that exert pressure on a group and help determine its successfulness. For example, a group that experiences many barriers, problems, and discouragement will likely fail if members cannot find a way to counterbalance these negative forces. Unconscious forces also exist that exert pressure on groups and influence the relationships between members in a social context, creating either unification or polarization

(Bales *et al.*, 1979). The term **valence** is used to describe the forces that create a push-pull dynamic on group process (Bion, 1961; Martin, 2003).

Other concepts that are important in field theory include group norms, roles, power, cohesion, leadership, and consensus. All groups operate with expected, collective rules and expectations about behavior (norms), and members are expected to fulfill certain functions and status in the group (roles). Further, power exists in groups to help influence members to fulfill roles and expectations, and groups, to be successful, must concur on groups' goals and functions (cohesion). Leadership is needed in groups to help them achieve their goals, but leadership styles can vary greatly among groups and influence how groups function. Leadership could be viewed on a continuum from authoritarian, where leaders exert control over decisions and actions with little input from members, to democratic, where all members have equal input on decisions and actions, to laissez-faire, where leadership is lacking and nondirectional. Finally, groups can differ on the amount of consensus they allow or achieve, which determines the extent to which members agree on goals and other group processes.

Social Exchange Perspectives

Social exchange perspectives help us to understand how people's circumstances influence their willingness to participate in the exchange of knowledge and practices (Emerson, 1976). These perspectives view groups from the level of members' interpersonal interactions and how rewards and costs influence group processes. Rewards include the amount of satisfaction, enjoyment, and positive aspects members derive from group membership and involvement. Costs include the negative aspects of group involvement such as time, energy, and loss of rewards that occur because of group ineffectiveness. Interactions of members include all of the behaviors and actions that occur between members and can be evaluated by how behaviors are rewarded or punished. Groups are successful insofar as members continue to derive pleasure from their interactions or are rewarded for their behaviors in the group context.

Whereas field theory considers the group as a whole as more important to group functioning than individual members' actions, social exchange perspectives view individual members' patterns of relationships and interactions as more important. The weakness or strength of members' social ties is a key contributor to group process and functioning (Granovetter, 1973). Networks of exchange, in which members are willing to share or exchange information and resources, are crucial components of group process. Further, strong emotional connections between members, where members know and trust each other well, can help to increase members' satisfaction and overcome resistance to work toward group goals. Factors including feelings of power and inclusion in decision making can also influence the success of a group from these perspectives (Cook & Emerson, 1978).

Empowerment and Feminist Perspectives

Groups conceptualized from empowerment perspectives aim to change oppressive conditions, both on micro and macro levels, that prevent people from achieving control over their lives and accessing resources needed to make changes (Breton, 2004). Empowerment approaches in group work rely on several dimensions to achieve change. One is social justice, which contends that structural forces oppress certain groups of people and action is needed to remove barriers that cause oppression and marginalization. Another is consciousness raising, which is focused on raising people's awareness of themselves, others, and environmental circumstances that create various situations. It promotes critical thinking to help deconstruct stereotypes about people and situations to empower people to make change based on factual information and realistic expectations. Mutual aid focuses on how members of groups can support one another by providing information, resources, and feedback. It views members as equal partners who can learn from one another. Another dimension of these perspectives is multicultural socialization, which places emphasis on identifying, honoring, and working with the differences exhibited by group members. Diversity among group members often promotes creative thinking generated by diverse perspectives on situations and issues (Breton, 2004; Finn & Jacobson, 2008).

Feminist perspectives in group work tend to be focused on women's self-determination, securing equal rights for women in institutions, and changing institutional structures to create more just and equitable environments for women. Groups using feminist perspectives may view issues and tasks through a gendered filter, using women's plights and issues as the foundation for group work. Group work often takes a pro-woman stance, where women's histories, strengths, and other considerations are used in group work. Empowerment and consciousness raising are important considerations in feminist perspectives, as is the emphasis on group process to ensure equity in group work. Diversity, validation of diverse viewpoints, and acknowledgment that the personal is political are also key components of feminist perspectives in group work (Bricker-Jenkins & Netting, 2009).

Applying Conceptualizations of Group Work

Our group of social work students could be viewed from many different perspectives. For instance, from field theory, we might view the group in the context of the campus environment. Forces from the administration, faculty, staff, and student body will exert pressure on the group, creating both opportunities for the group to achieve its goals and barriers to impede success. We might want to look at how unconscious forces affect individual group members to create conflict or unification in the group's work. We would also want to look at the group's norms, roles, power, cohesion, leadership, and consensus to gain a perspective on group dynamics and the nature of the group's work to determine if they are moving toward success.

The task group of social work students that has formed could also be viewed through a social exchange perspective. We would want to look at the students' circumstances—being social work majors in a cohort that spends a great deal of time together and shares many views on social issues—to better understand how the group functions and how willing members are to participate in the group. If there is a great deal of cohesion among members, they are likely to share information and resources and work together toward the group's goals. We could examine members' interpersonal interactions and analyze how rewards and costs are influencing the group process. For example, it could be that a few members do not get along or that one or two students are losing a great deal of study or social time by participating in the group. These factors could jeopardize the success of the group as a whole. Or, it could be that members gain a great deal from participating in the group, such as feeling more energized or motivated to take what they are learning from the group and apply it in their coursework. This could increase group cohesion and commitment of members to the group, increasing the likelihood that it will succeed in its goals.

GROUP WORK AND PROCESS

All groups, regardless of type and purpose, have processes and considerations that are important in developing and sustaining successful groups. Some of these considerations were mentioned earlier, but in this section, we will discuss in more detail some of the issues that need to be addressed before starting groups and during the time groups are functioning.

Both task and treatment groups share similar considerations and processes in the development and running of groups. However, given their different purposes, they each also have unique characteristics that need to be addressed. Let us take a look first at some of the characteristics that they share, and then we will discuss the ways in which they differ.

Shared Characteristics of Task and Treatment Groups

With regard to considerations, both groups share the requirement of thinking about composition of members. The purpose of the group will help determine who is appropriate to join the group. For example, task group members should share common interests, motivations, and goals; and treatment group members should share similar problems and issues on which they want to work. Before beginning a group, social workers need to think about the context in which the group will take place. Where will it be located? Can members easily get to the meeting location? At what time and how often should the group meet? Should the group meet in a confidential location? How will external forces, like a neighborhood or agency, feel about a group taking place in their space? For example, a confidential group for GLBT students probably will not want to meet in a public space on campus or even in a place where other students might see them gathering in a room. A task group that is focused on neighborhood improvement might be welcome to use space in a community center, whereas a group for convicted sex offenders likely would not, especially if children are present in the building. And, what if the group is held virtually? How can technology and confidentiality best be handled?

The size of the group is also important. Depending on the purpose, a group that is too large might generate too many differing opinions to get work accomplished. Conversely, a group that is too small may not have sufficient resources to achieve goals. For treatment groups, size is important to think about with regard to issues around trust, intimacy, support, and sustainability, depending on the problem that is the focus of the group. For survivors of sexual abuse, a large group may not be conducive to the development of trust among members. A group focused on self-improvement, however, might benefit from more members to generate more creative ideas and interactions with others.

Still other considerations to keep in mind include issues around group norms, leadership, cohesiveness, and confidentiality. Here too, the purpose of the group will help you decide on which characteristics to focus with these aspects. Norms of a group help members decipher what is appropriate behavior within the context of the group. In many treatment groups, for example, it is expected that members will share intimate information at some point. In task groups, it is usually expected that members will not share such information. Often norms are communicated in formal ways through ground rules of the group, but often they are unstated and communicated through the culture of the group (Dumler & Skinner, 2008). Rules about confidentiality are important; members must agree upon rules and abide by them. Again, depending on the purpose and activities of a group, the importance of confidentiality will differ. A task group working on neighborhood improvement, for example, may not be as concerned with confidentiality of the group's work as a treatment group dealing with experiences of sexual abuse. Group norms and rules around confidentiality help groups achieve cohesiveness, which is important to the success of groups.

Leadership, and the related power it often brings, is extremely important to groups. Sometimes leadership develops within the context of a working group; in other cases, leaders are appointed or elected to lead groups. Groups led by appointed individuals are generally more structured and controlled. Groups with no one individual in control of group processes and decisions are often less structured and more informal (Jacobs, Masson, Harvill, & Schimmel, 2012). Further, there are many styles of leadership and different characteristics that effective leaders can possess. Depending on the type and purpose of the group, some styles and characteristics work better for different types of groups than others. Often, leaders who are both task- and relationship-oriented tend to be more effective than leaders who have just one orientation or the other (Northouse, 2012). Characteristics of effective leaders include intelligence, determination, trustworthiness, self-confidence, and an ability to relate to others (Jacobs *et al.*, 2012).

The cohesiveness of the group, or how connected members feel to one another and the group's purpose, is normally dictated by the goals and nature of the group. If members feel a part of the group and are dedicated to its cause, attendance at meetings is usually consistent and there is a sense that members are working at each meeting (Dumler & Skinner, 2008). Conversely, if cohesion is not strong, members often will not show up at meetings, there may be a sense of consistent conflict among members, and a sense of trust and commitment may be low.

Confidentiality is an issue that can affect many aspects of groups, including cohesiveness and communication, particularly in treatment groups. Members who are expected to share intimate information that can leave them with a sense of vulnerability need to trust that information will remain confidential within the context of the group. If there is danger that information will not be kept confidential, the group will have difficulty building trust, intimacy, and commitment to the group. Breaches of confidentiality, depending on the group setting, can be serious violations of ethical conduct that can be emotionally, psychologically, socially, and sometimes physically and financially harmful to group members and leaders and to the health and success of the group as a whole (Corey, Corey, & Corey, 2010). The seriousness of confidentiality for a group can be communicated through group rules as well as group norms and culture.

The diverse characteristics of group members and leaders also need to be addressed, both in terms of how they contribute to group goals and process as well as how they can create barriers for group work. Factors such as age, ethnicity, religion, language, cultural background, socioeconomic status, sexual and gender identity, perceived or real power differences, and experiences with discrimination, oppression, and privilege all impact the group process and relationships between members.

Group leaders need to be aware of and work with their own personal beliefs, attitudes, prejudices, and worldviews; how factors of diversity can affect group process; and utilize skills that are appropriate for and respect the experiences of group members (DeLucia-Waack, 2010). Often, having discussion about these issues with group members before and during group work can help prevent problems and barriers in group work and maximize the trust, safety, and commitment members feel with other members and the group as a whole (Corey, Corey, & Corey, 2010).

Exhibit 15.3 displays some of the characteristics that social workers need to consider when developing and running groups.

Unique Processes of Task and Treatment Groups

Here we will explore some of the unique characteristics and processes of task and treatment groups. Some of these will overlap with what we discussed above, but they may play out in unique ways depending on the purpose of the group.

EXHIBIT 15.3

Shared Characteristics and Considerations of Task and Treatment Groups

- Group considerations
- Composition of members
- Context and location
- Size
- Norms
- Leadership
- Cohesiveness
- Confidentiality
- Diversity of members

Characteristics and Processes of Task Groups Communication is important for all groups, but how communication happens in task groups is a main focus for social workers, and it has unique characteristics. Communication in task groups needs to be open, allowing all members to participate. Members need regular and useful feedback on their ideas and performance to ensure the group is moving toward its goal efficiently and effectively. This feedback is often used deliberately to help inform, guide, and improve the work of the group (Wheelan, 1999). Nonverbal communication, as in treatment groups, can offer members a great deal of information about what is happening for other members during the group process. However, it is important to keep in mind that there may be many cultural differences affecting both verbal and nonverbal communication that could be misinterpreted by others. It is important for social workers and group members to check in with members about communication processes as they occur.

Task groups tend to proceed through five stages that differ slightly from treatment groups (Toseland & Rivas, 2009); these are described below.

- Composition stage: This is the stage in which the group's purpose, context, membership, and size are determined.

- Beginnings stage: Members become acquainted with one another and the groups' purpose. Members begin to establish rules and norms for the group and identify tasks needed to accomplish goals.

- Assessment stage: While assessment is categorized as its own stage, it is really an ongoing process of evaluating and re-evaluating the group process. Members assess how the group is performing with regard to achieving goals but also how the group is managing with regard to cohesion, commitment, communication, and other factors that affect group process.

- Stabilization and working stage: This stage is characterized as the most productive stage of the group process. There tends to be consensus on roles, structure, and group work that help the group work effectively.

- Endings and evaluation stage: This is the time when a group either disbands because it accomplished its goals or it was unable to achieve its goals. Even when groups are ongoing, endings still occur when members leave or changes happen to the group that create shifts in its functioning. As with any group, attempts should be made to facilitate endings so that members can reach closure and help protect the health of the group if it is ongoing. This can be done by asking members to process feelings and review successes. Members can also comment on aspects of their work they most appreciate and lessons they have learned by working with the group. This process is also helpful for evaluating the work of the group and learning from what works and what does not.

Characteristics and Processes of Treatment Groups   Treatment groups tend to differ somewhat from task groups in structure, process, and dynamics. This is often because of the intimate nature of the problems people bring to treatment groups and the fact that members often feel vulnerable in treatment groups, depending on the nature of the problem on which the group is focused. Decisions need to be made about the structure of the group given the purpose. For example, will the group be open or closed? Open groups allow new members to join at any time, whereas closed groups begin with a preselected group of members who stay with the group until its end. A group's open or closed status can impact the trust and cohesion of the group. Will the group be ongoing or time-limited? Groups that are formed to teach skills often need only a set amount of time to accomplish goals, whereas groups that address ongoing psychological concerns could continue indefinitely. Related to this, decisions need to be made about how often groups will meet. Groups dealing with serious problems that can cause a great deal of distress or physical or emotional crises (e.g., suicidal feelings; eating disorders) might meet a few times a week, whereas groups focused on less intense or chronic issues might meet once a week or twice a month. And, as was mentioned earlier, issues such as size of the group and the safety and accessibility of the group meeting location can be extremely important for treatment groups, particularly if the issues being dealt with are sensitive and could leave members feeling vulnerable or at risk.

Treatment groups also are more likely than task groups (again, depending on the purpose of the group) to screen members before the group begins. Screening helps to ensure that the composition of members will maximize cohesiveness and trust among members and that members have similar needs and compatible goals with one another and the purpose of the group. Screening often takes place as a one-on-one interview between the group leader and each potential group member. Sometimes group leaders will hold a pre-group meeting with members to clarify leader and member expectations, set up and clarify ground rules for the group, and discuss group expectations and procedures. Group leaders must also decide if they will run a group alone or with a co-leader. Co-leaders can help one another with the logistics of preparing for, starting, and running groups, and they can also benefit the group in many other ways. Different leadership styles may benefit members and balance out group dynamics, and paying attention to group process and problem solving is easier with two leaders. However, to help avoid problems and ensure groups run smoothly, co-leaders should spend time before a group begins to share their leadership styles, theoretical orientations and perceptions on group work, cultural and ethnic backgrounds and how these might affect their work, and general strengths and weaknesses that they might bring to the group process (Corey, Corey, & Corey, 2010).

Often in treatment groups, much attention is paid to process during group meetings because the process contains information about what is happening with individual members and the group as a whole in relation to the problem of focus. In other words, attending to the group process is therapeutic in and of itself. Aspects of group process that might be of interest to a group leader include:

- participation (e.g., who is participating; who is not; how silence is treated by others; who talks to whom),

- influence (e.g., who has it; who does not; does influence cause conflict),

- how members' styles of influence and communication play out in group and influence one another,

- how decisions are made (e.g., are decisions made by consensus; does one member seem to dominate in decision making; how do decisions affect members),

- how tasks of the group are carried out (e.g., do one or two members do most of the work; how are suggestions and feedback handled),

- how relationships are maintained,

- what the group atmosphere is like (e.g., how are unpleasant feelings handled; how is conflict handled),

- membership (e.g., how cohesive is the group),

- how feelings are expressed and handled, and

- what the norms are for the group.

The stages of treatment groups tend to differ slightly from those of task groups, again, usually because of the intimate environment and process that treatment groups foster. Below is a description of the four stages of treatment groups (Corey, Corey, & Corey, 2010).

- Initial stage: Process is focused on group orientation and exploration. Members get acquainted with one another, learn group norms and functions, explore fears and expectations, identify personal goals, and develop trust.

- Transition stage: Process is focused on members' conflict, anxiety, resistance, defensiveness, and need for control. Members must learn to trust and self-disclose, or the group will become stuck. Leaders often must put forth a lot of effort in this stage to "remain curious" about members' anxiety and gently push members to begin the work of the group.

- Working stage: Process is characterized by group members' commitment to exploring problems and working toward goals. Members are engaged, trusting, and motivated to participate in the group process. Members take on responsibility for the work of the group, and the group is cohesive.

- Final stage: Process is focused on closing the group and processing members' feelings about ending and reflecting on successes and growth. This stage is a time for members to practice new skills and find new resources for support.

Applying Group Characteristics and Processes

How might group considerations affect our task group of social work students? The group is formed by social work students who share similar values and views on GLBT issues, so that will help maximize group cohesion and determine the group's composition. They will need to think about where and when to meet. Depending on the campus culture, they may want to find a confidential location where they will not encounter any resistance or trouble from other students. Size may be an issue. The group may become so big that the number of members will make communication, decision making, or assignment of tasks difficult. On the other hand, the group should not be too small, as they will need quite a few people to carry out different tasks to achieve goals. Early on, the group may want to discuss ground rules, roles, norms, purpose, and goals to ensure everyone is in agreement about how the group should run. They may also want to talk about the extent to which group processes and information should be kept confidential. If information is shared too soon, say, through the university's newspaper, it may undermine their efforts. If it is shared too late, they may find their message does not reach the student body in a timely manner to motivate others to join their cause. Further, the group should consider the diversity of the membership and how diversity factors might shape group dynamics and process. If the group lacks diversity, they may miss out on crucial ideas or insights or have trouble gaining credibility with the campus community. If they have a diverse membership, they are likely to generate different points of views and ideas that can make their efforts more effective.

How might the stages play out in this task group? In the beginning stage, members likely already know one another well. But, this would be the time to clarify the purpose of the group and what they want to accomplish. It likely will be a time when members discuss the tasks that will need to be completed and which members are best suited for each task. As the group works, they will need to continually assess how group process and progress is moving forward. If problems are identified, they need to address those problems before moving on. As the group continues with its work, they will probably find that group processes move smoothly and that they are able to make good progress with their goals. Finally, when they have reached the end of their work, for example, when they gain acknowledgement from the university community about the problem and programming is being implemented by university administration, they can evaluate their progress and determine the extent to which their goals have been achieved. The group might decide they have more work to do, or they may feel that they have done all they can do and disband the group. Either way, the group will want to reflect on their accomplishments and the skills they have learned along the way.

CONCLUSION

Social workers work extensively with families and groups. The changing nature of families and the issues and problems they face means that social workers must find flexible and unique ways to approach their work with families. Just as with other issues in human behavior, there are many theories and perspectives that can be utilized in family work. Social workers must be cognizant of how viewing families and problems from different perspectives affect the families with which they work.

Social workers also engage in work with groups of all sizes. There are many types of groups, and how social workers approach their work with groups depends on groups' purposes. The type and purpose of groups also determines the considerations social workers must take into account when developing and running groups as well how the process of the group will occur. Being aware of these factors is an important part of group work.

MAIN POINTS

- The definition of family is changing; it is becoming more and more broad and diverse as different forms of families emerge.

- There are many theoretical and other perspectives from which to view families.

- Family systems are becoming more diverse and complex, and they are situated within broader, even more complex cultural, political, historical, and socioeconomic contexts. Social workers must attend to the diverse characteristics, situations, and issues that affect individual behavior and family systems.

- Work with families, like other areas of social work, brings with it many ethical considerations that can impact the process.

- Groups are defined as two or more people who identify and interact with one another in ways that are influenced by group norms and that influence behavior.

- There are many types of groups with many purposes. Groups can be considered as primary or secondary. They can also be categorized as task or treatment groups.

- As with families, there are many theoretical perspectives that help social workers conceptualize group work and processes.

- Task and treatment groups share many characteristics and considerations in terms of developing and running groups. These include group composition, context, size, norms, leadership, cohesiveness, confidentiality, and diversity of members.

- Task and treatment group both have unique considerations and processes because of their different purposes.

EXERCISES

1. *Sanchez family interactive case at* www.routledgesw.com/cases. Review the Sanchez family and the situations of each family member and their interactions with the environment. Then, answer the following questions:
   a. In what ways does this family fit and defy traditional definitions of family? Explain your answer and give examples.
   b. Discuss a few issues faced by this family that impacts its functioning. How are these issues affecting family dynamics and functioning? How does diversity affect the family?
   c. Choose one of the conceptualizations of family discussed earlier in the chapter. Apply it to the Sanchez family, describing how the family would be viewed through this lens.
   d. What might be some ethical issues to consider, using the above discussion as a guide?
2. *Brickville interactive case at* www.routledgesw.com/cases. Review information on the Stone family and respond to the questions above in item #1.
3. *Carla Washburn interactive case at* www.routledgesw.com/cases. Read Carla's case file and those of the people with whom she interacts. Discuss the following:
   a. How might family be defined in Carla's situation? Who might be considered family, and what challenges and opportunities does Carla face with regard to family?

   b. What issues of diversity apply in Carla's case? Be specific and discuss these in some detail.
   c. Which conceptualization of family might be best applied in Carla's case and why? Describe how this conceptualization might help a social worker to better understand and work with Carla.
4. *Brickville interactive case at* www.routledgesw.com/cases. Review the situation in Brickville and respond to these questions:
   a. Explain how the youth leadership group might be conceptualized using one of the lenses discussed above.
   b. Looking at the considerations for groups, discuss these in some detail as they might be applied to the youth leadership group. For example, what would be an ideal size? What issues might arise from confidentiality? Where should it be located? How long should it run? How might members be chosen? Be sure to discuss all of the important considerations.
   c. What issues of diversity need to be considered?
5. *Hudson City interactive case at* www.routledgesw.com/cases. Read the information provided for the RAINN case and respond to the following:
   a. Thinking about the issues presented in the Hudson case, think of both a task and treatment group that could be developed to work with issues. What would the purpose of both types of groups be?
   b. Choose one of the groups you discussed above and describe what factors would be important to consider before running such a group. Be sure to discuss aspects of diversity that would be important to consider.
   c. Thinking of the choice you made in item b., which group conceptualization might be best applied to group work in this case?
   d. What ethical dilemmas might be posed by running such a group?

CHAPTER 16

Social Organizations and the Social Environment

New Horizons is a methadone clinic located in a mid-sized city in the Midwest. The main focus of the clinic is to address substance use and abuse issues, particularly heroin addiction. The clinic offers counseling, prevention services, and outpatient methadone and medical treatment. The clinic also offers a small inpatient program through which clients who have been incarcerated for drug-related offenses can serve their remaining time in intensive treatment. Non-incarcerated individuals can also request treatment through the inpatient program. The clinic serves a large, geographically diverse region, including urban, suburban, and rural areas of the state.

New Horizons operates from an empirically based, integrated biopsychosocial model to address prevention of and risk factors for substance abuse. It attempts to address individual factors related to substance abuse as well as issues surrounding the families and communities of those who enter treatment. It is staffed with an interdisciplinary team consisting of nurses, physicians, and pharmacists, as well as licensed psychologists, counselors, social workers, and marriage and family therapists. It is primarily funded through local and state government entities and grants from private nonprofit groups.

The clients of New Horizons come from diverse backgrounds, and the clinic attempts to hire employees that reflect the diversity of the clientele, but the majority of the staff consists of white males, particularly in administration and positions of power. The clinic is organized in a hierarchical structure, with a few top administrators making decisions about clinic functions. While employees are encouraged to provide input into the clinic's processes, employees do not feel very empowered to raise issues, ask questions, or make changes.

The philosophy and some of the functions of New Horizons can sometimes pose ethical issues for its employees, funders, and the community where it is located. For instance, some funders and medical and other professionals disagree with replacing heroin with another drug, such as methadone. However, the viewpoint of the clinic is that offering clients a controlled replacement for heroin, which has been empirically supported as effective, not only helps to keep clients medically stable once they stop using heroin, but it also helps reduce some clients' criminal activity because they do not need money to buy heroin.

> *Further, some employees of the inpatient program have complained of the some-times sexist and unethical behavior of the male employees and their misuse of power. One female employee complained to the clinic directors that her male superiors would judge prospective female clients' eligibility for the program based on their physical appearance. While the directors seemed sympathetic to her complaints, processes for intake at the inpatient facility did not change, and the employee was told to take a "subordinate role" while at the inpatient facility. This employee quit after only a few months at the clinic.*
>
> *Another issue is that the inpatient facility is located in a residential neighborhood close to a park and elementary school. Some of the neighborhood residents complain about having a drug treatment program located close to areas where young children play and study.*

A S THE CASE STUDY OF NEW HORIZONS DEMONSTRATES, social organizations are complex entities that must deal with a variety of dynamics at different levels. Social organizations are one of the primary employers of social workers, so social workers play a vital role in the health and success of organizations. In this chapter, we will take a look at what social organizations are and some of the complex dynamics that are often found in organizations.

WHAT ARE SOCIAL ORGANIZATIONS?

Social organizations play a large and important role in our communities and larger society and affect many aspects of everyday lives. They provide the building blocks of modern societies and allow action to occur. Organizations are not only providers of services for people and communities served by social workers, but they also act as employers for many social workers. Organizations are a vital part of our social service delivery system, and social workers need to know how to work them to be effective in their work for others.

Definition and Characteristics of Social Organizations

Social organizations are socially constructed systems that provide and maintain boundaries around human activity (Aldrich, 1999). They are systems that are developed and established to achieve specific purposes and goals (Perrow, 1961). These organizations are artificially derived systems that are often established to address social problems or serve various populations or communities.

Most organizations articulate their purpose through mission statements, goals, and objectives. Mission statements help establish the parameters around which an organization will work, which populations it will serve, and the types of needs it will attempt to meet (Kettner, Moroney, & Martin, 2008).

Organizational goals flow from its mission. They state explicitly what the organization does to fulfill its mission. Goals help articulate the outcomes the organization would like to achieve or the problems it wants to address (Kettner *et. al.*, 2008). Goals help to guide an organization in its work, offer legitimacy to an organizations' existence, and offer a way in which people outside the organization can assess its success (Etzioni, 1964).

The goals that are stated in an organization's mission and that are publicized through documents like organizational brochures and annual reports or communicated to clients, boards, and the community are called **official goals**. Social organizations also have a set of goals that are **operative**, meaning they are not publicly articulated, but they reflect how organizations operate and function on a day-to-day basis, regardless of the officially stated goals (Perrow, 1961). For example, an organization may state its official goals are to provide safe and quality care to people with Alzheimer's disease, but its operative goals may be to locate patients who can pay for care out of pocket (vs. people who might rely on Medicaid to pay for care, which would bring less money to the organization). Understanding the difference between these two types of goals is important because sometimes organizations are guided more by operative goals than official goals. This can sometimes lead organizations into disarray or cause problems for staff, clients, and stakeholders. In our example of the care organization for Alzheimer's patients, allowing operative goals to guide the organization could lead staff to feel that profits are more important than patient care, which could compromise patient safety and well-being. And, depending on the service location, it could mean that many people with Alzheimer's disease are unable to access care. It could also lead to mistrust of the organization by the community and stakeholders.

Sometimes, social organizations are successful in achieving their goals, which is referred to as **goal succession**. In this case, organizations can either cease to exist or they can envision a new purpose and develop new goals. Sometimes, though, organizations experience **goal displacement**, meaning organizations move in a different direction than originally intended or articulated in the official goals (Etzioni, 1964).

When goal displacement occurs, organizations may end up using resources for purposes other than those publicly stated; they may also focus on problems or populations about which they lack expertise. An example of goal displacement would be when an agency that is set up to provide mental health treatment to clients with chronic and persistent mental illness begins to work on low-cost housing options for the community. Sometimes goal displacement occurs when staff members pursue personal or professional goals at the expense of organizational goals. However, goal displacement can sometimes occur through positive changes in goals and purpose. A frequently cited example of this is the March of Dimes, whose original purpose and goal was to eradicate polio. Once a vaccine for polio was developed, the organization turned its focus to preventing birth defects, premature birth, and infant mortality.

While goals provide a framework for an organization's purposes and guide its operations and daily functioning, a statement of goals is usually not specific enough to help an organization determine how to achieve them. Goals are often written so broadly that they cannot be measured and do not allow the organization to evaluate the degree to which they are being successful in achieving goals. Rather, organizations usually develop a set of objectives that flow from goals and offer language that refers to specific, realistic, time-limited, measurable steps that can be subject to observation and data collection. This data then can be used to determine how well an organization is following and achieving its stated goals.

Objectives can be approached in several different ways to reflect different types of goals (Brody, 2005):

- **Impact objectives** articulate organizational outcomes based on program activities, like enabling 50 older adults to remain in their homes independently or placing 30 incarcerated individuals in residential programs.

- **Service objectives** focus on assistance activities provided by an organization, such as providing group therapy to 100 GLBT youth in a year or offering one community parenting workshop a month to a particular school district.

- **Operational objectives** reflect activities to help improve the functioning of an organization. Examples would be to allocate $300.00 per employee each year for continuing education or to decrease staff members' caseloads by 20 percent

- **Product objectives** focus on outcomes that benefit specific populations or communities. These could be to develop and distribute social service referral and resource manuals for community members or to secure a grant to provide programming for youth and older adults.

Social organizations are important because they allow us to accomplish things collectively that we could not do individually. Organizations not only provide shape and structure to society, they also reflect the values and context of the societies in which they are created. Social workers are often a significant part of social organizations since they play such an important role in helping people get their needs met (Aldrich, 1999).

Applying Definitions of Organizations

The information in the New Horizons case study provides a basic sense of the clinic's mission, goals, and objectives. Given the variety of services the clinic offers—from prevention to outpatient and inpatient treatment—and the rather wide clientele focus—individuals, families, and communities—it likely has a broad mission. To help the clinic maintain focus, its goals and objectives should be refined and specific enough that it can carry out and evaluate its various programs effectively and avoid goal displacement due to straying from the mission.

The official goals of New Horizons likely reflect its efforts to increase prevention of substance abuse and familial and community problems caused by it as well as to treat clients for substance abuse within their biopsychosocial and environmental contexts. While the clinic's operative goals probably help support these activities, they also likely help the clinic function on another level that is not explicitly stated. For example, the clinics' staff and local judges and law enforcement personnel probably maintain mutually beneficial relationships that help refer individuals from jails and prisons into treatment at the clinic, which in turn helps prevent the local criminal justice system from becoming overcrowded. And by providing services to the community, the clinic may be able to maintain a good relationship with neighbors, who have the power to push the clinic out and into another location.

Depending on how New Horizons wants to articulate its goals, it could conceivably develop all four types of goals. For example, an impact objective could be for the clinic to reduce the number of people in the local jail for drug offenses by 10 percent by placing them in the inpatient facility for treatment. A service objective might be to serve 1,000 clients per year in the outpatient clinic. An operational objective might be to secure a large grant to improve clinic facilities. And a product objective could be to develop and conduct community programs to prevent substance abuse.

A BRIEF HISTORY OF SOCIAL ORGANIZATIONS IN THE UNITED STATES

Social organizations have not always played the integral role in society they do today. It was not until around the turn of the 17th century that organizations were viewed as bringing structure and order to society and that they were established in any significant way.

Before the 1800s, most social services were provided through religious voluntary associations, many of which still exist today (Berger & Neuhaus, 1996; Skocpol, 1998). Throughout the 19th century, many clubs and professional organizations were formed. With government assistance, they worked together on a national level, along with existing religious organizations, to develop initiatives to provide social services (Gamm & Putnam, 1999). During the Civil War period, many private organizations were formed to help administer governmental support for veterans; they also worked to provide support for people living in poverty, emancipation of slaves, and support for mothers and children. The Progressive Era, between 1885 and 1910, saw the establishment of settlement houses—better known today as community centers or neighborhood centers—institutions in inner-city areas providing services and activities for local individuals and families. At the same time, there was rapid growth in social organizations, including the formation of a whole host of new organizations for youth (e.g., YMCA and YWCA Boy Scouts and Girl Scouts, 4-H clubs and Future Farmers of America) and adults (e.g., Kiwanis International, National Association for the Advancement of Colored People [NAACP], National Urban League, Rotary International, U.S. Chamber of Commerce) (Fatout & Rose, 1998).

The Great Depression and the New Deal of the 1930s saw increased governmental involvement in social organizations, and the growth of voluntary organizations continued, many with the support of governmental funding. New Deal programs brought support for many, including farmers, veterans, and older adults (Skocpol, 1998). This trend continued in the World War II era. Then, from the 1950s until the turn of the 21st century, the number of social charity and advocacy organizations, public interest groups like the Sierra Club and Environmental Defense Fund, and business corporations grew significantly (P. D. Hall, 2005).

Today, even with reduced membership, social organizations remain a central part of society, providing important roles and services for everyone (P. D. Hall, 2005). While the nature of social organizations is changing, given the changing social landscape and social issues we will continue to see, they will remain a vital part of society.

CONCEPTUALIZATIONS OF SOCIAL ORGANIZATIONS

Since social organizations came into existence, different ways to conceptualize their purpose and function have been developed. Indeed, a great deal of research has gone into better conceptualizing and understanding organizations in an effort to improve them and make them more effective. And, as organizations have changed over time, so have our theories and perspectives about what they are and how they function. Here, we will take a look at a few of the contemporary conceptualizations on organizations.

Classic organizational theory, which evolved around the turn of the 20th century, focused on scientific management, bureaucracy, and people's behavior based on economic incentive. Many organizations still operate in ways to maximize efficiency, predictability, and control. However, changes in technology and the increase in global, dynamic organizations have necessitated new ways to look at them. Consequently, there are numerous theories and perspectives on how organizations are formed, maintained, and interact with inside and outside forces (Drucker, 1974).

Systems Theory

Systems theory (Bertalanffy, 1972) is one approach that recently has been applied to organizations. A foundational theory in social work, systems theory views organizations as open systems that continually interact with their environment and adapt to changes in the environment to maintain homeostasis (Scott, 1981). A more complete discussion of systems theory can be found in the core HBSE book, Chapter 2.

Concepts in systems theory such as rules, roles, norms, input, feedback, boundaries, and subsystems can all be applied to organizations to better understand how they function. For example, all organizations consist of norms and rules for how they operate, and employees usually understand these without being told. They help to guide employees' behavior and help the system function smoothly. Organizations get input and feedback from clients, employees, and outside groups about how they are meeting their mission and whether they are being successful in the work they do. Organizations construct boundaries that differentiate them from other organizations, and boundaries help define roles, relationships, hierarchies, and identities of employees and clients. And, often, coworkers form subsystems within organizations that help support their relationships and work. All of these factors work together to help organizations maintain homeostasis and function consistently on a daily basis. Concepts of differentiation and entropy also apply to organizations. As the organization matures and adapts, it differentiates. Employees also differentiate as they gain experience within the organization. If organizations cannot adapt to differentiation, they are at risk for entropy, or failure and death. Conversely, many organizations successfully adapt to change and differentiation, for example through altering their mission or methods of service provision. Through such alterations they can find a new, more adaptive level of homeostasis.

Ecosystems Perspective

Another perspective on organizational function is ecosystems or organizational ecology; ecosystems theory is also discussed in the core HBSE book, Chapter 2. Similar to systems theory, the ecosystems perspective places emphasis on how organizations operate within the context of the environment. If organizations are to survive and thrive, there must be a good fit between them and the environment. Because the environment is always changing, organizations themselves must change and adapt to meet shifting needs and demands of the people they serve as well as to the workers they employ. Social organizations must find ways to compete with other organizations that serve similar populations or focus on similar needs. This also applies to the ways in which organizations are funded. Funding sources change and disappear; organizations must remain flexible and adaptable enough to weather changes in the financial environment.

Further, ecosystems and organizational ecology perspectives look at how organizations change and develop over time. They examine the processes of development, growth, and decline in the context of social, political, and economic systems that affect organizations. These perspectives are concerned with how organizations respond to and change in response to environmental pressures and dynamic contexts (Hannan & Freeman, 1989).

Feminist Perspectives

Feminist perspectives on organizations have been in practice since the 1960s. While there are many branches of feminism, as discussed in the core HBSE book in Chapter 4, here we will look at the broad principles of feminist perspectives and how they apply to organizations.

Feminist perspectives focus on creating equality, community, and participation in organizations (H. Brown, 1992) and eliminating hierarchy that can disempower people working within organizations (Iannello, 1992). Organizations that are structured from feminist perspectives incorporate the following structures and processes (Iannello, 1992; Rothschild, 1992):

- Participatory decision making

- Power sharing

- Community building

- Rotation of duties and leadership

- Consensus building

- Promoting nurturing, caring, and empowerment

- Valuing relationships.

The feminist perspective on organizations pays attention to process over outcome. Rather than focusing on competition and getting ahead, which tends to be valued in mainstream society, feminist perspectives attempt to revalue all that is considered to be feminine, making these characteristics important to the functioning of organizations. It aims to rid organizations of gender stereotypes that hurt men and women and deprive organizations of the talents and skills of employees (Tong, 1989).

Some researchers and theorists argue that feminist perspectives are rooted in women's movements that only benefit white, heterosexual, middle-class women. As such, they lack critical analysis of how mainstream organizations also perpetuate practices that disempower people of color and others from minority populations. The argument continues that we cannot separate gender from other characteristics such as ethnicity and sexual identity if we are to change the nature of organizations and make them more equitable for everyone (hooks, 1981; Giddings, 1984).

Organizational Justice Theory

Organizational justice theory is concerned with how employees view fairness and justice within the organization and in relationship to their employers (Colquitt, Greenberg, & Zapata-Phelan, 2005). Justice and fairness from this perspective have a wide range of meanings, depending on the perspective of the employee. For example, an employee might be concerned with distributive justice, or the fairness of outcomes in the workplace. Another employee might be focused on procedural justice, or the fairness of workplace processes (Adams, 1965; Greenberg, 2009). Still another employee might be concerned with interactional justice, which involves fairness in decision making by superiors and a sense of belonging and importance to the organization (Bies, 2005).

A focus on interpersonal relationships and a sense of community are of primary importance in organizational justice theory. For organizations to be successful, this theory promotes fair treatment of employees; equitable and transparent processes and outcomes; and the support of employee's feelings of control, meaning, and self-regard in the organization (Cropanzano, Byrne, Bobocel, & Rupp, 2001). Organizational justice theory espouses that employees need to feel attachment to one another as well as a sense of working toward common goals. This work needs to be viewed as moral and ethical, and employees need to feel a sense of pride in the organization and the work they do.

Applying Organizational Conceptualizations

Two useful ways to conceptualize New Horizons and its functions are through systems and ecosystems theories. From systems theory, the rules, roles, norms, input, feedback, boundaries, and subsystems could be analyzed to help explain the processes, strengths, and limitations of the clinic. For example, from the case description, it sounds like there are strict boundaries between administration and other staff that not only define each employee's role but that also shape rules and keep decision making within an administrative subsystem and dictate the norms of conformity among non-administrative personnel. Employees have few opportunities to provide input and feedback into the system; however, the clinic receives a great deal of input and feedback from the community, which tends to guide its operations. While clinic administrators probably create rigid rules, boundaries, and subsystems to maintain homeostasis, the clinic likely experiences high employee turnover because these rules and boundaries create a sense of disempowerment and disengagement among employees, which can lead to entropy of the clinic over time.

From an ecosystems perspective, the clinic could be viewed within the context of its environment. In many ways, the clinic faces obstacles in terms of fitting in with its environment because of the nature of the issues with which it works. However, the clinic has learned to adapt to the environment by forming and nurturing mutually beneficial relationships with the communities and organizations that could potentially create problems for the clinic. The clinic is able to change its operations depending on the shifting needs of clients, community members, and funding sources. However, the agency seems to have more difficulty remaining flexible enough to be sensitive to employee needs and the ethical dilemmas faced by the clinic. This rigidity could lead to problems with the clinic adapting over time, and it may face legal or hiring problems or a damaged reputation if the clinic cannot adequately deal with these issues and accommodate the needs and desires of the staff.

TYPES AND FUNCTIONS OF SOCIAL ORGANIZATIONS

Many different types of organizations have been developed over the centuries, and their functions along with their dynamics have diversified as the different types of organizations have evolved. In this section, we will take a look at some of the types of organizations, how their dynamics shape and impact their effectiveness, and how social workers can operate with them.

Social organizations can be categorized into three distinct types. One type is the public/government organization; these include organizations like public universities, police and fire departments, and child welfare agencies. A second type is the private (meaning non-governmental), nonprofit/voluntary organization; examples include the United Way, Salvation Army, and American Civil Liberties Union. The third type is the private, for-profit organization, which could be owned by individuals, families, stockholders, and so on. Examples of these organizations include most businesses and companies that produce goods and services like realtors, restaurants, and retail chains. Further, many hospitals, skilled nursing and adult living facilities, and health and mental health agencies are owned by large, for-profit corporations. As a social worker, you could be employed by any of these types of organizations.

In addition to categorizing organizations into these three broad types, organizations can also be categorized according to their function or purpose. Exhibit 16.1 lists these categorizations along with a brief description of their purpose.

Social organizations also can be thought of in terms of their settings and whom they employ. **Primary settings** are those in which social workers make up the majority of employees for the organizations. Social workers usually are the administrators and the staff who provide services. Because social workers make up the majority of personnel in primary settings, they generally share the same values and goals. Examples of a primary setting might be an adoption agency or a homeless shelter. **Secondary settings** are usually staffed by personnel from a variety of professions, social work being one of them. Depending on the organization and focus of service provision, you may find psychologists, physicians, psychiatrists, and so on. Generally, social workers in secondary settings are part of interdisciplinary teams and must be knowledgeable about characteristics from a variety of professions. For example, in a hospice agency, you will find nurses, doctors, counselors, accountants, nursing assistants, and physical therapists in addition to social workers. Often in secondary settings, social workers must be able to talk about what social workers do to help educate those in other professions with whom they work on an interdisciplinary team. Further, social workers in secondary settings may find that other employees do not share the same values or goals, so conflict between employees

ORGANIZATION	PURPOSE	
Service-providing organizations • Social service organizations • Faith-based organizations	To provide social services, education, and research to address and alleviate social needs. Examples are health and human service organizations and churches.	**EXHIBIT 16.1** *Categories of Social Organizations*
Social advocacy organizations	To provide venues through which advocacy activities can be conducted that promote the health and well-being of individuals, families, communities, and society. Examples include the NAACP and political action committees.	
Intermediary organizations • Social intermediary organizations • Funding intermediary organizations	To support social organizations and the communities they serve through financing, consulting, administration, community development, and the like. They often act as convening and brokering agents. Examples include the Robert Wood Johnson Foundation and the Community Development Corporation.	
Social enterprise organizations • Commercial social enterprise organizations • Community wealth corporations	Neither private, for-profit or nonprofit, governmental organizations, they offer goods and services as a business would but for social purposes. Examples include Network for Good, which helps nonprofits raise funds through online platforms and Chrysalis, which helps low-income and homeless individuals find stable employment.	

may occur around service provision goals and processes. Social workers need to be skilled in handling these types of conflicts.

Social Organizational Dynamics

Organizations, like many other facets of human and social life, have cultures, structures, and processes of functioning in daily life. These factors have a great deal of impact on the roles and behavior of the employees working within organizations as well as the ability for employees to carry out the goals and purpose of organizations and effectively meet the needs of the people they serve.

Social Organizational Culture and Structure Earlier, we talked about conceptualizing organizations through systems theory. This theoretical lens is useful in thinking about organizational culture. Every organization has a culture made up of values, beliefs, norms, rules, roles, artifacts, boundaries, traditions, and assumptions about how things should be done and how employees (and even clients of the organization) should act (Chatman & Eunyoung Cha, 2003; Hellriegel & Slocum, 2009). An organization's culture is reflected in its mission, rituals, stories and language, rules and policies, and even in its physical environment.

Organizational culture has a lot do with how employees function, understand their place within the organization, and function in their jobs on a daily basis. Examples of organizational culture are the ways employees are expected to dress, how the employees interact with one another, how employees interact with administrators, and the freedom employees have in their daily work. For example, a substance abuse clinic may encourage their employees to dress casually to help clients feel more comfortable. Employees may have a great deal of freedom to come and go and control their own schedules depending on client needs. And administrators may keep an "open door" policy, encouraging employees to talk freely to their supervisors. Even the types of office decoration say much about the organization's culture. Signs that encourage clients to talk about abuse they may be experiencing or that state the organization does not tolerate discrimination create a sense of equality and safety for clients and employees. Artwork that reflects the diversity of the clientele and employees also sets a tone that reflects the organization's culture.

The extent to which employees are a good "fit" with the organizational culture has a lot to do with how satisfied they are in their jobs as well as their longevity with an organization (O'Reilly, Chatman, & Caldwell, 1991). And, organizational culture has a lot to do with the success of the organization itself (Marcoulides & Heck, 1993). For example, a social enterprise organization, with a mission that espouses innovation in community development, should cultivate a culture that values creativity, flexibility, and innovation if it wants to succeed. Employees, too, should value this type of environment if they want to feel a sense of belonging and commitment to the organization. Conversely, if this same organization has a culture of rigidity that stifles creativity in the face of market pressure to produce innovation in community development, both the agency and the employees are likely to suffer and possibly fail. The stronger an organization's culture, the bigger the impact it has on employees' behavior. Often, organizations' cultures are strengthened over time and are shaped by the larger context of consumer and social values (Chatman & Eunyoung Cha, 2003).

Much research has been conducted, particularly in the business arena, on organizational culture and its effects on employees, clients, and organizational success. One particularly useful typology to help explain organizational culture is the Organizational Culture Profile (OCP) (O'Reilly, Chatman, & Caldwell, 1991). This profile helps to describe organizational culture from seven distinct values, which in turn allows for organizational culture to be measured and managed more effectively. Below is a description of each of the seven types of organizational culture as articulated by the OCP.

- **Innovative cultures:** These organizations are characterized by adaptable and flexible values that encourage innovation and experimentation. They generally have flat hierarchies that allow for equality in power and influence in organization processes. As was mentioned in the above example, social enterprise organizations might espouse this type of culture. Many other social organizations also do this, particularly those guided by feminist values.

- **Aggressive cultures:** Characterized by competitiveness, these organizations often rely on aggressive language and practices to achieve their goals. Many businesses like Microsoft and car sales companies could be described as having an aggressive culture, where the goal is to beat all competition. Organizations with aggressive cultures sometimes find themselves in legal trouble because of the values of competition they embrace.

- **Outcome-oriented cultures:** In these organizations, values of action, results, and achievement are important. Employees are held accountable for the success, or lack thereof, of the organization, and they are trained specifically to achieve successful outcomes. The performance and compensation of the employees is tied to their output. While this type of culture can lead to better success over other types of cultures, it can sometimes lead employees to engage in unethical behavior to achieve goals. Some social organizations cultivate this type of culture. Indeed, some mental health agencies support an outcome-oriented model, for example holding employees accountable for how many clients they see in a day rather than the quality of services provided. Further, many funders of social organizations require a tally of the number of clients served or programs delivered in a particular time frame for agencies to continue to receive funding.

- **Stable cultures:** A bureaucratic, rule-focused, predictable environment characterizes this culture. Status quo is the norm; employees may find little opportunity for creativity, innovation, or thinking "outside the box" in these organizations. Many public organizations have stable cultures, which can be frustrating for many employees who face hierarchical red tape in decision making or attempts to improve or change organizational functioning.

- **People-oriented cultures:** Organizations with this type of culture tend to cultivate a sense of fairness, equality, and respect among their employees. Individual rights and employee support and empowerment are important in this culture. A people-oriented culture can be found in many social organizations, particularly in small, non-governmental agencies.

- **Team-oriented cultures:** These cultures value collaboration, particularly among employees and between employees and supervisors. Many social organizations, including private and public entities, tend to support and cultivate team-oriented cultures.

- **Detail-oriented cultures:** As the name suggests, these cultures value attention to detail and precision. Employees are trained to focus on customer service. Many service-oriented organizations like hotels and restaurants are characterized by this culture. Few social organizations in which social workers are employed are dominated by this culture.

The reality is that most social organizations have some combination of these cultures. It is important for social workers to be aware of which culture dominates in the organization where they are employed; whether the culture(s) matches the values of employees and clients and the mission of the organization; and ways in which the culture could change to improve services, working conditions, and the organization's success.

Social Organizational Structure Organizations' **formal structures** refer to the process through which they function: the tasks, policies, reporting mechanisms, hierarchies and authority through which decisions are made, and the formal ways in which management thinks things should be done (Griffin & Moorhead, 2010). Organizational charts are one way in which the formal organizational structure is communicated. These charts depict the hierarchy of communication and decision making and the ways in which organizations may be compartmentalized into smaller divisions or departments.

Organizations also have informal structures that are not depicted in policies or organizational charts. **Informal structures** refer to the ways in which employees may circumvent formal process or create informal pathways and methods to meet their needs or get tasks accomplished. For example, when questions arise, some employees may rely on more experienced colleagues for answers instead of consulting a supervisor. Both the formal and informal structure of an organization reflect how power, authority, and communication play out in the organization and affect its functioning.

Funding of Social Organizations Many social, political, and economic forces shape the development and functioning of social organizations. The extent to which organizations are able to hire employees, develop programs, expand service provision, allocate funds, and support employees depends on the type of program and the restrictions placed on it from funding sources. For example, organizations funded through governmental entities or grants often face strict rules and restrictions that guide the allocation of resources and accountability on how the funds are spent. Employees may have little flexibility in decisions around agency functioning because of these restrictions. Conversely, other funding sources like private foundations may allow organizations more freedom to make decisions around how funds are spent. Further, most organizations operate utilizing multiple sources of funding, which can make organizational functioning complex. For instance, one agency may simultaneously receive funds from a county government, private donations and gifts, and external grants and contracts—and they all may be disbursed and accounted for on different timetables. Employees in charge of budgeting, who are often social workers, must be knowledgeable about rules and restrictions on funding, including potential conflicts of funding that can occur when multiple funding sources are utilized. Specifically, some funders have rules that restrict organizations from soliciting funds from particular sources.

Much of the operating process depends on who is funding the organization, where the funds originate, and what external rules are in place to monitor the expenditure of funds. Because the funding of organizations can be complex, social workers need to understand how to navigate funding processes such as locating potential funding sources, grant writing, budgeting, and reporting.

Social Workers' Roles in Social Organizations

From the time when the social work profession was first established, social workers have played important roles in organizations. Social workers can be found in positions in every realm of organizations, from founders to board members to administrators to frontline workers. Early social workers often found themselves caught between the needs of clients in organizations and the needs of the organizations themselves (Kerson & McCoyd, 2013). Of course, this is still the case today. Social workers may find they are unable to effectively do their work within the confines of an organization's resources or that community demands and values are incompatible with those of the organizations for which they work. This is particularly true for social workers who find themselves in organizations that serve vulnerable populations. Sometimes organizational goals are in conflict with or create barriers to social action, a core value of the social work profession (Gates, 2014). Being a part of an organization brings benefits and challenges with which social workers need to be prepared to work.

Social workers have many opportunities to meet individual and community needs and create change through organizations. This includes needs and changes for the people they serve as well as the organizations themselves. However, social workers often find themselves in organizations that work with difficult and complex problems and that are entrenched in contexts with multiple stakeholders to which organizations are accountable (e.g., boards, courts, community leaders). These conditions can be stressful, demoralizing, ethically challenging, resistant or slow to change, and even detrimental to the people they serve (Glisson *et al.*, 2008).

Social workers often serve in administrative and leadership roles in organizations. This means that social workers need to be knowledgeable about and understand how organizations function and how to go about changing organizational structure and processes when needed (Rwomire, 2011). Social workers often must call upon the skills, knowledge, and values of the profession to provide good leadership and guidance to organizations. While working in leadership and administrative positions can be challenging because of the conflicts mentioned earlier, they can also bring opportunities for social workers to help make organizations more ethical and effective for employees and the people and communities they serve.

Lee (1937) recognized that organizations and the work we do within them could be in conflict with our calling to change systemic structures that perpetuate social problems, including those inflicted by organizations meant to address these problems. Consequently, new forms of organizations are becoming increasingly popular that help to address this conflict. For example, hybrid organizations, or organizations that incorporate several different organizational designs, structures, or approaches, are being developed for social service provision. They could be used to generate profit or community change while providing social services. Social workers bring many qualifications and skills that equip them to be leaders in developing innovative organizations that better serve our changing social, individual, and community needs.

Applying Organizational Functions

New Horizons is a private, non-profit organization, funded through a variety of sources both governmental and nongovernmental. Thus, the clinic must be sensitive to the competing needs and goals, values, and needs of the various funding sources. The clinic could be described as a service-providing organization, and because it relies on an interdisciplinary staff, including social workers, it can be considered a secondary setting. From the case description, it seems as if the clinic maintains a stable culture. The clinic is described as operating from a hierarchical, bureaucratic, rule-driven framework in which employees have little say or independence in their work.

SOCIAL ORGANIZATIONAL DIVERSITY

As with other aspects of society, organizations are becoming more diverse, particularly with regard to characteristics such as age, gender, ethnicity, and sexual orientation (Mor Barak & Travis, 2010). A diverse representation of employees in social organizations is important not only to offer organizations more creative and diverse viewpoints on organizational decisions and processes, but also to reflect the diversity of clients that organizations serve (Miranda, 1994). Indeed, recall our earlier discussion on feminist perspectives on organizations. The perspectives would support the idea that to successfully carry out an organization's mission, effectively serve clients, and increase employees' well-being and job satisfaction, an organization should fully integrate employees with diverse backgrounds into all aspects of the organization, including leadership positions (Cox, 1994).

However, philosophies inherent in our culture have important detrimental consequences for how organizations function in the face of diversity. The narrative that the United States is a meritocracy—that everyone has equal opportunities if they work hard enough—distracts from the historical and contemporary institutional discrimination that is embedded in our organizations and hurts minority individuals and groups. The notion that the United States is a melting pot suggests that people who immigrate to the United States have given up and should give up their unique cultural identities. And, the idea of colorblindness suggests that we ignore or not notice differences like skin color or other physical or cultural differences of people (Thomas, Mack, & Montagliani, 2004). What these philosophies do is to normalize majority group behavior and white privilege as well as perpetuate and maintain discriminatory behavior in organizations.

To help combat the effects of these philosophies in organizations, federal affirmative action and equal employment opportunity mandates have been established over the years. While many organizations may attend to diversity factors in their formal structures, like mission statements and policies, in practice many still continue to carry out, intentionally and unintentionally, discriminatory practices through their informal structures and processes (Thomas & Plaut, 2008).

The extent to which organizations attend to diversity in their practices and have cultivated a cultural identity can be grouped into three categories: monolithic, plural, and multicultural (Cox, 1991; Thomas & Ely, 1996). **Monolithic organizations** outwardly display little diversity or concern for achieving diversity goals; they are made up mostly of white men. If these organizations employ people with diverse characteristics, like women or people of color, they are found in lower-level, lower-paying positions in the organization. Monolithic organizations support the philosophies of colorblindness and assimilation, with the idea that treating employees the same will achieve fairness and equity. The cultural identity of **plural organizations** is more diverse than that of monolithic organizations, but they often fail to fully integrate diverse individuals into the organization. For example, minority individuals are likely to be employed in low-paying, low-power positions within the organization. While plural organizations may support diversity, they do not implement it fully in their practices (Cox, 1991). Finally, **multicultural organizations** tend to support diversity goals both in philosophy and practice. These organizations understand the value and resource in a diverse environment and are mindful of how they view diversity, incorporate it into their structures, and demonstrate their commitment to diversity goals (Thomas & Ely, 1996). Everyone involved in the organization is empowered to contribute their unique talents, skills, and perspectives to the organization.

Of particular importance in organizations is attention they give to ethnic diversity. While a colorblind approach to organizational functioning has been the dominant one in many cultures, like the one described in monolithic organizations above, today more attention is being paid to color cognizance, or multiculturalism, as was described in multicultural organizations and their impacts on organizational processes (Cox, 1994; Plaut, 2002). Research indicates that colorblindness, or the behavior of ignoring difference, tends to be detrimental to interactions among diverse employees, whereas color cognizance tends to enhance these interactions (Ely & Thomas, 2001; Evans, 2007).

However, some organizations may foster a plural climate as described above, where they acknowledge difference, but downplay the effects of it. One study of child welfare workers captured this phenomenon of color minimization (Foldy & Buckley, 2014). Teams of welfare workers were interviewed about their decisions around child placement, with a particular focus on racial and ethnic difference. The study found that while workers acknowledged and discussed factors of ethnic difference in placement decisions, most workers did not use these factors in their actual placement behavior and decisions. Specifically, workers were cognizant of color differences and their potential effects on children and families, but workers tended to minimize race and ethnicity in their decision-making process in their work. Workers engaged in color minimizing behaviors and justified these behaviors to the researchers.

Colorblindness and color minimization may feel safe, even egalitarian, for some, but these approaches tend to only create barriers for communication and positive outcomes within organizations (Norton, Sommers, Apfelbaum, Pura, & Ariely, 2006). Identifying these biases and behaviors among employees and helping them to overcome them can make organizations function more effectively and create better work conditions for employees. Organizations that can help workers to make sense of how they think about and act upon difference and how it affects their work are more likely to enhance relationships among employees and between employees and clients. These efforts help to undermine institutional discrimination in social organizations, bringing them closer to egalitarian, empowered environments that are socially just. Suggestions toward creating more just workplaces include making injustices known publicly; incorporating justice-oriented goals in organizational policy; creating spaces for dialogue and small group discussions between and among employees; holding public forums on justice-related topics; and encouraging employees to interact as individuals, not as representatives of an entire group (Bergsieker, Shelton, & Richeson, 2010).

Applying Organizational Diversity

New Horizons could be considered a plural organization because of its acknowledgment of the importance of diversity without subsequent action to create it among the employees. The clinic has mostly white employees and white men in its administrative and decision-making positions. Further, it seems that the administration of the clinic does not value the diversity of opinions and viewpoints of its employees, so it is failing to capitalize on the innovation and creativity that diversity can bring to organizations.

ETHICAL CONSIDERATIONS IN ORGANIZATIONS

Social organizations come with their strengths and limitations, and social workers need to be prepared to work with both. Sometimes, issues arise in organizations that create ethical dilemmas for employees or that move into the realm of illegal behavior that could put clients or employees at risk for harm. In this section, we will look at some of the issues that can arise in the context of organizations that social workers might need to address.

Discriminatory and Oppressive Behavior in Organizations

Earlier we discussed diversity considerations in organizations. Diversity, or lack of it, in organizations plays a large role in the extent to which organizations experience discrimination, oppression, stereotyping, or other negative behaviors by employees, administrators, boards and committees, and other stakeholders involved in organizations. Even with laws in place that make discriminatory behavior unlawful, individual and institutional factors make this behavior inevitable and sometimes difficult to spot and change. For example, we talked about monolithic organizational cultures in a previous section. These types of cultures, because of their inherent and often active refusal to acknowledge diversity, can easily cultivate and perpetuate stereotypical values, beliefs, and behaviors of those involved in these organizations. Those who experience discrimination will have few options and little support when calling attention to the discriminatory behaviors of others or advocating for change. Further, organizations that have few employees of color or who come with other diverse backgrounds likely will not cultivate an environment of inclusion or trust that can help recruit, promote, and retain a diverse employee pool. Often, these organizations lack representation of a diverse workforce in their upper administration positions and other positions of leadership. This type of situation often perpetuates institutional discrimination and keeps people of color and others with diverse characteristics from moving into management and other positions of power that can bring about change (Andersen & Taylor, 2013).

While overt discrimination has lessened over the past several decades, covert discrimination still remains and often leads to **tokenism**, or the hiring of a few people to represent diverse populations, to demonstrate that organizations are adhering to equal opportunity laws and policies. However, tokenism does not lead to systemic change, and it often perpetuates discrimination and stereotypes as the behavior and performance of a few become representative of the particular population as a whole (Henslin, 2014). Tokenism can also exaggerate differences between groups and reinforce stereotypes of those within diverse groups. These employees may be relegated to working with clients of similar backgrounds or be spokespersons for all things diversity related for the organization. Yet, these same employees are often shut out of informal networks, mentoring or leadership opportunities, or other avenues leading to advancement in organizations (Padavic & Reskin, 2002; Simon & Akabas, 1993).

Power and Politics

All social organizations are political, and power dynamics play an important role in organizational functions. Whether they want to or not, social workers need skills in understanding politics and power and how they influence organizations and employees as well as the clients they serve.

Power is an important concept to understand within organizations because it has ramifications for how work is accomplished and how people function within organizations. Different kinds of power exist within organizations, and some are more legitimate and beneficial than others. For example, supervisors and managers can have **legitimate power**, or power that is recognized by the organization because of one's position within it. Legitimate power can be used justly and fairly to promote the mission of the organization and well-being of workers and clients, or it can be misused to intimidate and undermine employee's work. **Coercive power**, on the other hand, is power that is used to punish or control others' behavior. Supervisors could hold this type of power, but other employees who have the capability to exert control over others can also use it. For example, one co-worker might undermine another co-worker by withholding important information, reporting minor mistakes made by the co-worker, or deliberately interfering with the co-worker's work to make the co-worker appear incompetent (Daft, 2010). Determining who has power and how it is being used or undermined can be difficult in social organizations, but power is an important element of how organizations function.

To maintain a sense of control or power, employees of social organizations may resort to destructive or unethical behaviors such as lying, self-promotion, face-saving, back stabbing, or distortion of the truth. Behaviors such as these not only undermine relationships and morale among workers, but they can undermine the goals of the organization and service to clients. Dynamics such as these need to be addressed and managed. Dealing directly with the people who are engaging in the behaviors is important to heal relationships and uncover deeper problems within the organization that may be promoting such behaviors.

Politics in social organizations play out on different levels. Politics could refer to larger social forces like laws, policies, and philosophies held by lawmakers and stakeholders associated with the service provision goals of the organization. Conversely, politics can refer to the daily functions and interactions of the employees within an organization and how these dynamics impact service provision. For example, being political in an organization can mean being mindful and sensitive to the views of important stakeholders as tasks are carried out, or it can mean behaving in ways that are congenial and professional even when disagreements between workers exist or personality issues create conflict among workers. In these cases, attending to politics can be advantageous to the workings and goals of an organization (Aldag & Kuzuhara, 2005).

However, politics can play a negative role in organizations and impede the work of its employees. Departments within an organization may compete with one another to achieve disparate goals, or the values of stakeholders may be contradictory to the mission of the organization or the needs of the clients it serves (Griffin & Moorhead, 2010). Being able to identify and work with political processes is an important skill for social workers to ensure that politics do not become a negative or destructive force within an organization. Indeed, social workers can be very skillful at the political process to help empower organizations and employees.

Crime and Exploitation

Social organizations, like businesses and other types of organizations, are vulnerable to crime and exploitation. For example, issues around individual and institutional discrimination and misuse of power and politics can create conditions that allow for criminal and exploitative behaviors among those who work for organizations. A good example of this is the misuse of power against minority populations within police departments across the United States. Our nation has a long history of police brutality and violation of human rights. Efforts to curb it—like the passage of the Violent Crime Control and Law Enforcement Act of 1994 and public protests like those in response to the police shooting of an unarmed black teenager in Ferguson, Missouri, in 2014—have brought attention to this misuse of power, but they have not been successful in eradicating it (Holmes, 2014).

Employee theft is another issue that social organizations face. Behaviors can range from the unethical, such as use of organization resources for personal reasons, to more criminal acts like theft of supplies and embezzlement. Sometimes these behaviors are the result of a lack of training on or awareness of professional behavior, boundaries, and policies, and sometimes they are deliberate acts for personal gain. Sometimes organizations that are staffed by employees with a lack of training and oversight can be at risk for theft and other problems (Zack, 2003). For example, school boards are usually staffed by parent or community volunteers with little to no training in their roles on the board. A school board treasurer may have unlimited access to school funds with no real accountability to other members, who may not know what to look for with regard to criminal behavior.

The most common forms of embezzlement activities in organizations include forging checks, keeping cash meant for deposit, issuing extra paychecks to oneself or others, submitting fraudulent expense reports and invoices, misusing organizational credit cards, and using organizational resources for personal reasons (Marquet, 2011). Often employees commit crimes because there is a perceived pressure or incentive to do so, such as when an employee has personal debts or addictions that need to be financed; there are opportunities to commit a crime because of a lack of oversight, such as the example cited above with the school board; or the crime is easy to rationalize (Zack, 2003). Issues around cybertheft are becoming increasingly relevant as organizations become more reliant on technology, leaving them vulnerable to data theft, confidentiality breaches, and other crimes by employees and people outside of the organization (Arlitsch & Edelman, 2014). Procedures such as governmental and organizational oversight, regulation, and accounting practices, as well as community and stakeholder involvement, have been suggested as ways to counter criminal and exploitative behaviors among employees (Holmes, 2014).

Whistle Blowing

When employees in an organization discover crime or unethical behavior, they may become **whistle blowers**, or people who report the illegal or unethical behaviors of other employees to people in authority (Near & Miceli, 1985). While whistle blowing can have positive effects on an organization, such as instigating organizational change, it can also bring stressful, negative consequences to the whistle blower. Indeed, whistle blowers may experience public alienation, decreased social support, and apathy on the part of the organization, even though they may experience support by others on a more personal, individual level (McGlynn & Richardson, 2014; K. Thompson, 2012). Often, whistle blowing is viewed by others as disloyal, disruptive, destructive, and a betrayal of trust (Dandekar, 1991).

Increasingly, whistle blowing is viewed as a form of advocacy in the social work profession, particularly because it has received attention in the context of ethical decision making (Reamer, 1998). However, it is rare that people are willing to be whistle blowers in organizations, mostly because of the perceived and real consequences of disclosing the unethical behavior of others, as discussed above. To help encourage advocacy behavior through whistle blowing, the Whistleblower Protection Law of 1989 was passed to protect federal employees who divulge information about unethical or illegal behavior (Congressional Information Service, 1986). In addition, in 1993, the National Association of Social Workers (1996) established the Jack Otis Whistle-Blower Award to recognize those who advocate for just practices in organizations through whistle blowing. Further, the Code of Ethics (National Association of Social Workers, 2008) articulates several standards of collegial behavior and responsibilities to employers that are related to whistle blowing. These include attending and responding to impairment, incompetence, and unethical conduct of colleagues as well as commitment to employers.

In deciding whether or not to disclose questionable behavior to employers, there are many steps social workers can take to help with decision making and the process of whistle blowing. Questions to ask oneself in the process include (Reamer, 1990):

- Is the behavior severe enough to warrant intervention?

- Are the benefits of whistle blowing worth the potential harm to relationships and reputations of individuals and the organization?

- Is there sufficient and credible evidence of wrongdoing?

- What are my own motivations for reporting the behavior?

- Can I accept the situation if I don't report the behavior?

- Can I manage the consequences of reporting the behavior?

The Code of Ethics (2008) and other experts and researchers in professional ethics (Greene & Latting, 2004; Reamer, 1990) also offer guidelines in handling unethical or illegal behavior of colleagues or organizations. Steps include:

- **Begin with the colleague whose behavior is in question:** If possible, social workers should speak directly with the colleague whose behavior is concerning. Sometimes, though, this may not be fruitful or possible depending on the nature of the situation and the disposition of the offending colleague.

- **Establish a record of credibility:** Approaching the issue with care and thought are important in these situations. Seeming proactive rather than reactive can help establish credibility in making claims about others' behavior.

- **Assume others are concerned:** Approaching the situation from a unified stance is helpful. This can be done by assuming others in the organization are aware of or would like to know about questionable behavior but have not been able to act for a variety of reasons.

- **Establish evidence and support and keep records:** Before taking action, it is useful to collect information about the questionable behavior and investigate the situation thoroughly. Be sure to document conversations and observations that occur in relation to the situation.

- **Utilize the administrative hierarchy:** It is advisable to adhere to organizational policies and structures for communication and filing grievances. This helps with communication, transparency, checks and balances within the system, and ensuring that people with authority are kept in the loop.

- **Get advice and document it:** Obtain consultation with others like supervisors, other colleagues, the code of ethics, and relevant laws, statutes, and policies. Document the consultation process and the outcomes and decisions you make based on that consultation.

Applying Ethics

What potential and current ethical issues do you see happening with New Horizons? The lack of diversity in the clinic, as discussed earlier, could create conditions leading to discrimination and tokenism. And, given that power seems to be concentrated among those in administration, any coercive use of power may be difficult to challenge. Coercive power also could become a problem between employees and clients since many clients can only remain out of jail through positive reports from employees to judges and probation officers. And, given that controlled substances such as methadone are kept at the clinic, there is the potential for theft by clients and employees. The disempowerment of employees could create a feeling of competition between employees, leading to behaviors like lying, self-promotion, face-saving, or backstabbing as employees attempt to gain favor with those in positions of power. Finally, New Horizons seems to have some issues with employees discriminating against and sexually harassing some of the potential clients. While there did not seem to be any immediate negative consequences for the employee who disclosed this behavior to clinic directors, the employees involved in the behaviors were not disciplined, and it does not appear that changes were made to the intake process. Ultimately, the employee did not feel supported and did not agree with the behaviors of her co-workers, but because of inaction on the part of the clinic, she felt her only course of action was to resign from the clinic. The culture of the organization, and its resistance to change, is sometimes enough to pressure employees to conform to norms or leave.

CONCLUSION

Social organizations not only help to bring order and structure to society, but they provide crucial services to individuals, families, and communities. Social workers play important roles in social organizations, and they are influential in their development and function, including the development and carrying out of organizations' mission, goals, and objectives.

Social organizations can be viewed through many lenses to help describe how they function and their impacts on employees and clients. Organizations can be described by characteristics related to structure, funding, mission, and the ways in which they operate through formal and informal channels. Organizations develop and operate with their own unique cultures that include rules, roles, norms, boundaries, and subsystems that shape employees' and clients' behaviors and influence service delivery. Organizations also have their own ways of dealing with and incorporating diverse characteristics of employees and clients, which also affect the culture of the organization and behavior of employees and clients. Organizations also deal with unique ethical issues that arise because of the nature of the work they do and the multitude of stakeholders often involved in the functions of organizations.

MAIN POINTS

- Social organizations are socially constructed systems that provide and maintain boundaries around human activity and help to address social problems.

- Social organizations are guided by mission statements, goals, and objectives that articulate how activities of the organization will be carried out and lend themselves to evaluation to determine whether goals have been achieved.

- Social organizations became important to society around the turn of the 17th century. Before this time, services were provided primarily through religious and other private, voluntary associations.

- Social organizations and their structures and functions can be viewed through a multitude of lenses and perspectives including systems, ecosystems, feminist, and organizational justice perspectives. Each offers a unique view on how organizations are developed and organized as well as descriptions about their processes.

- Social organizations can be described by the nature of their funding and purpose. They can be public/governmental or private depending on their funding, and their purposes dictate whether they are service-providing, social advocacy, intermediary, or social enterprise organizations. Further, organizations can be described by their settings, where primary settings are staffed by social workers and secondary settings are staffed by interdisciplinary teams including social workers.

- Social organizations have a culture made up of values, beliefs, norms, rules, roles, artifacts, boundaries, traditions, and assumptions about how things should be done and how employees (and even clients of the organization) should act. Several different types of cultures have been identified based on their characteristics including innovative, aggressive, outcome-oriented, stable, people-oriented, team-oriented, and detail-oriented cultures.

- Social organizations function through formal structures, or the tasks, policies, reporting mechanisms, hierarchies and authority through which decisions are made, and the formal ways in which management thinks things should be done. They also function through informal structures, or processes not depicted in policies or organizational charts. These could include the ways in which employees may circumvent formal process or create informal pathways and methods to meet their needs or get tasks accomplished.

- Social, political, and economic forces shape the development and functioning of social organizations. The extent to which organizations are able to hire employees, develop programs, expand service provision, allocate funds, and support employees depends on the type of program and the restrictions placed on it from funding sources.

- Social workers play important and influential roles in social organizations. They can be found in positions in every realm of organizations, from founders to board members to administrators to frontline workers.

- Social organizations differ a great deal with regard to how they deal with and incorporate diverse characteristics of employees and clients. The categories of monolithic, plural, and multicultural organizations help to describe how organizations address diversity. While the United States has laws in place to prevent and deal with discrimination, and many organizations have policies in place to address discrimination, many organizations still have serious issues related to discrimination.

- Social organizations have their own set of unique ethical issues that affect their functioning and well-being of employees and clients. These include issues around discrimination, oppression, power, politics, crime, exploitation, and whistle blowing.

EXERCISES

1. *RAINN interactive case at* www.routledgesw.com/cases. Review information on the RAINN case and answer the following questions:
   a. Describe the type and structure of the organization including whether it is private or public, profit or nonprofit; its funding sources; and what you can gather about its formal structures.
   b. How well are RAINN's mission, goals, and objectives articulated on the website? Are the objectives measurable? What more information do you need to ascertain the organization's purpose and whether their approaches are effective?
   c. From RAINN's website, what can you tell about the organization's culture?
   d. What ethical issues, including problems with discrimination, might be relevant or problematic for this organization?
2. *Hudson City interactive case at* www.routledgesw.com/cases. Take some time to explore the Hudson City case and the environmental context in which this case is situated. Then answer the following:
   a. What organizations are available in the area to provide services?
   b. Describe the different types and structures of these agencies. What are some of the strengths and limitations of these agencies with regard to serving the community based on their types, funding, structures, and the like?
   c. What other service organizations might be needed by the community and why?

3. *Carla Washburn interactive case at* www.routledgesw.com/cases. Explore Carla's case and her community. Then respond to the following:

   a. Given Carla's situation and presenting problems, what types of social services would benefit her?

   b. Looking at her community, which social organizations seem to be the best fit for Carla and why?

   c. In what ways might these organizations be problematic or create barriers for Carla based on culture, structure, and other factors related to diversity?

   d. In what ways could these organizations be changed to be more multicultural or responsive to diverse characteristics of clients?

CHAPTER 17

Communities and the Social Environment

Washington Elementary School is a small Spanish-immersion charter school located in a suburban area outside of a mid-sized metropolitan western city. The city's political climate is not welcoming to alternative educational arrangements. The school has been in operation for about five years after being established by a community of parents who wanted a language immersion option for their children. The school began with about 50 children, grades 1st through 5th, and it has since grown to over 200 children, grades 1st through 8th.

Since the school opened, it has moved locations three times, had four principals, and has seen a high turnover of teachers each year. Much of this instability is due to the school's inadequate funding: charter schools only receive 80 percent of the funding that is allocated for public schools. As a community, the families at Washington Elementary School must all participate in fundraising and volunteering to keep the school running and help make up the fiscal shortfall.

The school enjoys a tight-knit community even though families come from geographically diverse areas around the city. Some families travel more than 30 miles so their children can attend. In addition to fiscal issues, the community has had to deal with several challenges. For example, a few years ago, the principal was accused by parents and the school board of falsifying test scores so the school's funding would not be endangered; the school relies heavily on volunteerism by people not trained in tasks like budgeting, planning, running meetings, and effective communication; and children who need special services at Washington Elementary do not have access to the same level of services as children in public schools. Further, families, with limited help from the principal, are charged with recruiting and retaining Spanish-speaking teachers, many of whom arrive from other countries with no connections or resources in their new community and minimal English-language skills. This can be challenging for these teachers given the low pay, relocation costs, and tasks needed to become licensed to teach in a new country, among other adjustments they must make. The school community feels a great deal of guilt and responsibility when teachers decide not to stay in their positions after the sacrifices they had to make to come to the school.

In addition to minimal support with student needs, the school district offers little assistance with planning, standardized testing, finding a permanent home for the

school, or legal issues the community might face, such as the situation with the
principal who submitted false test scores. Many of the community's problems have
created such severe stress that most of the founding families have left the school.
Even if teachers stay in spite of low pay, many subsequently leave due to stress, lack
of support, and sense of chaos felt in the community.

T HE CASE OF THE WASHINGTON ELEMENTARY SCHOOL community shows
just how important community is to human behavior and well-being. It is also
an important element of the social work profession. Indeed, a focus on community
has been part of social work since its beginning, when community development
and settlement houses were utilized to improve human conditions. Many of social
work's theoretical underpinnings and approaches continue to incorporate community, making the concept of human behavior in the social environment a central
tenet in the profession.

In this chapter we will explore what makes a community, including definitions,
characteristics, and types of communities. We will look at ways social workers conceptualize and make sense of communities as well as ways we can assess and intervene with communities. We will also discuss ethical issues and dilemmas that can
come with community work.

WHAT ARE COMMUNITIES?

Social workers often speak of "community" in their work, and it can mean many
different things to different people, depending on the context in which the word is
being used. In this section, we will explore the meaning of community most often
used in the profession and some of the characteristics of community you likely will
encounter.

Definition and Characteristics of Communities

What is community? Is community marked by geographical lines and physical
spaces, or is it more about psychological and emotional aspects that bind a group
of people together? How do we "cultivate" community? How do people form a
sense of belonging to a community? These questions help point out the different
meanings of community and the ways they are used in social work.

One common theme or aspect of community entails the spaces, people, identity,
and interactions that take place between members (Hillery, 1955; Netting, Kettner, &
McMurty, 2004). Given these common factors, we can look at specific components
to help us identify characteristics of community and ways to work with them.

In Chapter 5 of the core HBSE book, two definitions of communities were offered: communities that are territorial in nature and bound by geography; and relational communities, bound together by common values, beliefs and culture. Here, we will look at a few more definitions of community. One specific way to define community is through identification. **Identificational communities** can be thought of as groups of people bound together by similar values, connections, struggles, and shared traditions (Gilbert, 2003; Harrison, 1995). Members are self-identified based on perceived shared characteristics like race, ability, religion, culture, ethnicity, or lifestyle. For example, many minority groups form identificational communities such as the GLBT community, the Mexican–American community, the caregiver community, the Jewish community, or the refugee community.

Communities can also be defined through location. **Locational communities** are those that exist in shared spaces like neighborhoods, towns, cities, or regions. These can also be referred to as space, territorial, or geographical communities (Netting *et al.*, 2004). Often, official geographical boundaries, like city limits, define these communities, and money and resources are determined by these boundaries. Some locational communities are defined by natural markers like rivers, or manmade markers like major highways; in other cases, signs that specify city limits can serve to define locational communities.

Communities can also be formed through shared interests. **Interest communities** are those in which people are brought together by common goals and interests in causes or activities (Fellin, 2001). Interest communities may, for example, include professional organizations or social clubs whose members have specific objectives around helping the community in certain ways. While interest communities are based on shared identification, they are usually more specific and narrow in their focus than identificational communities.

Virtual communities are newer types of communities formed through means of electronic communication and platforms. These could include any community developed via the Internet such as LISTSERVs and similar email discussion lists, social networking sites, and discussion and chat rooms. Virtual communities are reshaping the ways people interact with one another, and they pose some interesting ethical and logistical questions, particularly around access, safety, confidentiality, and human connectedness, which we discuss later in this chapter.

Functions of Communities

Communities exist, ideally, to help promote the health, safety, and well-being of their members and to meet members' needs. Warren (1978) specified five main functions of communities that help to support members. These functions revolve around socialization; social control; social participation; mutual support; and production, distribution, and consumption.

Socialization. Community membership and participation are avenues through which members are socialized. Children, for example, learn roles, rules, norms, and cultural values through their parents and families, but they also learn them from other members of the community like their peers, teachers, religious leaders, and the media. Different sectors of communities share, pass along, and reinforce beliefs, customs, teachings, traditions, and behavioral expectations.

Social control.   Socialization can be thought of as one way to control human behavior and create conformity or social control. Communities help promote social control by influencing members' behavior through established rules and norms that guide behavior and consequences for violating those rules and norms. These rules and norms can be formal in nature, like laws and policies that specify boundaries of behavior and consequences for violating them, like fines or jail time. Rules and norms can also be informal, like members' expectations that place subtle pressure on other members to conform. Subtle enforcement of rules and norms could include nonverbal indications of disapproval, verbal warnings or statements of disapproval, or even excommunicating or ostracizing members from communities.

Social participation.   Communities provide opportunities for members to socialize and interact with other members. These opportunities can be formal, like when organizations hold events, activities, or socials. Examples include neighborhood parties, professional conferences, and organized sports events. Opportunities can also be informal, such as when members form friendships or subgroups outside of formal events or when related members gather and provide social support.

Mutual support.   One important function of communities is to provide support to other members. This support could be social, economic, or service-related, for example. Often in times of crisis, community members band together to help those affected by the crisis. It is not unusual for communities to provide food, shelter, health care, and other resources to members during natural disasters or other events like death, divorce, or job loss. Communities may have formal networks established to provide resources to members in times of need, or more informal networks may develop that are employed whenever a need arises. For example, neighbors may look out for one another's property and well-being by shoveling snow for older neighbors or bringing meals to those who are ill, disabled, or caring for a newborn baby.

Production, distribution, and consumption.   Over the past century, communities have been reliant on others, like farmers and businesses, to provide and distribute goods necessary for survival. While goods and services were once provided largely by families, communities now look to others often located in other geographical regions to provide food and other necessities. These providers are reliant on other communities to consume these goods to remain financially viable. This relationship has shaped the way our economy functions and the ways in which we view services and goods. Currently, many communities are shifting back to providing goods and services on a more local level. For example, many neighborhoods host farmers' markets that sell local produce and other goods, helping to sustain local economies and a healthier environment.

Applying Definitions and Functions of Communities

Given the information in the case study, it seems that the Washington Elementary School community has been brought together and is held together by mutual interests of the families who attend the school. The families all share the same interest of giving their children an opportunity to be immersed in a second language and to be exposed to certain curricular characteristics that are not offered in their neighborhood public schools. Families also share an interest in giving their children opportunities to interact with children from diverse backgrounds.

Like school communities in general, the Washington Elementary School community serves several functions for the families and their children. The school provides an environment in which the children can be socialized and engage in social participation, both with their peers and also in a bilingual environment that emphasizes cultural diversity. This context also allows for socialization among families who can interact with others from their own and different cultural, geographical, and socioeconomic backgrounds. Of course, the community provides a context in which to provide social control, teaching the children about rules, safety, responsibility, and mutual respect. Families find mutual support in this community in many ways, including collaboration on building and shaping the school to support their academic goals, especially in a hostile political environment that is not welcoming to charter schools; contributing to school administrative tasks; offering opportunities for families to gather in social contexts for support; and creating networks through which families can meet transportation and child care needs.

CONCEPTUALIZATIONS OF COMMUNITIES

The ways in which we view communities have direct implications for how we work with them. As with other areas of human behavior, theories help to guide the ways we view behavior, problems, and approaches to work with issues. In this section, we will discuss a few theoretical lenses through which to view communities.

Critical Race Theory and Social Justice

In Chapter 4 of the core HBSE book, we introduced critical practice theory, which views social problems as caused by oppressive societal structures and the cultural and moral assumptions generated and maintained by dominant groups. Critical race theory is similar in that it seeks to examine human behavior and change in light of how structures of racism and white privilege enforce and perpetuate inequality and how these structures can be disrupted to work toward social and economic justice.

Critical race theory can be used to conceptualize communities and their functions. From this perspective, social and cultural capital might be examined to determine how concepts of race and class may be used to perpetuate inequality and oppression and create barriers for those in minority groups, particularly with regard to assuming positions of power and decision making in a community. This lens also helps to examine how identificational and geographical definitions of community may promote colorblind views of community that disenfranchise certain members from accessing social capital and other resources (Bonilla-Silva, 2013; LeChasseur, 2014). Critical race theory focuses on the social construction of community: who is included; who is excluded; and how its members' conceptualizations of community make room for power, racism, privilege, and injustice (LeChasseur, 2014; Sonn & Quayle, 2013). These analyses can inform community interventions that lead to transformed perceptions of community, increased inclusion of all members, and greater social and economic justice.

Concepts used in critical theories also can be helpful in thinking about community problems and change. For instance, examining community members' experiences of injustice and their current reality can help social workers and community members act upon environmental structures that perpetuate oppression and discrimination. Through raising awareness of oppressive social structures and creating egalitarian relationships among community members, they can better understand their circumstances and devise strategies to create long-term change (Freire, 1970; Held, 1980; McKerrow, 1989).

Systems Theory

Systems theory was discussed in some detail in Chapter 2 of the core HBSE book. Here, we will take a look at how constructs from this theory can be applied to communities.

From a systems perspective, communities themselves are really just formal and informal systems made up of smaller parts; these parts, in turn, help them function. Like other systems, communities are made up of subsystems with boundaries, rules, and norms that help define relationships between and among members and that help communities maintain homeostasis. Boundaries could include geographic lines established to differentiate where one community ends and another begins. Or, boundaries could consist of the particular goals and tasks on which a community is focused, which give it definition and identity. For example, boundaries of a professional organization may dictate that it focus strictly on health service provision and not educational activities. Given a community's boundaries then, roles, rules, and norms are established to help guide members' behaviors. A rural community may have flexible, relaxed boundaries, which allow community members to feel close to one another and to know a great deal about other members' lives. Community members may feel comfortable with, even entitled to, ask personal questions of others and become involved in the personal matters of their neighbors. Conversely, communities with rigid boundaries may foster a strong sense of privacy among members so that neighbors or community members do not interact often, preferring to "mind their own business."

Communities also receive input from other members and outside sources like governments, organizations, and funding sources. Communities receive information, communication, and resources from other systems that can help support their members and improve quality of life. Communities also generate output through energy expended on community development and investment and the ways in which members respond to input.

As is the case with other systems, communities continually strive to maintain homeostasis or a status quo in their functioning, even when this functioning may be detrimental to the well-being of the community and its members. A neighborhood with a great deal of poverty and crime may have a desire to create change and improve the conditions of the area, but this tendency to preserve the status quo may mean that it is resistant to change efforts simply because of the natural resistance systems create against change. This resistance can lead to entropy—a process in which the community's energy becomes increasingly negative and degraded, ultimately leading to the death of the community. This is a challenge for community members and the social workers who work with them to overcome.

The Strengths Perspective

Also discussed in Chapter 2 of the core HBSE book is the strengths perspective and how it can be used as a lens to view human development and behavior. Many social workers also use it to conceptualize communities.

From the strengths perspective, communities are viewed from the assumption that they have the capacity for growth, change, and adaptation (Weick, Rapp, Sullivan, & Kisthardt, 1989). Regardless of the dysfunction of a community or the problems it faces, community members have the skills and capabilities to change the functioning of the community. Further, community members are viewed as the experts on their situations, so their perceptions on community problems and functioning are key to creating community change. This perspective presumes that community members have endured adversity, they are resilient, and they inherently desire positive change.

From the strengths perspective, social workers and community members call upon the resources and talents of a community and its members to plan for and carry out interventions leading to change. This approach does not deny the fact that structural oppression and discrimination likely exist in communities, which can create barriers to change. However, social workers and community members can assess these barriers and devise strategies to overcome barriers and change structures to minimize or eradicate oppressive practices. Often this task involves assessing how communities have overcome barriers in the past and adapted to less than optimal conditions so that these strengths can be used to solve current and future problems.

This perspective guides social workers' work with community members to identify strengths, resources, expertise, and talents among community members that can be employed to solve problems. Rather than focusing solely on problems, the focus is on empowering community members to view problems as catalysts for change and mobilization.

Applying Community Conceptualizations

From a critical race perspective, the Washington Elementary School community could be viewed as a marginalized group in need of empowerment. Because it is a charter school, the school district treats the school in a discriminatory manner, reflected in the fact that the school receives less funding, support, and resources than standard public schools. The treatment of the school by the district means that families, even those with few resources related to time or money, must carry the burden to ensure that the school survives. Further, many families complain that the school suffers from communication problems in which families often are not included in decision-making processes. As a result, the school board is able to hold on to power by making all the decisions with very little input from the community. Many families feel disenfranchised by the inadequate communication and lack of opportunities to offer input into school processes. Families also complain that the current principal will not listen to parents' concerns or ideas. Further, many of the families in the community are from vulnerable populations who are accustomed to institutional discrimination and feel hopeless about positive change occurring. Attending Washington Elementary School, for these disenfranchised families, is an opportunity for their children to participate in a language immersion program that they might not have access to otherwise. From this perspective, social workers would want to attend to the processes taking place that perpetuate families' feelings and perceptions of marginalization and disempowerment, helping families to advocate for their community, sustained access to resources and opportunities, and the changes they want to implement to improve the community.

From a strengths perspective, the resources and strengths inherent in the community would be the focus of community work. The fact that the school was established and has survived for five years is an important strength this community brings. The commitment of the families who established the school and their continued investment of time, money, and energy into the school are also strengths. The community is able to adapt to challenges and changes and has the "people resources" to survive the many barriers that the school district and community dysfunction create. Further, the common interests and goals of the community members have created strong loyalty to the school that helps motivate members when difficult situations arise. The curriculum is strong, and most of the students are thriving, so this helps to reinforce families' commitment to their goals. Social workers can identify the many strengths this community possesses and utilizes to persevere in working with the members to find ways to move forward.

COMMUNITY ASSESSMENT AND INTERVENTION

Social work with communities comes with its own unique approaches and processes. As with micro and mezzo social work, there are many different philosophies about community work and ways to work with communities. In this section, we will explore some of the ways social workers approach community work.

Community Assessment

As with work with individuals and families, work with communities requires assessment processes to help determine needs, problems, strengths, resources, and approaches to move toward community improvement. Social workers can approach community assessment in many different ways, depending on the goals of the work.

Community assessment can involve activities as broad as collecting membership, governmental, census, or other data to describe a community; at the other end of the spectrum, it may involve immersing oneself in a community to collect detailed information and observations about it. Often, social workers use a combination of methods to better understand communities, including their needs, problems, functions, strengths, resources, and members. For example, a community assessment might include observations and descriptions of a community, a community profile using existing data sources, interviews with key informants in the community, attendance at community meetings (Johnson, 2001; Sherraden, 1993; Timm, Birkenmaier, & Tebb, 2011), and photo documentation to help tell members' stories in pictures. Important characteristics that social workers should understand about a community before working with it include demographics of the members and the community itself; the history of the community and its members; how the environmental context impacts the community including the political and economic environment; and the culture of the community including aspects like norms, beliefs, attitudes, practices, and language (Netting, Kettner, & McMurty, 2008).

In the assessment process, sometimes social workers focus on communities' needs, engaging in needs identification to describe what a community is lacking along with needs assessments that determine the importance of those needs (Siegel, Attkisson, & Carson, 2001). Conversely, social workers might engage in assessing a community's assets and strengths. Mapping assets help social workers determine a community's capacities and skills. Social workers can identify positive aspects of a community such as people, resources, and opportunities available to help improve the community (Kretzmann & McKnight, 1993). Along with this, social workers may engage in capacity building to increase community members' leadership and other skills that can be invested in the community and its efforts to change (Gamble & Hoff, 2005). Often, social workers may combine both a needs approach and a strengths approach in their work with communities.

Community Planning

In addition to assessment, planning is an important part of engaging community members, instigating community change, and increasing the well-being of community members. **Community planning**, sometimes referred to as social or neighborhood planning, is planning in and with the community to gather information and plan programs and evaluation processes that help improve communities (Rothman, 1974). Community planning is often viewed as a particular practice realm within community work. Interdisciplinary in nature, community planning is often thought of as an area of practice that requires specific skills and technical knowledge related to planning. Since it tends to be less process focused than community development and organization, discussed below, some professionals argue that practitioners do not need to be particularly skilled at communication and relationship building, as they do in community development and organization (Gilbert & Specht, 1977).

Community planning has a long history in the United States. Indeed, community planning is viewed by many as the beginning of the social work profession (Forester, 1989). Beginning with the Progressive Era, charity organizations and settlement houses engaged in local community planning to improve service provision and living conditions of community members (Kurzman, 1985). During the Great Depression and World War II, community planning was crucial in providing services on a local level to help support community members hit hard by economic problems. In the 1960s, the Great Society initiative of the Lyndon Johnson administration spurred the development of community action agencies to improve local service provision (Pine, 1986). After Johnson's presidency ended in 1969, neighborhood planning councils took over this function. Since then, we have seen a continuation of planning efforts, many of them turning to citizen-based efforts and more comprehensive models that include community development, advocacy, and empowerment in addition to service provision (Smock, 1997).

As is reflected in the rich and diverse history of community planning, social workers can engage in community planning in many different ways. For example, social workers may serve as advocates for communities and may view their role as an expert who acts for, instead of with, community members. In this approach, social workers likely do not include community members in the planning process; instead, they conduct planning in concert with local governments, policies, and laws. This planning approach is more likely than other approaches to disenfranchise community members, however, giving them little or no input into planning or decision-making processes (Bella, Madsen, Sullivan, Swidler, & Tipton, 1985; Lasswell, 1971).

Conversely, social workers may take a more social action approach, which was discussed in Chapter 5 of the core HBSE book in the discussion on community organizing. We will take a look at this approach in more detail in the next section of this chapter. With regard to planning, however, social workers may view their role in planning as more of a helper; that is, one in which community members are seen as experts on their communities, including their strengths, weaknesses, and needs. Thus, social workers allow community members to take the active lead in planning, and focus on the social aspect of planning. In this approach, social workers help to empower community members by fostering leadership, democracy, and goal-directed work among community members (Brueggemann, 2013).

Community Development and Organizing

As with community planning, community development and organizing can be viewed as distinct processes in which social workers might engage, and they can flow from community assessment and planning. Community development and community organizing share many characteristics, and the terms might be used synonymously. However, they are different processes that are characterized by different activities.

The main difference between community development and community organizing lies in their focus. Community development tends to be focused on physical aspects of a community such as buildings and infrastructure, or on specific economic or social projects. Because of this, the development process is usually conducted with the cooperation of people in power and those with technical expertise such as government officials, development corporations, and those with specific knowledge sets. Community organizing, on the other hand, is more focused on building power and promoting change within a community, so it involves community members directly impacted by problems in its processes and work for community change (Parachini & Covington, 2001; Stoecker, 2001). However, it is important to keep in mind that a wide variety of definitions exist for community development and organizing. Here we will take a look at both concepts and how they can be used to help communities.

Community development. As was mentioned above, **community development** tends to be focused on physical or infrastructure development or on specific economic, political, or social projects that require the assistance of others with specific skills or knowledge. Community development also can be seen as both process and product. Not only is community development concerned with producing an outcome like the building of a recreation center or the establishment of literacy programs in a community, it is also focused on the process of community development in areas such as improvement, empowerment, and advancement of communities (Wise, 1998).

Community development has a long history, but currently, it is generally informed by interdisciplinary fields, including social work, and grouped into three areas of practice: new community economic development, community political development, and community social development. While these areas all have the common goal of strengthening and improving communities, they use different methods and approaches to attain that goal. Technology and social media are enhancing areas of practice in community development, allowing for creative and innovate ways for institutions, organizations, and practitioners as well as community members to participate in the development process and provide access to resources and collaboration that were not available before (Brueggemann, 2013). For example, rural communities can link up with urban communities to access resources and information, and community members can plan and organize using social media.

Unique to community development are community development corporations, or CDCs. **Community development corporations** are non-profit organizations often located in low-income neighborhoods that are charged with developing profitable enterprises such as businesses and housing projects that can enhance communities (Twelvetrees, 1996). In general, CDCs are small in scope, operating on small budgets with minimal staff and focusing on targeted areas. However, they do have the power to instigate powerful community change (Smock, 1997).

Community organizing. It is difficult to find one, unifying definition of community organizing because it can mean different things to different people, even within the social work profession. However, a comprehensive definition may help us to better understand how social workers often approach community organizing. According to Stoecker and Beckwith (1992), **community organizing** is about building power in communities by working with community members who define the community's problems along with the methods and solutions they want to pursue in solving those problems. Community organizing involves democratic processes to help build leadership and empower community members for future problem-solving efforts. Further, it can be viewed as a value-based process in which community members, usually those who are disenfranchised and excluded from decision making, come together to take action to improve their community (Parachini & Covington, 2001). Community organizing as macro practice in social work relates to the methods and processes employed to address unjust policies, systems, and practices in communities and to promote community health and well-being (Gamble & Weil, 2010).

Chapter 5 of the core HBSE book offered a brief history of community organizing along with ways in which community organizing views communities, and models used to conduct community organizing. Here, we will look at some additional ways in which community organizing takes place in social work.

Community organizing can be placed into three general groups. Although in real-world practice these groups often overlap, they can be differentiated according to their approaches (Parachini & Covington, 2001):

- **Direct/Individual Membership Groups:** These groups are generally small and made up of community members from low- to moderate-income backgrounds. These groups typically focus on community improvement or specific issues like crime or access to specific resources within the community.

- **Issue-Based Coalitions:** These coalitions serve to activate existing groups like unions or interest groups to influence policy or work on specific problems.

- **Institution-Based Organizing:** This group brings together faith-based or religious institutions to work on community problems.

With regard to models of community organizing, a few other broader models exist in addition to the ones discussed in Chapter 5 that help guide organizing work. Often, social workers use various components of several models in their work with communities. Here we will explore power, development, and information models of community organizing.

Power models of community organizing focus on the economic and other inequities among community members and are built on the ideas of Saul Alinsky, which were discussed as they applied to the social action model in Chapter 5 and above in the Community Planning section. Characteristics of the social action model are similar to the power models of community organizing. Power models focus on organizing rather than issues; they seek to empower communities to become political leaders and stakeholders and become part of the decision-making process so that communities can solve their own problems. To empower communities, power models focus on developing relationships among community members and providing opportunities for members, particularly those who are disenfranchised, to participate in community processes and have access to more powerful members. It is not uncommon for power models to use tactics like demonstrations and protests to deliver messages and achieve goals (Stoecker, 2001).

Development models of community organizing, in contrast to power models, focus more on issues than organizing. Development models focus on helping community members build coalitions and call on resources that will help to establish programs and services and address problems. These models stem from asset-based community development, with the goal of rebuilding a community's infrastructure, which may include physical structures, as is the case in community development (Kretzmann & McKnight, 1993). However, development models go further than community development in that the goal is to mobilize community members to identify needs, problems, resources, and potential coalitions that can be formed to help the community achieve its goals. Development models see the importance of building coalitions with people and organizations outside of the community such as banks, governmental entities, service providers, and other groups who might bring resources or expertise that can support the community. Relationship building and political participation among community members are important in develop-ment models, but these models emphasize cooperation, volunteerism, and civic engagement over protest and unrest (Stoecker, 2001).

Finally, **information models** of community organization are built on the ideas of Paulo Freire (1970), whose focus was on popular education and political action. Myles Horton is another important person whose work in unions and civil rights movements has been incorporated in community organization (Horton & Freire, 1990). While many do not view Freire's and Horton's work as linked with commu-nity organizing, others view education, participatory research, and similar activities as part of community planning and organizing and instigating community change and social movements. Information models focus on the individual, community, and external factors that create problems. Information models employ creative methods and popular education activities like theater, drawing, songwriting, and role plays to help members express concerns unique to their contexts and cultures. And like developmental models, these models seek to create educational opportu-nities like literacy, legal awareness, and technology programs that help empower members and give them a voice in community concerns and efforts.

Social Workers' Roles in Communities

Communities are important for social workers to understand, regardless of whether they are engaged in micro, mezzo, or macro social work. Even if social workers are focused on individuals and families, these clients' social systems and environments, like the communities in which clients live and interact, are a crucial part of clients' functioning and well-being.

Community health is extremely important for all of us. Communities can be a resource and strength for our clients, but communities also can bring barriers, stressors, and problems. Social workers need to understand how communities affect the lives of our clients, both positively and negatively, how to conceptualize the role communities play in well-being, and how to work with communities and their members to utilize resources and promote change (Brueggemann, 2013).

Depending on the philosophy of macro social work that social workers hold and the types of communities with which they are working, social workers will take on different roles and varying levels of responsibilities when engaging with communities. Social workers who work with communities that are small, isolated, or poorly funded may take on many roles in their work because of the lack of exper-tise or limited number of people capable of taking on responsibilities. In a rural setting, for example, a social worker may be the only person who has the skills to negotiate with state government for the provision of services in the community, organize community members to advocate for resources, or provide expertise on community development to help the community improve. On the other hand, social workers may engage in community work that is highly specialized, requiring specific skills and knowledge. For example, a social worker may work with a service community that needs specific skills around gathering data on the needs of the older population in the community that the agency serves. The social worker needs to know how to research this information, where to find it, the scope of service needs, who the stakeholders and other providers are in the community, and how to develop a report that will inform and guide the work of the service community.

So, as you can see, there are many ways in which social workers can engage in community work, whether that is to specialize in macro social work or include it as a part of micro or mezzo work. Regardless of the approach, social workers need to be well informed on the many theories, processes, and approaches of community work to be effective in their work with clients.

Applying Community Assessment and Intervention

With regard to assessment, what are some of the needs and strengths you see with the Washington Elementary School community? In the previous sections, we discussed how the community might be viewed from the strengths perspective, which helped us to think about all the assets and resources the community has as well as the ways in which the community has adapted and demonstrated resilience in the face of challenges. Assessing the community's strengths is an important part of community work.

Social workers also need to assess the needs and barriers with which the community is struggling. Some of the more readily apparent issues are inadequate funding to run the school properly; a lack of a permanent location for the school that provides adequate space to facilitate learning and support school growth; problems with clear, transparent communication among the school community, particularly between the school board, principal, and families; and a lack of resources to help support families and teachers in their work.

In the assessment process, social workers will want to attend to the history of the community and how the social, political, and economic environment are affecting the school. For instance, while the law mandates that the school receive less funding than neighborhood public schools, the culture of the city tends to be open and creative, which means there is support for the school even if it receives less from the governmental budget than the district's standard public schools. Social workers also will want to pay attention to the culture of the community, such as its values, beliefs, and attitudes toward education and the school itself. The community has strong beliefs in language immersion, small class sizes, and maintaining control over the academic environment. These attitudes will be important to remember as community work goes forward.

Social workers could also help the school community in planning processes. Planning could involve helping community members think about what changes need to happen and establish goals for the school. In the planning process, social workers might take a social action approach, where they help community members develop leadership skills and foster a democratic environment in which planning and change can happen.

The Washington Elementary School community already has accomplished a great deal with regard to community development. The establishment of the school is a product of the development process. Much of the work that needs to be accomplished now involves activities to improve the school and the relationships among community members and between members and the school district. Social workers could employ a development model to community organizing, for example, where they work with community members to build coalitions with the school district and state legislature to increase funding and secure a permanent location for the school. The community could also work to improve programs and the administrative infrastructure and mobilize members to advocate for their needs.

DIVERSE COMMUNITY PROBLEMS AND STRENGTHS

As we discussed earlier in the chapter, communities are formed in different ways and serve different purposes for their members. Depending on the type of community, its goals, functions, and culture, and the ways in which it is situated in the environmental context, a community faces unique problems and barriers as well as resources and strengths that can be utilized to address issues. In this section, we will explore just a few types of communities and some of their unique characteristics that need to be considered in macro social work, particularly with regard to empowering and strengthening communities and their identities.

Rural Communities

Rural areas are common in the United States, with about 15 percent of the U.S. population living in a rural community (Cromartie, 2013). For U.S. Census purposes, the term *rural* is considered anything that is not urban. *Urban*, in turn, is defined as areas consisting of 50,000 or more people or urban cluster areas consisting of between 2,500 and 50,000 people (Health Resources and Services Administration, n.d.).

Because of geography, economics, and other factors, rural communities have unique problems and barriers as well as strengths and resources. Rural communities deal with some of the highest poverty rates in the nation (Richgels & Sande, 2009) as well as low education levels and high unemployment (Arsenault, 2006). Many rural communities face inadequate public services like roads, housing, and schools, (Willits, Bealer, & Timbers, 1990); less access to health insurance and specialized health and mental health care; and poorer health, chronic illness, and more health and mental health disparities compared to their urban counterparts (Johnson *et al.*, 2014; Rasheed & Rasheed, 2003).

Industries such as mining, forestry, and agriculture formerly gave rural communities a solid economic base, but in recent years many of these industries have been replaced by large meat processing plants, hydraulic fracturing ("fracking"), and the like. At the same time, many rural areas are increasingly threatened by urban sprawl and "ranchette" suburbs (Carter, 2007; Safford, Henly, Ulrich-Schad, & Perkins, 2014). Further, many employers that supported rural economies because of low-wage labor have moved their plants abroad (Chittum & Hilsenrath, 2004), and rural communities have experienced a consistent decline in population, which further affects their health and well-being (Cromartie, 2013). Many rural communities are sustained by government-funded industries like universities, military bases, and prisons (Huling, 2002); or by private institutions like prep schools, colleges, and drug-rehabilitation centers.

Sub-communities in rural areas also face unique issues. For example, child poverty rates are high in rural communities, particularly those on Native American reservations (Arsenault, 2006). Older adults and those in GLBT communities face issues related to work, housing, transportation, health care, long-term care, end-of-life care, and other social service challenges because of discrimination, lack of service providers, and lack of community planning (Hash, Jurkowski, & Krout, 2015).

Conversely, rural communities also enjoy strengths and resources. For example, while Latino immigrants who settle in rural communities often face language barriers, acculturation issues, and loss of support networks and family roles, they also bring strengths like a strong work ethic and strong connections with family, friends, and community that sometimes are easier to develop and maintain in a rural setting (Raffaelli & Wiley, 2012).

Often, problems in rural communities call for creative and innovative solutions, which necessitate collaborative efforts, like those between public services, non-profit organizations, and community members to reach rural communities and integrate services (Richgels & Sande, 2009). Rural communities can offer opportunities for macro social workers to be creative and utilize natural resources of rural communities like churches, schools, family ties, community resilience, supportive relationships, and informal care networks, which in some ways can make community organization easier and more dynamic than in urban areas (Lewis, Scott, & Calfee, 2013). For example, social workers can utilize informal care systems like the helping tradition in African–American communities to help fill service gaps (Rasheed & Rasheed, 2003). One small rural community in Oregon saw its agricultural industry decline, which caused concern about the continued existence of the community. Community members began a community planning and organizing process that allowed them to harness resources of nonprofit organizations and create partnerships with nearby communities to help fund and revitalize the community (Irvine, 2014). As another example of community organizing efforts, the

U.S. Department of Agriculture Rural Development has offered financial assistance to rural businesses, including cooperatives (S. Thompson, 2012), and businesses that once went overseas, like call centers, are establishing themselves in rural communities (Chittum & Hilsenrath, 2004). Community organizing is one way to bring about changes and positive community growth, particularly in rural areas.

Tribal Communities

Tribal communities have a long, unique history, particularly in relation to mainstream U.S. institutions' attempts to destroy their culture, family, history, customs, traditions, schools, language, religious practices, and other systems (Reyhner & Eder, 1992). Institutional racism, oppression, violence, and forced assimilation and marginalization have had and continue to have extensive, devastating effects on tribal communities, including consequences on health; mental health; interpersonal relationships; and social, economic, and spiritual well-being (Deloria, 1988; Heinrich, Corbine, & Thomas, 1990). Young children were removed from their homes to spend as many as eight years in boarding schools where they were only allowed to speak English and were disoriented from their tribal religious and cultural traditions. Upon returning to their communities, these children often felt no sense of being either "white" or "Indian," causing generational and cultural rifts that linger today (Garrett & Pichette, 2000; Sue & Sue, 1990). It was not until 1978, with the passage of the American Indian Religious Freedom Act, that tribal communities were granted autonomy with regard to culture and religion (Deloria, 1988). Currently, some federal- and tribal-run boarding schools still exist, though there is much debate about whether these schools should exist at all and who should administer them (Reyhner, 2013).

The effects of institutional oppression and violence are reflected in many of the issues with which tribal communities continue to struggle. Unemployment and poverty rates among tribal communities are some of the highest in the nation (Hodgkinson, 1990). Tribal communities have experienced dramatic shifts in diet and physical activity, resulting in high obesity rates, especially among children (Noonan *et al.*, 2010; Ogden *et al.*, 2006), as well as high rates of other health and mental health problems such as anxiety, asthma, depression, alcoholism, tuberculosis, obstructive pulmonary disease, and posttraumatic stress disorder (Sprague, Bogart, Manson, Buchwald, & Goldberg, 2010). These communities have also seen increased gang activity (Freng, Davis, McCord, & Roussell, 2012). Many tribal communities experience high suicide rates, particularly among some Alaska Native groups, where rates for suicide among males aged 15 to 24 are eight times higher (142.9 per 100,000) than among males in the same age range (17.4 per 100,000) (Wexler, Silveira, & Bertone-Johnson, 2012).

Even with the seemingly insurmountable historical and institutional discrimination and oppression tribal communities have faced, they also have a long history of coping, adapting, and maintaining resilience in the face of daunting, horrific experiences. Researchers, practitioners, and others who work with these communities often overlook strengths of tribal communities. For example, research suggests that culture, family, spirituality, personal characteristics, supportive relationships, and community connectedness are all factors that cultivate strength and resilience for Native American youth (Filbert & Flynn, 2010; Stiffman *et al.*, 2007). Native American elders are viewed and honored as teachers and keepers of community and spiritual wisdom, culture, and tradition as well as resources for younger community members (Holkup, Salois, Tripp-Reimer, & Weinert, 2007). Further, tribal communities have ancient traditions and practices around spirituality, healing, and supporting community members. Many of these strengths are ignored or overlooked in favor of a view that tribal communities are only a social problem group (Garrett & Garrett, 1994).

Faith and Spiritual Communities

Characteristics of faith and spiritual communities are complex, as are the issues relating to them. What are faith and spiritual communities? How do they form? What are their purposes, functions, issues, and strengths? As with other types of communities, faith and spiritual communities can form in many ways. For example, some faith and spiritual communities could be considered locational communities as when congregations are formed based on proximity to places of gathering or worship. In this case, members usually choose the community in which they participate because of common belief systems. Conversely, approximately 80 percent of people around the globe claim to hold religious or spiritual beliefs (O'Brien & Palmer, 2007), but only a small percentage report attending any kind of formal service or gathering related to their beliefs (Dinham, 2010). This suggests that many people may feel part of a larger community based not on location or regular gathering and interpersonal contact, but rather on beliefs, values, history, interests, and the like (MacIntyre, 1981). Faith and spiritual communities may also be based on solidarity and feelings of interdependence, common activities, and political participation, including group actions and decision making (Barber, 1984; Dinham, Furbey, & Lowndes, 2009).

Regardless of beliefs or definitions of faith, religion, or spirituality, many people belong to or are connected with a faith or spiritual community. Membership in faith and spiritual communities can bring members many health, social, economic, and psychological benefits, and these communities can have profound impacts on the well-being of the larger social environment. Members of faith and spiritual communities are often regarded by society as people who are compassionate and caring, and who contribute to the welfare of their communities. However, faith and spiritual communities can also be viewed as insular, attending only to their own members and their interests (Dinham, 2010).

Faith and spiritual communities are sometimes referred to as the "first community developers" because of their historical role in providing for those in need

(Clarke & Donnelly, 2009). **Faith-based organizing** employs methods to work with faith communities on problems and concerns of the community and to strengthen and vitalize congregations. Religious institutions, in particular, are often well organized, and well funded, and are often in positions of responding to community members' needs, sometimes better than governmental or other nonprofit institutions (James, 2009). For example, People Improving Communities through Organizing (PICO) uses faith-based values to address problems, and the Jeremiah Project enlists young community members to engage in community projects. Further, faith and spiritual communities have long engaged with other communities to help promote the well-being of not only their own members but of society as a whole. For example, religious organizations have long-standing partnerships with public health and health care organizations to address health care issues, services, and disparities (Levin, 2012, 2013). And, for those in the African–American community, faith-based and spiritual communities can be especially helpful in supporting members through situations of adversity, facilitating better health and mental health outcomes (Cannon, 1995). And, those with mental illness tend to fare better with regard to achieving positive mental health outcomes when they feel they have the support of a faith community (Basky, 2000).

Military Communities

Military communities, including service members and their families and loved ones, are characterized and defined by the many demands of military lifestyle. These often include relocations for both service members and their families, as well as separation of active service members from family and geographical communities. The military lifestyle requires a great deal of adjustment for service members and their families as service members are deployed and return home, often to be redeployed (Wright, Burrell, Schroeder, & Thomas, 2006). Further, many military community members—both military personnel and their family members—experience unique social, economic, health, and mental health issues related to military experiences and adjustment to family and community life pre- and post-deployment. Community is of great importance to military personnel and their families to help support and meet the needs of community members (Wright, Foran, & Wood, 2014).

Research has articulated many of the unique challenges and needs of military communities. For example, from a social work perspective, primary needs revolve around mental health issues (e.g., depression, anxiety, substance abuse, and post-traumatic stress disorder); sleep disorders; and chronic health conditions. Within the military community, there is a need to address stress, social support, and access to health and mental health services (Frey, Collins, Pastoor, & Linde, 2014). Further, Frey *et al.* (2014) suggested that needs depended on how many deployments military personnel and their families experience and whether crises arise pre- or post-deployment. For example, a service member's loved one may be dealing with a chronic health issue that strains social and financial resources. This situation could be made worse by the service member's deployment, particularly if the family experiences multiple deployments. Or, a returning service member who suffers from debilitating health and mental health problems because of adverse experiences during deployment may be faced with financial issues because of unemployment and inadequate access to health care services. These problems may contribute to added stress for the service member and her or his family as well as exacerbate the service member's physical and mental health issues.

Still, many in military communities show a great deal of resilience and adaptability to their circumstances (Bartone, 2006). Strengths among military community members include unit cohesion; camaraderie with other community members; structural support; free access to health care; and access to employment and other resources, benefits, and opportunities for service members and their family members (Pietrzak *et al.*, 2010; Wooten, 2013).

Virtual Communities

Over the past century, society has become increasingly mobile, resulting in shifts of what we perceive of as locational communities. Nowhere do we see this phenomenon more than in virtual communities. **Virtual communities** form on the basis of shared interests and develop a shared, clearly defined social identity among members who can be situated all over the globe. Virtual communities can be based on people with real identities or those with assumed identities. These communities allow people to develop a deep level of intimacy without ever meeting one another. Virtual communities can allow members to gain a sense of fulfillment, knowledge, and social support, much like real-life communities. Virtual communities are both an expression of self-identity and of social identity (Lord, 2002; Tonteri, Kosonen, Ellonen, & Tarkiainen, 2011), and research indicates that people's participation in virtual communities is comparable to that in real-world communities (Wasko & Faraj, 2000).

There are numerous ways people participate in virtual communities, from discussion boards to online gaming to LISTSERVs and similar e-mail groups (Lin, 2010). New technologies continually create new ways for people and organizations to communicate and form virtual communities around the globe. Indeed, in many ways, virtual communities are changing the nature of our interactions as well as the ways in which we organize, form communities, and solve problems. For instance, virtual communities and organizing allow people to do things without needing physical buildings or other costly resources, reducing the costs to communicate, collaborate, consult, and gather. Virtual communities can also change the structures and power of communities, as many of them do not have hierarchies or people in charge. Indeed, many businesses, governments, special interest groups, and other naturally formed communities have found a use for virtual communities. On the other hand, virtual communities and the technologies supporting them have seen new "pathologies of the internet" emerge, such as cyberbullying, internet addictions, and social isolation (Kirmayer, Raikhel, & Rahimi, 2013).

Many people wonder how virtual communities may aid—or undermine— traditional communities and community organizing, given how virtual communities have challenged established social structures and hierarchies. In many ways, virtual communities have empowered marginalized and vulnerable communities, allowing more people to participate in social and political life and creating new pathways toward democracy and equality. Conversely, however, virtual communities and the technology behind them have been used for nefarious purposes such as global organized crime and terrorism as well as to create social division and unrest. So, in an extreme sense, while virtual communities have the power to create transformative experiences and positive change for individuals and society, they also have the potential to weaken community by empowering individuals to express negativity and aggression, creating an unfettered freedom of expression that often lacks accountability, and fostering a disdain for authority and order (Mathews, 1997).

The International Community

What is the international community? Some scholars argue there is no "international community," but it is becoming increasingly difficult to argue against its existence. A broad definition of international community comes from the former United Nations Secretary General Kofi Annan, who described it as a shared vision of a better world and a shared vulnerability in the face of threats like nuclear war and climate change (Annan, 1999). A sense of international community can be felt in increased economic and social globalization, efforts of governments to establish international courts, coordinated aid to victims of natural disasters, and global peacekeeping efforts, for example. Efforts such as international civic engagement, collective conflict management, and international participatory development as well as the establishment of regional and international non-governmental and intergovernmental organizations, to name just a few, are ways in which the international community can respond, sometimes through community organization, to shared problems that threaten the well-being of us all (Boehmer & Nordstrom, 2008; Castelloe, Watson, & White, 2002; Crocker, Hampson, & Aall, 2014).

One example of the international community participating in global community organizing relates to the issue of gender disparities and inequality. While gender equity is an issue on local levels across the globe, it has become a focus of macro practice internationally, particularly related to the health and well-being of women. Concerns about civil rights violations like prostitution, female infanticide, sexual slavery, forced marriage, and bride burning, as well as low participation rates of women in health, economic, education, and political arenas, are prompting international efforts to create more equitable communities that promote structural and interactional changes that chip away at gender inequality. Even in locations that seem equitable with regard to gender, disparities still exist. Further, because of entrenched values, beliefs, and attitudes around gender and gender roles within social, religious, and cultural structures, change is slow (Lopez-Claros & Zahidi, 2005).

In response to gender-related issues, organizations like the United Nations established the Development Fund for Women in 1984 to help promote women's participation in all arenas of their communities. Other organizing efforts such as the 1995 Beijing World Conference on Women are attempting to address gender disparities in policy, research, advocacy, and community planning across the globe (Lopez-Claros & Zahidi, 2005). Often, social workers are part of these international efforts, bringing their expertise in community planning, development, and organizing and their values and ethics around social and economic justice to international work.

Empowering and Strengthening Unique Community Identities

Many in social work argue that focusing on strengths in our work is of primary importance. As was discussed earlier, the strengths perspective offers an important lens through which to approach community work. Here we will look at some of the ways in which strengths and similar perspectives can be used in empowering and strengthening communities.

When engaging with communities, it is important to emphasize assets and strengths rather than focusing primarily on problems and deficits. A strengths approach not only helps to empower communities in their efforts toward change by calling on members' expertise and experience, but it helps to avoid the application of irrelevant, inappropriate, or oppressive methods and policies to community problems when the assumption is that communities have nothing to offer, particularly poor and marginalized communities (Perkins, Crim, Silberman, & Brown, 2004).

Related to community strengths, when engaging in macro work, it is important to keep in mind that community ownership and participation are key to successful community planning, development, and organizing (Chambers, 2005). This is because those who are affected by community work (i.e., the community members) are the experts of the situation. They can identity goals, needs, values, problems, barriers, resources, strengths, and stakeholders that are important to the community as well as approaches and methods that are likely to succeed in working with community problems and ways to ensure the sustainability of change (Clarke, 2013).

One helpful concept to think about with regard to communities is the **social capital** they often bring, or the benefits community members receive through reciprocal, collective, and cooperative relationships they build with one another (Sartorius, 2003). Social capital consists of both process and structure. Process involves the ways in which community members establish benefits through the social networks and structures in a community (Portes, 1998). Structure refers to how social organizations and the norms, networks, and the level of established trust within them facilitate cooperation and coordination that lead to collective benefits for members (Putnam, 2000).

Social capital provided through community can be important and powerful. For example, the networks formed through informal gatherings and conversations in a neighborhood can provide protection from theft, criminal activity, and other problems. And, faith communities provide one of the most significant sources of social capital through emphasis on attending to the welfare of their members (Putnam, 2000). However, increasing ethnic diversity and immigration could pose short-term threats to the social capital provided by community but still provide long-term benefits to community. On the one hand, increased ethnic diversity can create feelings of isolation, enhance perceptions of difference, and foster a sense of distrust. On the other hand, increased diversity can help bridge gaps between those in different ethnic groups, reduce ethnocentric beliefs, and improve relationships among and between groups (Putnam, 2007).

Globally, we face an increasing loss of locational community through shifts such as displacement, use of technology, and migration due to war, violence, economics, climate change, and other factors. These changes have the potential to create feelings of social isolation and mistrust along with other social problems. Loss of community can also lead to the loss of community memory as well as trust (Boyles, 1997). And, in poor communities, member participation and engagement in community planning and development tend to be low because of trust and conflict issues as well as negative past experiences with governmental entities whose policies and practices have been detrimental to these communities (Annette & Creasy, 2007; Grimsley, Hickman, Lawless, Manning, & Wilson, 2005).

Part of the task in macro social work is thinking about how to empower communities and rebuild the trust and health that are needed for members' well-being. This includes helping communities establish political power and legitimacy that is often primarily held by those in seemingly legitimate governmental or other powerful positions, so that communities can make their own decisions about how to address community planning and development in the face of these shifts. To truly empower communities, community development, planning, and organizing needs to happen from the bottom up, where communities are mobilized to act and participate (Amdam, 2002; Paasi, 1986). Social workers can help communities learn brokering and advocacy skills and work with local and state governments, NGOs, and other organizations to develop "open door" policies that offer community members access to people in decision-making roles as well as facilitate communication and relationship building. This includes cultivating a welcoming and participatory culture in community meetings, creating formal and informal networks among community members and service employees, attending to the physical spaces community members use to conduct business, and evaluating community development processes to ensure that approaches are effective and inclusive (Morgan-Trimmer, 2013).

Empowering a Unique Community

The Washington Elementary School community, like all communities, has some unique characteristics that both help and hinder its progress and growth. The community enjoys a strong commitment to the school and its goals, and the members invest a great deal of time, energy, and money into the school to help insure its success. The community has demonstrated resilience and adaptation, which are important as the community moves forward to create change. Still, the community faces many problems and barriers, particularly around funding and communication. How can social workers help empower the community?

Given the inadequate economic support shown by the school district and state government as well as mistrust fostered by actions of the past principal and communication problems among members, social workers can help the community by first rebuilding trust to facilitate open communication and effective working relationships that are needed to work on other issues such as financial stability. This will take time and effort on the part of all community members as well as those in power at the school district. Part of the work of social workers will be to help community members develop political power through lobbying, writing letters, and mobilizing members that can influence decision makers at the state level. Social workers can also work with state officials to create a more welcoming environment that invites openness in communication and a spirit of creativity to solve problems.

ETHICAL CONSIDERATIONS IN COMMUNITY SOCIAL WORK

Community social work shares many of the same ethical concerns and issues with micro and mezzo social work. All social work practitioners are concerned with maintaining professionalism, carrying out best practices, empowering the people and communities with which they work, and working toward social and economic justice. However, given the nature of community practice, there are unique ethical dilemmas that this work can pose. In this section, we will explore some of the ethical situations that social workers may encounter in macro work with communities.

Unique Ethical Challenges of Community Practice

One important way that community social work differs from other types of social work is the level of involvement social workers often have with the community and its members. For example, for social workers to establish trust and truly understand the issues communities face and the perspectives of community members, it is often preferred for organizers to be part of the community with which they are working. However, social workers' engagement with the community can sometimes blur boundaries between their professional roles, their community memberships, and their relationships with other members. Community practitioners may be friends with other members, have more difficulty delineating between work and personal time, or want to strive toward equitable relationships with other members instead of taking on professional roles that might put them in positions of authority over other members (Hardina, 2004). While guidance around boundaries, dual relationships, and other ethical challenges often is more straightforward in micro and macro practice, guidance on these issues in macro practice can sometimes be unclear, contradictory, or nonexistent.

Sometimes the characteristics or nature of communities can bring ethical issues and dilemmas. Some communities may be viewed as promoting or supporting harmful behaviors, particularly among vulnerable members. For example, virtual communities can experience problems with members falsifying identities or joining communities to exploit others. Or, virtual communities can perpetuate controversial, problematic, unethical, or even criminal behavior. Examples include virtual communities like "pro-ana" (pro-anorexia) or "pro-mia" (pro-bulimia) sites whose members offer, among other things, advice and strategies on maintaining unhealthy eating behaviors. Many virtual communities are established to promote activities like gambling, child pornography, and suicide pacts (Lewis, Heath, St. Denis, & Noble, 2011). However, research suggests that some of these communities, like "pro-ana" and "pro-mia" communities, can help members by giving them insights into their behaviors and a safe and welcoming space to communicate with others who share similar concerns (Bell, 2007). Social workers whose clients are involved in controversial communities must work through the ethical questions they can bring for their work and their clients.

As with micro and mezzo social work practice, macro practitioners increasingly are relying on web-based technologies and platforms in their approaches to their work. These approaches bring with them potential ethical issues that are continually evolving as technology and its use evolves. In macro practice with communities, technology can be used in many ways including, but not limited to, fundraising, advocacy efforts, building online communities for activism, and mobilizing communities (Homan, 2011). The use of technology in community practice can be effective and efficient, particularly for reaching a wide audience and having a sweeping impact (McNutt & Menon, 2008). Technology can potentially allow many more people to become engaged in community change and connect large numbers of people to one another and to service organizations (Giffords, 2009). However, technology use in practice can bring ethical problems. These include maintaining control of the message and methods being used; ensuring all community members have access to the technology, including marginalized members like those living in poverty, older adults, and those who speak other languages; and managing ethical and professional boundaries (Mattison, 2012). Another question that is raised around the use of technology in community practice is whether these approaches help develop and support human relationships and interconnected collective action (Hill & Ferguson, 2014).

Ethical dilemmas are a part of the social work profession, and community practice brings unique ethical issues that are sometimes nebulous and difficult to resolve. Social workers play an important role in continually working with and developing the NASW Code of Ethics, in conjunction with consultation work with other professionals, to address these challenges in ways that do not undermine the work of community practice and the empowerment of community members.

Applying Ethics

What potential ethical issues do you see happening with the Washington Elementary School community? Some of the more obvious ethical situations include the falsification of test scores by the past principal and the inequity of funding for charter schools, which disadvantage students and create unfair burdens for the families in terms of money and time. Social workers could argue that the added stress on staff and parents caused by inequity, in part, has led to drastic actions such as those demonstrated by the past principal and the communication problems among members. Part of the ethical dilemma that faces this community is based in the discrimination that occurred from the beginning of the process when the community set out to establish the school.

From an empowerment perspective, social workers may choose to address the inequity that exists in the school funding structure before working on specific situations that are eroding the trust of the community. This approach gets at the values in the Code of Ethics around social and economic justice, but it also supports the community's right to self-determination to establish a learning community that is in line with their values and beliefs about creating a context where their children can learn in a multicultural, bilingual environment.

CONCLUSION

Community practice is an important part of social work with roots going back to the foundation of the profession. Community practice has a rich history along with its own set of theories, methods, and approaches that can create powerful change for communities and their members. Social workers, regardless of the context in which they work, must understand communities and how they affect people, their behavior, and well-being and incorporate this knowledge into their work. But, many social workers choose to focus on macro practice with communities to become agents of environmental and structural change and to empower community members.

Given the variety of communities—their definitions, characteristics, needs, cultures, perspectives, and ethical dilemmas—as well as the variety of approaches to community work, it can be challenging but also very exciting and rewarding. Community work demands an array of social work skills and roles that are needed for micro and macro work including brokering, advocating, active listening, and relationship building, among others. And, given the marginalization and isolation of so many communities and their members, locally and globally, community work is more important than ever.

MAIN POINTS

- In social work, there are a variety of definitions and meanings of the term *community*. For the purposes of community practice, social workers often define communities based on how they are formed, whether it be by how members identify with a community, are geographically located in a community, or share common interests with other community members.

- Communities serve many functions for members and society including socialization; social control; social participation; mutual support; and production, distribution, and consumption of goods and resources.

- Communities and community practice can be conceptualized through many theoretical lenses and perspectives. Often social workers take a strengths or empowerment approach to view communities along with other perspectives to help guide their work.

- Social work with communities comes with its own unique approaches, processes, and philosophies. Depending on the goals of the work, social workers might engage in community assessment, development, planning, or organizing. Each of these activities has specific aims, goals, and methods for carrying out community change.

- Social workers can take on a variety of roles in community work. Consequently, they need to be skilled in not only foundational social work skills but in the unique methods and approaches of community practice.

- Communities come with a wide range of diverse characteristics, strengths, and needs. There are many kinds of communities: rural, tribal, faith and spiritual, military, virtual, and international are among the major categories. Social workers need to be aware of unique aspects of communities to be effective in working with them and to ensure that their members are empowered to create change.

- Community work comes with unique ethical challenges and situations that are not easily resolved. These often differ from micro and mezzo social work in the areas of boundaries and professional roles.

EXERCISES

1. *Sanchez family interactive case at* www.routledgesw.com/cases. Review the information on the Sanchez family, paying particular attention to their community. Then answer the following questions:
   a. Describe the different communities in which the Sanchez family (or members of the family) participates. For example, are they based on identification? Location? Interest? A mix of these?
   b. What functions do these different communities serve?
   c. Pick a community in which the Sanchez family (or members) are a part. How might this community be viewed through a theoretical perspective?
   d. What are the strengths and needs of this community?

2. *Riverton interactive case at* www.routledgesw.com/cases. Take some time to explore the Riverton case and the environmental context in which this case is situated. Then answer the following:
   a. What are some of the strengths, needs, and unique characteristics of this community?
   b. Choose a theoretical perspective from which to view this community and describe what the community looks like using that perspective.
   c. If you were the social worker working with this community, based on your responses to item "a" above, how would you go about helping the community to plan? How might you approach community development and organizing?
   d. How might you go about helping to empower the community members?
   e. What types of potential ethical dilemmas might you identify in working with this community?

3. *Hudson City interactive case at* www.routledgesw.com/cases. Explore the community. Then respond to the following:
   a. What are some of the strengths, needs, and unique characteristics of this community?
   b. Choose a theoretical perspective from which to view this community and describe what the community looks like using that perspective.
   c. If you were the social worker working with this community, based on your responses to item "a" above, how would you go about helping the community to plan? How might you approach community development and organizing?
   d. How might you go about helping to empower the community members?
   e. What types of potential ethical dilemmas might you identify in working with this community?

References

Abar, B., Cater, K. L., & Winsler, A. (2009). The effects of maternal parenting style and religious commitment on self-regulation, academic achievement, and risk behavior among African American parochial college students. *Journal of Adolescence, 32*, 259–273.

Adams, J. S. (1965). Inequity in social exchange. In L. Berkowitz (Ed.), *Advances in experimental social psychology* (Vol. 2, pp. 267–299). New York: Academic Press.

Adler, A. (1925). *The Practice and Theory of Individual Psychology*. London: Routledge.

Adler-Baeder, F., & Higginbotham, B. (2004). Implications of remarriage and stepfamily formation for marriage education. *Family Relations, 53*(5), 448–458.

Ainsworth, M. (1979). Infant-mother attachment. *American Psychologist, 34*, 932–937.

Albertsen, E. J., O'Connor, L. E., & Berry, J. (2006). Religion and interpersonal guilt: Variations across ethnicity and spirituality. *Mental Health, Religion & Culture, 9*(1), 67–84.

Aldag, R. J., & Kuzuhara, L. W. (2005). *Mastering management skills*. Mason, OH: South-Western.

Aldrich, H. E. (1999). *Organizations evolving*. Thousand Oaks, CA: Sage.

Alexander, J. F., & Parsons, B. (1973). Short-term behavioral interventions with delinquent families: Impact on family process and recidivism. *Journal of Abnormal Psychology, 81*, 219– 225.

Alford, H. J., & Naughton, M. (2001). *Managing as if faith mattered: Christian social principles in the modern organization*. Notre Dame, IN: University of Notre Dame Press.

Amdam, R. (2002). Sectorial versus territorial regional planning and development in Norway. *Journal of European Planning Studies, 10*(1), 99–112.

American Cancer Society. (2013). Faith healing. [Online.] Retrieved on December 26, 2014, from http://www.cancer.org/treatment/treatmentsandsideeffects/complementaryandalternativemedicine/mindbodyandspirit/faith-healing.

Ammerman, N. T. (2013). Spiritual but not religious? Beyond binary choices in the study of religion. *Journal for the Scientific Study of Religion, 52*(2), 258–278.

Andersen, M., & Taylor, H. (2013). *Sociology: The essentials* (7th ed.). Belmont, CA: Wadsworth.

Annan, K. (1999). Secretary-General examine "meaning of international community" in address to DPI/NGO conference. [Online.] Retrieved on April 27, 2015, from http://www.un.org/press/en/1999/19990915.sgsm7133.doc.html.

Annette, J., & Creasy, S. (2007). *Individual Pathways in Participation*. ESRC Seminar Series: Mapping the Public Policy Landscape. Swindon, U.K.: ESRC.

Aponte, H. J. (1994). *Bread and spirit: Therapy with the new poor—Diversity of race, culture, and values*. New York: Norton.

Archard, D. (2012). The future of the family. *Ethics and social welfare, 6*(2), 132–142.

ARDA. (2010). US religious traditions 2010. [Online.] Retrieved on December 30, 2014, from http://www.thearda.com/rcms2010/r/u/rcms2010_99_US_name_2010.asp.

Argyle, M., & Beit-Hallahmi, B. (1975). *The social psychology of religion*. London: Routledge.

Arsenault, S. (2006). Implementing welfare reform in rural and urban communities: Why place matters. *American Review of Public Administration*, 36, 173–188.

Arlitsch, K., & Edelman, A. (2014). Staying safe: Cyber security for people and organizations. *Journal of Library Administration*, 54(1), 46–56.

Ashmos, D. O., & Duchon, D. (2000). Spirituality at work: A conceptualization and measure. *Journal of Management Inquiry*, 9(2), 134–145.

Austin, D. M. (1986). *A history of social work education*, Social work education monograph series. Austin, TX: School of Social Work at the University of Texas at Austin.

Avis, J. M. (1986). Feminist issues in family therapy. In F. P. Piercy, D. H. Sprenkle, & Associates (Eds.), *Family therapy sourcebook* (pp. 213–242). New York: Guilford.

Bales, R. F., Cohen, S. P., & Williamson, S. (1979). *SYMLOG: A System for the multi-level observation of groups*. New York: Free Press

Banks, S. (2001). *Ethics and values in social work* (2nd ed.). New York: Palgrave.

Barber, B. R. (1984). *Strong Democracy: Participatory Politics for a New Age*. Berkeley, CA: University of California Press.

Barker, E. (2008). The church without and the God within: Religiosity and/or spirituality? In E. Barker (Ed.), *The centrality of religion in social life: Essays in honor of James A. Beckford* (pp. 187–202). Aldershot, UK: Ashgate.

Bartone, P. T. (2006). Resilience under military operational stress: Can leaders influence hardiness? *Military Psychology*, 18(Suppl), S131–S148.

Basky, G. (2000). Does religion speed recovery in mental illness? *Canadian Medical Association Journal*, 163(11), 1497.

Bell, V. (2007). Online information, extreme communities and Internet therapy: Is the Internet good for our mental health? *Journal of Mental Health*, 16(4), 445–457.

Bella, R. N., Madsen, R., Sullivan, W. M., Swidler, A., & Tipton, S. M. (1985). *Habits of the heart: Individualism and commitment in American life*. Berkeley, CA: University of California Press.

Bellah, R. N. (1967). Civil religion in America. In R. N. Bellah & W. G. McLoughlin (Eds.), *Religion in America* (pp. 3–6). Boston, MA: Beacon Press.

Benore, E., Pargament, K. I., & Pendleton, S. (2008). An initial examination of religious coping in children with asthma. *The International Journal for the Psychology of Religion*, 18(4), 267–290.

Berger, B. L. (2011). Key theoretical issues in the interaction of law and religion: A guide for the perplexed. *Constitutional Forum*, 19(2), 41–52.

Berger, P. L., & Neuhaus, R. J. (1996). *To empower people: From state to civil society*. Washington, DC: AEI Press.

Bergsieker, H. B., Shelton, J. N., & Richeson, J. A. (2010). To be liked versus respected: Divergent goals in interracial interactions. *Journal of Personality and Social Psychology*, 99(2), 248.

Bertalanffy, L. von. (1972). The history of general systems theory. In G. J. Klir (Ed.), *Trends in general systems theory* (pp. 21–41). New York: Wiley-Interscience.

Bhaskar, R., Arenas-Germosen, B., & Dick, C. (2010). Demographic analysis 2010: Sensitivity analysis of the foreign-born migration component. [Online.] Retrieved on December 30, 2014, from http://www.census.gov/population/www/documentation/twps0098/twps0098.pdf.

Bies, R. J. (2005). Are procedural justice and interactional justice conceptually distinct? In J. Greenberg & J. A. Colquitt (Eds.), *Handbook of organizational justice* (pp. 85–112). Mahwah, NJ: Erlbaum.

Bion, W. R. (1961). *Experiences in groups and other papers*. New York: Basic Books.

Bitter, J. R. (2014). *Theory and practice of family therapy and counseling* (2nd ed.). Belmont, CA: Brooks/Cole.

Blane, D. (2006). The life course, the social gradient and health. In M. Marmot & R. G. Wilkinson (Eds.), *The social determinants of health* (2nd ed., pp. 54–77). New York: Oxford University Press.

Blumer, H. (1969). *Symbolic interaction: Perspective and method*. Englewood Cliffs, NJ: Prentice-Hall.

Boehmer, C., & Nordstrom, T. (2008). Intergovernmental organization memberships:

Examining political community and the attributes of international organizations. *International Interactions*, 34, 282–309.

Bonilla-Silva, E. (2013). *Racism without racists: Color-blind racism and the persistence of racial inequality in America* (4th ed.). Lanham, MD: Rowman & Littlefield.

Borysenko, J. (1999). *A woman's journey to God: Finding the feminine path*. New York: Putnam.

Boston, R. (2010). 'No religious test' tested. Americans united for separation of church and state. Retrieved on January 1, 2015, from https://www.au.org/church-state/february-2010-church-state/featured/%E2%80%98no-religious-test%E2%80%99-tested.

Bottoms, B. L., Nielsen, M., Murray, R., & Filipas, H. (2003). Religion-related child physical abuse: Characteristics and psychological outcome. In J. Mullins (Ed.), *The victimization of children: Emerging trends* (pp. 87–114). Binghamton: Hayworth.

Bowen, M. (1976). Theory in the practice of psychotherapy. In P. J. Guerin. (Ed.). *Family therapy*. New York: Gardner.

Bowers, R., Minichiello, V., & Plummer, D. (2010). Religious attitudes, homophobia, and professional counseling. *Journal of LGBT Issues in Counseling*, 4(2), 70–91.

Bowie, R. (2011). Human rights and religion in the English secondary RE curriculum. *Journal of Beliefs & Values*, 32(3): 269–280.

Bowlby, J. (1969). *Attachment and loss* (Vol. I). London: Hogarth Press.

Boyles, A. (1997). The meaning of community. [Online.] Retrieved on April 30, 2015, from http://www.bahai.org/documents/essays/boyles-ann/meaning-community.

Braam, A. W., Sonnenberg, C. M., Beekman, A. T. F., Deeg, D. J. H., & Van-Tilburg, W. (2000). Religious denomination as a symptom-formation factor of depression in older Dutch citizens. *International Journal of Geriatric Psychiatric*, 15, 458–466.

Brady, L. L. C., & Hapenny, A. (2010). Giving back and growing in service: Investigating spirituality, religiosity, and generativity in young adults. *Journal of Adolescent Behavior*, 17, 162–167.

Brelsford, G. M. (2013). Sanctification and spiritual disclosure in parent–child relationships: Implications for family quality. *Journal of Family Psychology*, 27(4), 639–649.

Brenner, M. J., & Homonoff, E. (2004). Zen and clinical social work: A spiritual approach to practice. *Families in Society*, 85, 261–270.

Breton, M. (2004). An empowerment perspective. In C. D. Garvin, L. M. Gutierrez, & M. J. Galinsky (Eds.), *Handbook of social work with groups* (pp. 58–75). New York: Guilford.

Bricker-Jenkins, M., & Netting, F. E. (2009). Feminist issues and practices in social work. In A. R. Roberts (Ed.), *Social workers' desk reference* (2nd ed., pp. 277–283). New York: Oxford.

Briggs, M. K., & Dixon, A. L. (2013). Women's spirituality across the life span: Implications for counseling. *Counseling and Values*, 58, 104–120.

Briggs-Myers, I., & Briggs, K. C. (1985). *Myers-Briggs Type Indicator (MBTI)*. Palo Alto, CA: Consulting Psychologists Press.

Brody, R. (2005). *Effectively managing human service organizations* (3rd ed.). Thousand Oaks, CA: Sage.

Bronfenbrenner, U. (1979). *The ecology of human development*. Cambridge, MA: Harvard University Press.

Brown, E., Orbuch, T. L., & Bauermeister, J. A. (2008). Religiosity and marital stability among Black American and White American couples. *Family Relations*, 57, 186–197.

Brown, H. (1992). *Women organizing*. London: Routledge.

Brown, J., Cohen, P., Johnson, J. G., & Salzinger, S. (1998). A longitudinal analysis of risk factors for child maltreatment: Findings of a 17-year prospective study of officially recorded and self-reported child abuse and neglect. *Child Abuse and Neglect*, 22, 1065–1078.

Brown, S. M., & Porter, J. (2013). The effects of religion on remarriage among American women: Evidence from the national survey of family growth. *Journal of Divorce & Remarriage*, 54, 142–162.

Brueggemann, W. G. (2013). *The practice of macro social work* (4th ed.). Belmont, CA: Brooks/Cole.

Burris, J. L., Smith, G. T., & Carlson, C. R. (2009). Relations among religiousness, spirituality, and sexual practices. *Journal of Sex Research*, 46(4), 282–289.

Butler, J. (2002). Is kinship already always heterosexual? *Differences: A Journal of Feminist Cultural Studies*, 13 (1), 14–44.

Bygrave, C., & Macmillan, S. (2008). Spirituality in the workplace: A wake up call from the American dream. *Journal of Workplace Rights*, 13(1), 93–112.

Canda, E. R. (1988). Conceptualizing spirituality for social work: Insights from diverse perspectives. *Social Thought: The Journal of Religion in the Social Services*, Winter, 30–46.

Canda, E. R. (1991). East/West philosophical synthesis in transpersonal theory. *Journal of Sociology and Social Welfare*, 18(4), 137–152.

Canda, E. R., & Furman, L. D. (1999). *Spiritual diversity in social work practice: The heart of helping*. New York: The Free Press.

Canda, E. R., & Furman, L, D. (2010). *Spiritual diversity in social work practice: The heart of helping*. New York: Oxford University Press.

Cannon, K. (1995). Surviving the blight. In G. Wade-Gayles (Ed.), *My soul is a witness: African American women's spirituality* (pp. 19–26). Boston: Beacon Press.

Caplan, S., Escobar, J., Paris, M., Alvidrez, J., Dixon, J. K., Desai, M. M., Scahill, L. D., & Whittemore, R. (2013). Cultural influences on causal beliefs about depression among Latino immigrants. *Journal of Transcultural Nursing*, 24(1), 68–77.

Capps, D. (1995). *The child's song: The religious abuse of children*. Louisville: Westminster John Knox Press.

Carneiro, R. (2013). The impact of Christianity on therapy with Latino families. *Contemporary Family Therapy*, 35, 137–146.

Carter, B., & McGoldrick, M. (2005). Overview: The expanded family life cycle: Individual, family, and social perspectives. In B. Carter & M. McGoldrick (Eds.), *The expanded family life cycle: Individual, family, and social perspectives* (4th ed.). Boston: Allyn & Bacon.

Carter, N. E. (2007). Agriculture, communities and rural environmental initiative: Can small family farms and large agribusiness live peacefully in Pennsylvania? *Widener Law Journal*, 16(3), 1023–1051.

Castelloe, P., Watson, T., & White, C. (2002). Participatory change: An integrative approach to community practice. *Journal of Community Practice*, 10(4), 7–31.

Chambers, R. (2005). *Ideas for development*. London: Earthscan.

Chapple, P. E. (2003). Mental health and religion: A guide for service providers. [Online.] Retrieved December 15, 2014, from https://www.rcpsych.ac.uk/pdf/E.%20Paul%20Chapple%201.11.03%20Mental%20Health%20and%20Religion%20-%20a%20Guide%20for%20Service%20Providers.pdf.

Chatman, J. A., & Eunyoung Cha, S. (2003). Leading by leveraging culture. *California Management Review*, 45, 19–34.

Chaves, M. (2011). *American religion: Contemporary trends*. Princeton, NJ: Princeton University Press.

Cherlin, A. J. (2009). The Deinstitutionalization of American Marriage. *Journal of Marriage & Family*, 66, 848–61.

Child Trends. (2013). *World family map*. [Online.] Retrieved December 28, 2014, from http://worldfamilymap.org/2013/articles/world-family-indicators/family-structure.

Chittum, R., & Hilsenrath, J. E. (2004). Call centers phone home. *Wall Street Journal*, *243*(112), B1–B8.

Clarke, M. (2013). Good works and God's work: A case study of churches and community development in Vanuatu. *Asia Pacific Viewpoint*, *54*(3), 340–351.

Clarke, M., & Donnelly, J. (2009). *Learning from missionaries: Lessons for secular development practitioners*. Presented at Edinburgh 2010 Commission VII Forum, Edinburgh, 11–12 June.

Cnaan, R. A. (1999). *The Newer Deal*. Columbia University Press: New York.

Cohen, S. A. (2009). Facts and consequences: Legality, incidence, and safety of abortion worldwide. *Guttmacher Policy Review*, 12(4). [Online.] Retrieved on January 1, 2015, from https://www.guttmacher.org/pubs/gpr/12/4/gpr120402.html.

Colquitt, J. A., Greenberg, J., & Zapata-Phelan, C. P. (2005). What is organizational justice? A historical overview. In J. Greenberg & J. A. Colquitt (Eds.), *Handbook of organizational justice* (pp. 3–56). Mahwah, NJ: Erlbaum.

Congressional Information Service. (1986). *Abstracts of congressional publications* (Vol. 7, Nos 1–12). Washington, DC: U.S. Government Printing Office.

Cook, K. S., & Emerson, R. M. (1978). Power, equity and commitment in exchange networks. *American Sociological Review, 43*(5), 721–739.

Coontz, S. (Ed.). (2008). *American families: A multi-cultural reader* (2nd ed.). New York: Routledge.

Corey, M. S., Corey, G., & Corey, C. (2010). *Groups: Process and practice* (9th ed.). Belmont, CA: Brooks/Cole.

Cortright, B. (1997). *Psychotherapy and spirit: Theory and practice in transpersonal psychotherapy.* Albany: State University of New York Press.

Council on Social Work Education. (2015). Educational policy and accreditation standards. [Online.] Retrieved on December 4, 2014, from http://www.cswe.org/Accreditation/EPASRevision.aspx.

Cox, T. A. (1991). The multicultural organization. *The Executive, 5*(2), 34–47.

Cox, T. A. (1994). *Cultural diversity in organizations: Theory, research, and practice.* San Francisco, CA: Berrett-Koehler.

Crocker, C. A., Hampson, F. O., & Aall, P. (2014). A global security vacuum half-filled: Regional organizations, hybrid groups, and security management. *International Peacekeeping, 21*(1), 1–19.

Cromartie, J. (2013). *How is rural America changing?* [Online.] Retrieved on April 27, 2015, from http://www.census.gov/newsroom/cspan/rural_america/20130524_rural_america_slides.pdf.

Cropanzano, R., Byrne, Z. S., Bobocel, D. R., & Rupp, D. E. (2001). Moral virtues, fairness, heuristics, social entities, and other denizens of organizational justice. *Journal of Vocational Behavior, 58*, 164–209.

Cui, M., Fincham, F. D., & Pasley, B. K. (2008). Young adult romantic relationships: The role of parents' marital problems and relationship efficacy. *Personality and Social Psychology Bulletin, 34,* 1226–1235.

Curtis, K. T., & Ellison, C. G. (2002). Religious heterogamy and marital conflict: Findings from the National Survey of Families and Households. *Journal of Family Issues, 23*(4), 551–576.

Daft, R. L. (2010). *Management* (9th ed.). Mason, OH: South-Western.

Dandekar, N. (1991). Can whistle-blowing be fully legitimated? A theoretical discussion. *Business & Professional Ethics Journal, 10*, 89–108.

Dattilio, F. M. (2005). Restructuring family schemas: A cognitive-behavioral perspective. *Journal of Marital and Family Therapy, 31*(1), 15–30.

Dattillio, F. M., & Bevilacqua, L. J. (2000). *Comparative treatments for relationship dysfunction.* New York: Springer.

Deloria, V. (1988). *Custer died for your sins: An Indian manifesto.* Norman, OK: University of Oklahoma Press.

DeLucia-Waack, J. L (2010). Diversity in groups. In R. K. Conyne (Ed.), *The Oxford handbook of group counseling* (pp. 83–101). New York: Oxford University Press.

Derezotes, D. S. (2006). *Spirituality oriented social work practice.* Boston, MA: Pearson.

Derezotes, D., & Evans, K. E. (1995). Spirituality and religiosity in practice: In-depth interviews of social work practitioners. *Social Thought, 18*(1), 39–56.

de Shazer, S. (1991). *Putting differences to work.* New York: Norton.

Dillon, M., & Wink, P. (2007). *In the course of a lifetime: Tracing religious belief, practice and change.* Berkeley: University of California Press.

Dinham, A. (2010). What is a "faith community"? *Community Development Journal, 46*(4), 526–541.

Dinham, A., Furbey, R., & Lowndes, V. (Eds.). (2009). *Faith in the Public Realm: Problems, Policies, Controversies.* Bristol: Policy Press.

Dodson, L. (2013). Stereotyping low-wage mothers who have work and family conflicts. *Journal of Social Issues, 69*(2), 257–278.

Dodson, L., & Luttrell, W. (2012). Untenable choices: Taking care of low-income families. *Contexts: Understanding people and their social world, 10*(1), 39–42

Doherty, W. J. (1991). Family therapy goes postmodern. *Family Networker, 15*(5), 36–42.

Dollahite, D. C., & Thatcher, J. Y. (2008). Talking about religion: How religious youth and parents discuss their faith. *Journal of Adolescent Research, 23*, 611–641.

Drucker, P. F. (1974). *Management: Tasks, Responsibilities, Practices*. New York: Harper & Row.

Dumler, M. P., & Skinner, S. J. (2008). *A primer for management* (2nd ed.). Mason, OH: South-Western.

Dupuis, S. B. (2007). Examining remarriage: A look at issues affecting remarried couples and the implications towards therapeutic techniques. *Journal of Divorce & Remarriage, 48*(1/2), 91–104.

Durkheim, E. (1933). *The division of labor in society*. New York: Free Press.

Durkheim, E. (1965). *The elementary forms of the religious life*. New York: Free Press.

Dworkin, S. (1997). Female, lesbian, and Jewish: Complex and invisible. In B. Greene (Ed.), *Ethnic and cultural diversity among lesbians and gay men. Psychological perspectives on lesbian and gay issues* (Vol. 3, pp. 63–87). Thousand Oaks, CA: Sage Publications.

Dykstra, P. A. (2006). Off the beaten track: Childlessness and social integration in late life. *Research in Aging, 28*, 749–767.

Edwards, D. (2010). Planetary spirituality: Exploring a Christian ecological approach. *Compass, 44*(4), 16–23.

Eggebeen, D., & Dew, J. (2009). The role of religion in adolescence for family formation in young adulthood. *Journal of Marriage and Family, 71*, 108–121.

Ellison C. (1991). Religious involvement and subjective well-being. *Journal of Health and Social Behavior, 32*, 80–99.

Ely, R. J., & Thomas, D. A. (2001). Cultural diversity at work: The effects of diversity perspectives on work group processes and outcomes. *Administrative Science Quarterly, 46*(2), 229–273.

Emerson, R. M. (1976). Social exchange theory. *Annual Review of Sociology, 2*(1), 335–362.

Ephross, P., & Vassil, T. (2005). *Groups that work: Structure and process*. New York: Columbia University Press.

Erikson, E. (1950). *Childhood and society*. New York: W. W. Norton.

Etzioni, A. (1964). *Modern organizations*. Englewood Cliffs, NJ: Prentice-Hall.

Evans, A. E. (2007). School leaders and their sensemaking about race and demographic change. *Educational Administration Quarterly, 43*(2), 159–185.

Exline, J. J., Prince-Paul, M., Root, B. L., & Peereboom, K. S. (2013). The spiritual struggle of anger toward God: A study with family members of hospice patients. *Journal of Palliative Medicine, 16*(4), 369–375.

FACIT. (2007). *Functional Assessment of Chronic Illness Therapy*. [Online.] Retrieved on December 20, 2014, from http://www.facit/org/about/welcome.aspx.

Fallon, K. M., Dobmeier, R. A., Reiner, S. M., Casquarelli, E. J., Giglia, L. A., & Goodwin, E. (2013). Reconciling spiritual values conflicts for counselors and lesbian and gay clients. *Adultspan Journal, 12*(1), 38–53.

Fatout, M., & Rose, S. R. (1998). *Task groups in the social services*. Thousand Oaks, CA: Sage.

Fellin, P. (2001). *The community and the social worker* (3rd ed.). Itasca, IL: Peacock.

Fetzer Institute. (1999). *Multidimensional measurement of religiousness/spirituality for use in health research*. [Online.] Retrieved on December 22, 2014, from http://fetzer.org/resources/multidimensional-measurement-religiousnessspirituality-use-health-research.

Filbert, K. M., & Flynn, R. J. (2010). Developmental and cultural assets and resilient outcomes in First Nations young people in care: An initial test of an exploratory model. *Children and Youth Services Review, 32*, 560–564.

Finn, J. L., & Jacobson. M. (2008). *Just practice: A social justice approach to social work* (2nd ed.). Chicago: Lyceum.

Foldy, E. G., & Buckley, T. R. (2014). Color minimization: The theory and practice of addressing race and ethnicity at work. In K. M. Thomas, V. C. Plaut, & N. M. Tran (Eds.), *Diversity ideologies in organizations* (pp. 159–203). London: Routledge.

Forester, J. (1989). *Planning in the face of power.* Berkeley, CA: University of California Press.

Fowler, J. (1981). *Stages of faith: The psychology of human development and the quest for meaning.* San Francisco: Harper & Row.

Freedman, J., & Combs, G. (2000). Narrative therapy with couples. In F. M. Dattilio & L. J. Bevilacqua (Eds.), *Comparative treatments for relationship dysfunction.* New York: Springer.

Freire, P. (1970). *Pedagogy of the oppressed.* London: Penguin.

Freng, A., Davis, T., McCord, K., & Roussell, A. (2012). The New American gang? Gangs in Indian country. *Journal of Contemporary Criminal Justice, 28*(4), 446–464.

Freud, S. (1909). *Selected papers on hysteria and other psychoneuroses.* New York: The Journal of Nervous and Mental Disease Publishing Company.

Frey, J. J., Collins, K. S., Pastoor, J., & Linde, L (2014). Social workers' observations of the needs of the total military community. *Journal of Social Work Education, 50,* 712–729.

Gamble, D. N., & Hoff, M. D. (2005). Sustainable community development. In M. Weil (Ed.), *The handbook of community practice* (pp. 169–188). Thousand Oaks, CA: Sage.

Gamble, D., & Weil, M. (2010). *Community practice skills: Local to global perspective.* New York: Columbia University Press.

Gamm, G., & Putnam, R. D. (1999). The growth of voluntary associations in America, 1840–1940. *The Journal of Interdisciplinary History, 29*(4), 511–557.

Ganga, N. S., & Kutty, R. (2013). Influence of religion, religiosity, and spirituality on positive mental health of young people. *Mental Health, Religion, & Culture, 16*(4), 435–443.

Garcia-Zamor, J. C. (2003). Workplace spirituality and organizational performance. *Public Administration Review, 63*(3), 355–364.

Garnett, R. W. (2008, January 28). When Catholicism was the target. *USA Today,* p. 9A.

Garrett, J. T., & Garrett, M. W. (1994). The path of good medicine: Understanding and counseling Native American Indians. *Journal of Multicultural Counseling and Development, 22,* 134–144.

Garrett, M. T., & Pichette, E. F. (2000). Red as an apple: Native American acculturation and counseling with or without reservation. *Journal of Counseling & Development, 78,* 3–13.

Garvin, C. D., & Galinsky, M. J. (2008). Groups. In T. Mizrahi & L. E. Davis (Editors), *Encyclopedia of social work* (Vol. 2, pp. 287–298). Washington, DC: NASW Press.

Gates, A. B. (2014). Integrating social services and social change: Lessons from an immigrant worker center. *Journal of Community Practice, 22,* 102–129.

Gergen, K. J. (1985). The social construction movement in modern psychology. *American Psychologist, 40,* 266–275.

Gershoff, E. T., Miller, P. C., & Holden, G. W. (1999). Parenting influences from the pulpit: Religious affiliation as a determinant of parental corporal punishment. *Journal of Family Psychology, 13,* 307–320.

Ghanea-Hercock, N. (2010). *Religion and human rights: Critical concepts in religious studies.* London: Routledge.

Giddings, P. (1984). *When and where I enter: The impact of Black women on race and sex in America.* New York: Bantam.

Giffords, E. (2009). The Internet and social work: The next generation. *Families in Society, 90*(4), 413–418.

Gilbert, D. (2003). *The American class structure: In an age of growing inequality.* Belmont, CA: Wadsworth/Thomson Learning.

Gilbert, N., & Specht, H. (1977). *Dynamics of community planning.* Cambridge, MA: Ballinger Publishing Co.

Gilligan, C. (1982). *In a different voice: Psychological theory and women's development.* Cambridge, MA: Harvard University Press.

Gillum, F., & Griffith, D. (2010). Prayer and spiritual practices for health reasons among American adults: The role of race and ethnicity. *Journal of Religion & Health, 49*(3), 283–295.

Glazer, D. (2014). LGBT parenting: The kids are all right. LGBT transitions to parenthood. *Journal of Gay & Lesbian Mental Health, 18*, 213–221.

Glicken, M. D. (2007). *Social work in the 21st century.* Thousand Oaks, CA: Sage.

Glisson, C., Schoenwald, S. K., Kelleher, K., Landsverk, J., Hoagwood, K. E., Mayberg, S., & Green, P. (2008). Therapist turnover and new program sustainability in mental health clinics as a function of organizational culture, climate, and service structure. *Administration and Policy in Mental Health and Mental Health Research, 35*, 124–133.

Goeke-Morey, M. C., Taylor, L. K., Merrilees, C. E., Shirlow, P., & Cummings, E. M. (2014). Adolescents' relationship with God and internalizing adjustment over time: The moderating role of maternal religious coping. *Journal of Family Psychology, 28*, 749–758.

Goldenberg, H., & Goldenberg, I. (2013). *Family therapy: An overview* (8th ed.). Belmont, CA: Brooks/Cole.

Goldman, M. S. (2009). Averting apocalypse at Rajneeshpuram. *Sociology of Religion, 70*(3), 311–327.

Goldner, V. (1985). Feminism and family therapy. *Family Process, 24*, 31–47.

Goldstein, S., and Thau, S. (2004). Attachment theory, neuroscience, and couple therapy. *Psychologist-Psychoanalyst, 24*(1), 15–19.

Goldston, D. B., Molock, S. D., Whitbeck, L. B., Murakami, J. L., Zayas, L. H., & Nagayama Hall, G. C. (2008). Cultural considerations in adolescent suicide prevention and psychosocial treatment. *American Psychologist, 63*, 14–31.

Good, M., & Willoughby, T. (2014). Institutional and personal spirituality/religiosity and psychosocial adjustment in adolescence: Concurrent and longitudinal associations. *Journal of Youth and Adolescence, 43*, 757–774.

Granovetter, M. S. (1973). The strength of weak ties. *American Journal of Sociology, 78*(6), 1360–1380.

Greeff, A. P., & Thiel, C. (2012). Resilience in families of husbands with prostate cancer. *Educational Gerontology, 38*, 179–189.

Greenberg, J. (2009). Promote procedural and interactional justice to enhance individual and organizational outcomes. In E. A. Locke (Ed.), *Handbook of principles of organizational behavior* (2nd ed., pp. 255–271). Hoboken, NJ: Wiley.

Greene, A. D., & Latting, J. K. (2004). Whistle-blowing as a form of advocacy: Guidelines for the practitioner and organization. *Social Work, 49*(2), 219–230.

Griffin, R. W., & Moorhead, G. (2010). *Organizational behavior: Managing people and organizations* (9th ed.). Mason, OH: South-Western.

Grim, J. (2011). The roles of religions in activating an ecological consciousness. *International Social Science Journal, 62*(205/206), 255–269.

Grimsley, M., Hickman, P., Lawless, P., Manning, J., & Wilson, I. (2005). *Community involvement and social capital. NDC national evaluation: Data analysis paper 30.* Centre for Regional Economic and Social Research, Sheffield Hallam University.

Grotevant, H. D. (1989). The role of theory in guiding family assessment. *Journal of Family Psychology, 3*, 104–117.

Haley, J. (1963). *Strategies of psychotherapy.* New York: Grune & Stratton.

Halkitis, P. N., Mattis, J. S., Sahadath, J. K., Massie, D., Ladyzhenskaya, L., Pitrelli, K., et al. (2009). The meanings and manifestations of religion and spirituality among lesbian, gay, bisexual, and transgender adults. *Journal of Adult Development, 16*(4), 250–262.

Hall, G. (2012). Applying psychological-type theory to faith: Spirituality, prayer, worship and scripture. *Mental Health, Religion, & Culture, 15*(9), 849–862.

Hall, H. R., Neely-Barnes, S. L., Graff, J. C., Krcek, T., & Roberts, R. J. (2012). Parental stress in families of children with a genetic disorder/disability and the resiliency model of family stress, adjustment, and adaptation. *Issues in Comprehensive Pediatric Nursing, 35*, 24–44.

Hall, J. R. (2004). Jonestown in the twenty-first century. *Society, 41*(2), 9–11.

Hall, P. D. (2005). Historical perspectives on non-profit organizations in the United States. In R. D. Herman (Ed.), *The Jossey-Bass handbook of nonprofit leadership and management* (2nd ed., pp. 3–38). San Francisco, CA: John Wiley & Sons.

Hannan, M. T., & Freeman, J. (1989). *Organizational ecology*. Cambridge, MA: Harvard University Press.

Hardina, D. (2004). Guidelines for ethical practice in community organization. *Social Work, 49*(4), 595–604.

Harrison, W. D. (1995). Community development. In R. L. Edwards (Ed.), *Encyclopedia of social work* (19th ed., Vol. 1, pp. 555–562). Washington, DC: NASW Press.

Hash, K. M., Jurkowski, E. T., & Krout, J. A. (2015). *Aging in rural places: Policies, programs, and professional practice*. New York, New York: Springer.

Health Resources and Services Administration. (n.d.). *Defining the rural population*. [Online.] Retrieved on April 27, 2015, from http://www.hrsa.gov/rural-health/policy/definition_of_rural.html.

Heermann, M., Wiggins, M. I., & Rutter, P. A. (2007). Creating a space for spiritual practice: Pastoral possibilities with sexual minorities. *Pastoral Psychology, 55*(6), 711–721.

Heinrich, R. K., Corbine, J. L., & Thomas, K. R. (1990). Counseling Native Americans. *Journal of Counseling & Development, 69*, 128–133.

Held, D. (1980). *Introduction to critical theory: Horkheimer to Habermas*. Los Angeles: University of California Press.

Hellriegel, D., & Slocum, J. W. (2009). *Organizational behavior* (12th ed.). Mason, OH: South-Western.

Helminiak, D. (1987). *Spiritual development: An interdisciplinary study*. Chicago: Loyola University Press.

Henslin, J. M. (2014). *Sociology: A down-to-earth approach*. (12th ed.). Boston, MA: Pearson.

Hicks, D. A. (2003). *Religion and the workplace: Pluralism, spirituality, leadership*. Cambridge, UK: Cambridge University Press.

Hicks, S. (2011). *Lesbian, Gay and Queer Parenting: Families, Intimacies, Genealogies*. New York: Palgrave Macmillan.

Hill, K., & Ferguson, S. M. (2014). Web 2.0 in social work macro practice: Ethical considerations and questions. *Journal of Social Work Values and Ethics, 11*(1), 1–11.

Hillery G. A. (1955). Definitions of community: areas of agreement. *Rural Sociology, 20*, 111–124.

Hines, P. M., Preto, N. G., McGoldrick, M., Almeida, R., & Weltman, S. (1999). Culture and the family life cycle. In B. Carter & M. McGoldrick (Eds.), *The expanded family life cycle: Individual, family, and social perspectives* (3rd ed., pp. 69–87). Boston: Allyn & Bacon.

Hodge, D. R. (2001). Spiritual assessment: A review of major qualitative methods and a new framework for assessing spirituality. *Social Work, 46*, 203–214.

Hodge, D. R. (2005a). Spiritual lifemaps: A client-centered pictorial instrument for spiritual assessment, planning, and intervention. *Social Work, 50*, 77–88.

Hodge, D. R. (2005b). Spiritual assessment in marital and family therapy: A methodological framework for selecting between six qualitative assessment tools. *Journal of Marital and Family Therapy, 31*, 341–356

Hodge, D. R. (2013). Implicit spiritual assessment: An alternative approach for assessing client spirituality. *Social Work, 58*(3), 223–230.

Hodge, D. R., & Bushfield, S. (2006). Developing spiritual competence in practice. *Journal of Ethnic & Cultural Diversity in Social Work, 15*(3/4), 101–127.

Hodge, D. R., & Limb, G. E. (2011). Spiritual assessment and Native Americans: Establishing the social validity of a complementary set of assessment tools. *Social Work, 56*(3), 213–223.

Hodge, D. R., & Williams, T. R. (2002). Assessing African American spirituality with spiritual eco-maps. *Families in Society, 83*, 585–595

Hodgkinson, H. L. (1990). *The demographics of American Indians: One precent of the people, fifty percent of the diversity*. Washington, DC: Institute for Educational Leadership.

Holkup, P. A., Salois, E. M., Tripp-Reimer, T., & Weinert, C. (2007). Drawing on wisdom from the past: An elder abuse intervention with tribal communities. *The Gerontologist, 47*(2), 248–254.

Hollingsworth, L. D. (2000). Who seeks to adopt a child? Findings from the national survey of family growth. *Adoption Quarterly, 3*, 1–24.

Holmes, A. (2014). Bridging the information gap: The Department of Justice's "pattern or practice" suits and community organizations. *Texas Law Review, 92*(5), 1241–1276.

Holtzman, M. (2006). Definitions of the family as an impetus for legal change in custody decision making: Suggestions from an empirical case study. *Law & Social Inquiry, 31*(1), 1–37.

Homan, M. (2011). *Promoting community change: making it happen in the real world* (5th ed). Belmont, CA: Brooks/Cole.

Hong, Y. J. (2011). Developing a new human services management model through workplace spirituality in social work. *Journal of Workplace Behavioral Health, 26*, 144–163.

hooks, b. (1981). *Ain't I a woman.* Boston: South End Press.

Horton, M., & Freire, P. (1990). *We make the road by walking: Conversations on education and social change.* Philadelphia: Temple University Press.

Houtman, D., & Aupers, S. (2008). The spiritual revolution and the new age gender puzzle: The sacralization of the self in late modernity (1980–2000). In K. Aune, S. Sharma, & G. Vincett (Eds.), *Women and religion in the West: Challenging Secularization* (pp. 99–118). Burlington, VT: Ashgate Publishing Company.

Huling, T. (2002). Building a prison economy in rural America. In M. Mauer & M. Chesney-Lind (Eds.), *Invisible punishment: The collateral consequences of mass imprisonment* (pp. 197–213). New York: New Press.

Iannello, K. (1992). *Decision without hierarchy: Feminist interventions in organization theory and practice.* London: Routledge.

Idler, E., (1987). Religious involvement and the health of the elderly: some hypotheses and an initial test. *Social Forces, 66* (1), 226–238.

IPAS. (2009). Ensuring women's access to safe abortion. [Online.] Retrieved on November 19, 2015, from http://www.ipas.org/~/media/Files/Ipas%20Publications/MDGFLY3E11.ashx.

Irvine, S. (2014). Independence, Oregon: Weaving the fabric of a successful rural community. *National Civic Review, 103*(4), 25–32.

Jacobs, E. E., Masson, R. L., Harvill, R. L., & Schimmel, C. J. (2012). *Group counseling: Strategies and skills* (7th ed.). Belmont, CA: Brooks/Cole.

Jacobson, N. S., & Christensen, A. (1996). *Integrative couple therapy: Promoting acceptance.* New York: Norton.

James, R. (2009). *What is distinctive about FBOs? How European FBOs define and operationalise their faith.* Praxis Paper 22, INTRAC.

James, W. (1961). The *varieties of religious experience.* New York: Collier Books. (Original work published 1902).

Jayakody, R., & Stauffer, D. (2000). Mental health problems among single mothers: Implications for work and welfare reform. *Journal of Social Issues, 56*(4), 617–634.

Johnson, A. K. (2001). The community practice pilot project: Integrating methods, field, community assessment and experiential learning. *Journal of Community Practice, 8*(4), 5–25.

Johnson, D. B., Quinn, E., Sitaker, M., Ammerman, A., Byker, C., Dean, W., Fleischhacker, S., Kolodinsky, J., Pinard, C., Pitts, S. B., & Sharkey, J. (2014). Developing an agenda for research about policies to improve access to healthy foods in rural communities: A concept mapping study. *BMC Public Health, 14*(19), 550–572.

Johnson, D. W., & Johnson, F. P. (2000). *Joining together: Group theory and group skills* (7th ed.). Boston: Allyn & Bacon.

Johnson, S. M. (2004). *The practice of emotionally focused marital therapy: Creating connection* (2nd ed.). New York: Brunner/Routledge.

Johnson, S. M., & Greenberg, L. S. (1985). The differential effects of experiential and problem solving interventions in resolving marital conflicts. *Journal of Consulting and Clinical Psychology, 53*, 175–184.

Kaslow, F. W. (2010). A family therapy narrative. *American Journal of Family Therapy, 38*(1), 50– 62.

Kaufman, G. D. (2001). Re-conceiving God and humanity in light of today's evolutionary-ecological consciousness. *Journal of Religion and Science, 36*(2), 335–349.

Kempler, W. (1974). *Principles of Gestalt family therapy.* Costa Mesa, CA: Kempler Institute.

Kerson, T. S., & McCoyd, J. L. M. (2013). In response to need: An analysis of social work roles over time. *Social Work, 58*(4), 333–343.

Kettner, P. M., Moroney, R. M., & Martin, L. L. (2008). *Designing and managing programs: An effectiveness-based approach* (3rd ed.). Thousand Oaks, CA: Sage.

Kidd, S. M. (1995). *The dance of the dissident daughter.* San Francisco: HarperCollins.

Kim, J. (2009). Barriers to work among poor families: Health limitations, family structure, and lack of job opportunities. *Journal of Policy Practice, 8,* 317–334.

Kim-Spoon, J., Farley, J. P., Holmes, C. J., & Longo, G. S. (2014). Does adolescents' religiousness moderate links between harsh parenting and adolescent substance use? *Journal of Family Psychology, 28,* 739–748.

King, S. V., Burgess, E. O., Akinyela, M., Counts-Spriggs, M., & Parker, N. (2006). The religious dimensions of the grandparent role in three generation African American households. *Journal of Religion, Spirituality & Aging, 19*(1), 76–96.

Kirmayer, L. J., Raikhel, E., & Rahimi, S. (2013). Cultures of the internet: Identity, community and mental health. *Transcultural Psychiatry, 50*(2), 165–191.

Klein, M. (1932). *The psychoanalysis of children.* New York: Random House.

Koenig, H., McCullough, M., & Larson, D. (2001). *Handbook of religion & health.* New York: Oxford University Press.

Koenig, H. G., Meador, K. G., & Parkerson, G. (1997). Religion index for psychiatric research. *American Journal of Psychiatry, 154,* 885–886.

Kohlberg, L. (1976). *Stages in the development of moral thought and action.* New York: Hold, Rinehart, & Winston.

Koocher, G. P. (2008). Ethical challenges in mental health services to children and families. *Journal of Clinical Psychology: In Session, 64*(5), 601–612.

Kretzmann, J. P., & McKnight, J. L. (1993). *Building communities from the inside out: A path toward finding and mobilizing a community's assets.* Chicago: ACTA Publications.

Krumrei, E. J., Mahoney, A., & Pargament, K. I. (2009). Divorce and the divine: The role of spirituality in adjustment to divorce. *Journal of Marriage and Family, 71*(2), 373–383.

Kurzman, P. (1985). Program development and service coordination as components of community practice. In S. Taylor & R. Roberts (Eds.), *Theory and practice of community social work.* New York: Columbia University Press.

La Cour, P., & Götke, P. (2012). Understanding of the word "spirituality" by theologians compared to lay people: An empirical study from a secular region. *Journal of Health Care Chaplaincy, 18,* 97–109.

Lamis, D. A., Wilson, C. K., Tarantino, N., Lansford, J. E., & Kaslow, N. J. (2014). Neighborhood disorder, spiritual well-being, and parenting stress in African American women. *Journal of Family Psychology, 28,* 790–799.

Land, H. (2015). *Spirituality, religion, and faith in psychotherapy.* Chicago: Lyceum.

Lasswell, H. D. (1971). *A Pre-View of Policy Sciences.* New York: American Elsevier.

Lawler-Row, K. A., & Elliott, J. (2009). The role of religious activity and spirituality in the health and well-being of older adults. *Journal of Health Psychology, 1,* 43–52.

Lease, S. H., Horne, S. G., & Noffsinger-Frazier, N. (2005). Affirming faith experiences and psychological health for Caucasian lesbian, gay, and bisexual individuals. *Journal of Counseling Psychology, 52*(3), 378–388.

LeChasseur, K. (2014). Critical race theory and the meaning of community in district partnerships. *Equity & Excellence in education, 47*(3), 305–320.

Lee, P. (1937). *Social work as cause and function.* New York: Columbia University Press.

Leighninger, L. (2000). *Creating a New Profession: The Beginnings of Social Work Education in the United States.* Alexandria, VA: Council on Social Work Education.

Lewin, K. (1951). *Field theory in social science.* New York: Harper & Row.

Lewis, M. L., Scott, D. L., & Calfee, C. (2013). Rural social service disparities and creative social work solutions for rural families across the life span. *Journal of Family Social Work, 16*, 101–115.

Lewis, S. P., Heath, N. L., St Denis, J. M., & Noble, R. (2011). The scope of nonsuicidal self-injury on YouTube. *Pediatrics, 127*(3), 552–557.

Levin, J. (2012). A faith-based agenda for the Surgeon General: Challenges and recommendations. *Journal of Religion and Health, 51*, 57–71.

Levin, J. (2013). Engaging the faith community for public health advocacy: An agenda for the surgeon general. *Journal of Religion and Health, 52*, 368–385.

Levy, D. L., & Lo, J. (2013). Transgender, transsexual, and gender queer individuals with a Christian upbringing: The process of resolving conflict between gender identity and faith. *Journal of Religion & Spirituality in Social Work, 32*(1), 60–83.

Liechty, D. (2013). Sacred content, secular context: A generative theory of religion and spirituality for social work. *Journal of Social Work in End-of-Life & Palliative Care, 9*, 123–143.

Lin, C.-P. (2010). Learning virtual community loyalty behavior from a perspective of social cognitive theory. *International Journal of Human-Computer Interaction, 26*(4), 345–360.

Lloyd, J. B. (2007). Opposition from Christians to Myers-Briggs personality typing: An analysis and evaluation. *Journal of Beliefs and Values, 28*, 111–123.

Lopez-Claros, A., & Zahidi, S. (2005). *Women's empowerment: Measuring the global gender gap.* Geneva, Switzerland: World Economic Forum.

Lord, A. (2002). Virtual communities and mission. *Evangelical Review of Theology, 26*(3), 196–208.

Luepnitz, D. A. (2002). *The family interpreted: Psychoanalysis, feminism and family therapy.* New York: Basic Books. (Original work published 1988).

Lunn, J. (2009). The role of religion, spirituality and faith in development: A critical theory approach. *Third World Quarterly, 30*(5), 937–951.

MacIntyre, A. C. (1981). *After Virtue: a Study in Moral Theory.* London: Duckworth.

Macionis, J. J. (2014). *Sociology* (15th ed.). Boston, MA: Pearson Education.

Mahoney, A. (2010). Religion in families, 1999–2009: A relational spirituality framework. *Journal of Marriage and Family, 72*, 805–827.

Mahoney, A., & Cano, A. (2014). Introduction to the special section on religion and spirituality in family life: Pathways between relational spirituality, family relationships and personal well-being. *Journal of Family Psychology, 28*(6), 735–738.

Main, M., Goldwyn, R., & Hesse, E. (2003). *Adult attachment scoring and classification systems.* Unpublished manuscript, University of California at Berkeley.

Marcoulides, G. A., & Heck, R. H. (1993). Organizational culture and performance: Proposing and testing a model. *Organizational Science, 4*, 209–225.

Marler, P. L., & Hadaway, C. K. (2002). "Being religious" or "Being spiritual" in America: A zero-sum proposition? *Journal for the Scientific Study of Religion 41*(2), 289–300.

Martin, J. L. (2003, July). What is field theory? *The American Journal of Sociology, 109*(1), 1–50.

Marques, S., Lopez, S., & Mitchell, J. (2013). The role of hope, spirituality, and religious practice in adolescents' life satisfaction: Longitudinal findings. *Journal of Happiness Studies, 14*(1), 251–261.

Marquet, C. T. (2011). Embezzlement epidemic. *University Business, 14*(7), 89–94.

Maselko, J., & Kubzansky L. D. (2006). Gender differences in religious practices, spiritual experiences and health: Results from the US General Social Survey. *Social Science and Medicine 62*(11), 2848–2860.

Mathews, J. T. (1997). *Power shift.* [Online.] Retrieved on April 29, 2015, from https://www.foreign affairs.com/articles/1997-01-01/power-shift.

Mattison, M. (2012). Social work practice in the digital age: Therapeutic email as a direct practice methodology. *Social Work, 57*(3), 249–258.

McBride, D. F. (2013). Uplifting the family: African American parents' ideas of how to integrate religion into family health programming. *Journal of Child and Family Studies, 22*, 161–173.

McElwain, N. L., Booth-LaForce, C., Lansford, J. E., Wu, X., & Dyer, W. J. (2008). A process model of attachment-friend linkages: Hostile attribution biases, language ability, and mother-child affective mutuality as intervening mechanism. *Child Development, 79*(6), 1891–1906.

McGlynn, J., & Richardson, B. K. (2014). Private support, public alienation: Whistle-blowers and the paradox of social support. *Western Journal of Communication, 78*(2), 213–237.

McGoldrick, M., Carter, B., & Garcia-Preto, N. (2011). *The expanded family life cycle: Individual, family, and social perspectives* (4th ed.). Boston: Allyn & Bacon.

McGuire, M. B. (2008). *Religion: The social context* (5th ed.). Long Grove, IL: Waveland Press.

McKerrow, R. E. (1989). Critical rhetoric: Theory and praxis. *Communication Monographs, 56*(2), 91–111.

McLeod, P. L., & Kettner-Polley, R. B. (2004). Contributions of psychodynamic theories to understanding small groups. *Small Group Research, 35*(3), 333–361.

McNutt, J., & Menon, G. (2008). The rise of cyberactivism: Implications for the future of advocacy in the human services. *Families in Society, 89*(1), 33–38.

Meissner, W. W. (1978). The conceptualization of marriage and family dynamics from a psychoanalytic perspective. In T. J. Paolino & B. S. McCrady (Eds.), *Marriage and Marital Therapy: Psychoanalytic, Behavioral, and Systems Perspectives*. New York: Brunner/Mazel.

Menon, G. M. (2000). The 79 cent campaign: The use of on-line mailing lists for electronic advocacy. *Journal of Community Practice, 8*, 73–81.

Merton, R. K. (1968). *Social theory and social structure*. New York: Free Press.

Miller, E. J. (1998). A note on the protomental system and "groupishness": Bion's basic assumptions revisited. *Human Relations, 51*, 1495–1508.

Milliman, J., Czaplewski, A. J., & Ferguson, J. (2003). Workplace spirituality and employee work attitudes: An exploratory empirical assessment. *Journal of Organizational Change Management, 16*(4), 426–447.

Milliman, J., Ferguson, J., Trickett, D., & Condemi, B. (1999). Spirit and community at Southwest Airlines: An investigation of a spiritual values-based model. *Journal of Organizational Change Management, 12*, 221–233.

Mills, K. (1998). *Human rights in the merging global order: A new sovereignty?* Baingstoke: Macmillan.

Minuchin, S. (1974). *Families and family therapy*. Cambridge, MA: Harvard University Press.

Miranda, S. M. (1994). Avoidance of groupthink. *Small Group Research, 25*, 105–136.

Mitroff, I., & Denton, E. (1999). *A spiritual audit of corporate America: A hard look at spirituality, religion, and values in the workplace* (1st ed.). San Francisco: Jossey-Bass Publishers.

Mor Barak, M. E., & Travis, D. J. (2010). Diversity and organizational performance. In Y. Hasenfeld (Ed.), *Human services as complex organizations* (2nd ed., pp. 341–378). Thousand Oaks, CA: Sage.

Morgan-Trimmer, S. (2013). "It's who you know": Community empowerment through network brokers. *Community Development Journal, 49*(3), 458–472.

Muselman, D. M., & Wiggins, M. I. (2012). Spirituality and loss: Approaches for counseling grieving adolescents. *Counseling and Values, 57*, 229–240.

Mylek, I., & Nel, P. (2010). Religion and relief: The role of religion in mobilizing civil society against global poverty. *New Zealand Journal of Social Sciences, 5*(2), 81–97.

National Association of Social Workers. (1996). *Memorandum to the president of the national board of directors*. Washington, DC: Author.

National Association of Social Workers. (approved 1996, revised 2008). *Code of ethics*. Washington, DC: NASW.

National Association of Social Workers. (2008). *Code of ethics*. [Online.] Retrieved on December 4, 2014, from http://www.socialworkers.org/pubs/code/code.asp.

National Association of Social Workers. (2012). *Social work speaks: NASW policy statements, 2012–2014* (9th ed.). Washington, DC: NASW Press.

National Women's Law Center. (2012). *Pharmacy refusals 101.* [Online.] Retrieved on December 30, 2014, from http://www.nwlc.org/resource/pharmacy-refusals-101/.

Near, J. P., & Miceli, M. P. (1985). Organizational dissidence: The case of whistleblowing. *Journal of Business Ethics, 4,* 1–16.

Netting, F. E., Kettner, P. M., & McMurtry, S. L. (2004). *Social work macro practice* (3rd ed.). Boston: Pearson.

Netting, F. E., Kettner, P. M., & McMurty, S. L. (2008). *Social work macro practice* (4th ed.). Boston: Allyn & Bacon.

Nichols, M. P. (1987). *The self in the system: Expanding the limits of family therapy.* New York: Brunner/ Mazel.

Noguera, R. T. (2013). The narratives of children in armed conflict: An inference to spirituality and implication to psychological intervention. *International Journal of Children's Spirituality, 18*(2), 162–172.

Noonan, C. W., Brown, B. D., Bentley, B., Conway, K., Corcoran, M., FourStar, K., Freide, P., Hemlock, B., Wagner, S., & Wilson, T. (2010). Variability in childhood asthma and body mass index across northern plains American Indian communities. *Journal of Asthma, 47,* 496–500.

Northouse, P. G. (2012). *Introduction to leadership: Concepts and practice* (2nd ed.). Thousand Oaks, CA: Sage.

Norton, C. L. (2012). Social work and the environment: An ecosocial approach. *International Journal of Social Welfare, 21,* 299–308.

Norton, M. I., Sommers, S. R., Apfelbaum, E. P., Pura, N., & Ariely, D. (2006). Color blindness and interracial interaction: Playing the political correctness game. *Psychological Science, 17*(11), 949–953.

O'Brien, J., & Palmer, M. (2007). *The atlas of religion.* London: Earthscan.

O'Brien, L., Denny, S., Clark, T., Fleming, T., Teevale, T., & Robinson, E. (2013). The impact of religion on the risk behaviours of young people in Aotearoa, New Zealand. *Youth Studies Australia, 32*(4), 25–37.

Ogden, C. L., Carroll, M. D., Curtin, L. R., McDowell, M. A., Tabak, C. J., & Flegal, K. M. (2006). Prevalence of overweight and obesity in the United States, 1999–2004. *JAMA, 295,* 1549–1555.

O'Hanlon, W. H. (1993). Take two people and call them in the morning: Brief solution-oriented therapy with depression. In S. Friedman (Ed.), *The new language of change: Constructive collaboration in psycho-therapy.* New York: Guilford Press.

O'Reilly, C. A., Chatman, J., & Caldwell, D. F. (1991). People and organizational culture: A profile comparison approach to assessing person-organization fit. *The Academy of Management Journal, 34*(3), 487–516.

Orel, N. (2004). Gay, lesbian and bisexual elders: Expressed needs and concerns across focus groups. *Journal of Gerontological Social Work, 43*(2/3), 57–77.

Paasi, A. (1986). The institutionalization of regions: A theoretical framework for understanding the emergence of regions and the constitution of regional identity. *Fennia, 164*(1), 105–146.

Padavic, I., & Reskin, B. (2002). *Women and men at work* (2nd ed.). Thousand Oaks, CA: Pine Forge Press.

Parachini, L., & Covington, S. (2001). "Community organizing: The basics." *The community organizing toolbox.* Washington, DC: Neighborhood Funders Group.

Pargament, K. I., Koenig, H. G., & Perez, L. M. (2000). The many methods of religious coping: Development and initial validation of the RCOPE. *Journal of Clinical Psychology, 56,* 510–543.

Pargament, K. I., McCarthy, S., Shah, P., Ano, G., Tarakeshwar, N., Wachholtz, A., *et al.* (2004). Religion and HIV: A review of the literature and clinical implications. *The Southern Medical Journal, 97*(12), 1201–1209.

Parry, T. A. (1993). Without a net: Preparations for postmodern living. In S. Friedman (Ed.), *The new language of change: Constructive collaboration in psychotherapy.* New York: Guilford Press.

Payne, M. (1997). *Modern social work theory* (2nd ed.). New York: Palgrave.

Pearce, L. D., & Hayne, D. L. (2004). Intergenerational religious dynamics and adolescent delinquency. *Social Forces, 82,* 1553–1572.

Perkins, D. D., Crim, B., Silberman, P., & Brown, B. B. (2004). Community development as a response to community-level adversity: Ecological theory and research and strengths-based policy. In K. I. Maton, C. J. Schellenbach, B. J. Leadbeater, & A. L. Solarz (Eds.), *Investing in children, youth, families, and communities: Strengths-based research and policy* (pp. 13–30). Washington, DC: American Psychological Association.

Perls, F., Hefferline, R. F., & Goodman, P. (1973). *Gestalt therapy: Excitement and growth in the human personality.* Harmondsworth, Middlesex: Penguin Books.

Perrow, C. (1961). The analysis of goals in complex organizations. *American Sociological Review, 26,* 856–866.

Petts, R. J. (2014). Family, religious attendance, and trajectories of psychological well-being among youth. *Journal of Family Psychology, 28,* 759–768.

Pew Forum on Religion & Public Life. (2013). *U.S. religious landscape survey: Summary of key findings.* [Online.] Retrieved on December 31, 2014, from http://religions.pewforum.org/reports.

Pew Research Center. (2014). *Faith healing and the law.* [Online.] Retrieved December 26, 2014, from http://www.pewforum.org/2009/08/31/faith-healing-and-the-law.

Pew Research Center. (2015). The future of world religions: Population growth projections, 2010–2015. [Online.] Retrieved on September 4, 2015, from http://www.pewforum.org/2015/04/02/religious-projections-2010-2050/.

Piaget, J. (1952). *The origins of intelligence in children.* New York: International Universities Press.

Pietrzak, R. H., Johnson, D. C., Goldstein, M. B., Malley, J. C., Rivers, A. J., Morgan, C. A., ... Southwick, S. M. (2010). Psychosocial buffers of traumatic stress, depressive symptoms, and psychosocial difficulties in veterans of Operations Enduring Freedom and Iraqi Freedom: The role of resilience, unit support, and postdeployment social support. *Journal of Affective Disorders, 120,* 188–192.

Pine, L. R. (1986). Economic Opportunity Act (EOA). 1964. In P. M. Melvin (Ed.), *American community organizations.* New York: Greenwood Press.

Plaut, V. C. (2002). Cultural models of diversity in America: The psychology of difference and inclusion. In R. Schweder, M. Minow, & H. R. Markus (Eds.), *Engaging cultural differences: The multicultural challenge in liberal democracies* (pp. 365–395). New York: Russell Sage.

Portes, A. (1998). Social capital: Its origins and applications in modern sociology. *Annual Review of Sociology, 24,* 1–25.

Putnam, R. D. (2000). *Bowling alone: The collapse and revival of American Community.* New York: Simon & Schuster.

Putnam, R. D. (2007). E pluribus unum: Diversity and community in the twenty-first century. The 2006 Johan Skytte prize lecture. *Scandinavian Political Studies, 30*(2), 137–174.

Raffaelli, M., & Wiley, A. R. (2012). Challenges and strengths of immigrant Latino families in rural midwest. *Journal of Family Issues, 34*(3), 347–372.

Rasheed, M. H., & Rasheed, J. M. (2003). Rural African American older adults and the Black helping tradition. *Journal of Gerontological Social Work, 41*(1/2), 137–150.

Reamer, F. G. (1990). *Ethical dilemmas in social service* (2nd ed.). New York: Columbia University Press.

Reamer, F. G. (1998). *Ethical standards in social work: A critical review of the NASW code of ethics.* Washington, DC: NASW Press.

Regnerus, M., & Burdette, A. (2006). Religious change and adolescent family dynamics. *The Sociological Quarterly, 47*(1), 175–194.

Reid, K. (1997). *Social work practice with groups: A clinical perspective* (2nd ed.). Pacific Grove, CA: Brooks/Cole.

Renani, H. A., Hajinejad, F., Idani, E., & Ravanipour, M. (2014). Children with asthma and their families' viewpoints on spiritual and psychological resources in adaptation with the disease. *Journal of Religion and Health, 53,* 1176–1189.

Reyhner, J. (2013). A history of American Indian Education. [Online.] Retrieved on August 6, 2015, from http://www.edweek.org/ew/projects/2013/native-american-education/history-of-american-indian-education.html.

Reyhner, J., & Eder, J. (1992). A history of Indian education. In J. Reyhner (Ed.), *Teaching American Indian students* (pp. 33–58). Norman: University of Oklahoma Press.

Reynolds, A. L., & Constantine, M. G. (2004). Feminism and multiculturalism: Parallels and intersections. *Journal of Multicultural Counseling and Development, 32*, 346–357.

Richgels, J., & Sande, C. (2009). Collaboration is key for rural challenges. *Policy & Practice, 67*(5), 17–19.

Rida, A., & Iram, F. (2014). Role of personality and spirituality in nonviolent behavior in young adults. *Journal of Behavioural Sciences, 24*(1), 1.

Rodriguez, E., & Oullette, S. (2000). Gay and lesbian Christians: Homosexual and religious identity integration in the members and participants of a gay positive church. *Journal for the Scientific Study of Religion, 39*, 333–347.

Roehlkepartian, E. C., & Syvertsen, A. K. (2014). Family strengths and resilience: Insights from a national study. *Reclaiming Children and Youth, 23*(2), 13–18.

Rogers, C. R. (1951). *Client-centered therapy: Its current practice, implications, and theory.* Boston: Houghton Mifflin.

Roof, W. C. (1993). *A generation of seekers: The spiritual journeys of the baby boom generation.* San Francisco: Harper.

Rothman, J. (1974). *Planning and organizing for social change.* New York: Columbia University Press.

Rothschild, J. (1992). *Principles of feminist trade union organizations.* Paper presented at the workshop on feminist organizations. Washington, DC.

Rwomire, A. (2011). The role of social work in national development. *Social and Society: International Online Journal, 9*(1). [Online.] Retrieved on March 16, 2015, from http://www.socwork.net/sws/article/view/10/39.

Safford, T., Henly, M., Ulrich-Schad, J., Perkins, K. (2014). Charting a future course for development: Natural resources, conservation, and community character in coastal Alaska. *The Journal of Rural and Community Development, 9*(3), 21–41.

Saroglou, V. (2002). Religion and the five factors of personality: A meta-analytic review. *Personality and Individual Differences 32*, 15–25.

Sartorius, N. (2003). Social capital and mental health. *Current Opinion in Psychiatry, 16*(Suppl2), S101–S105.

Satir, V. (1967). *Conjoint family therapy* (3rd ed.). Palo Alto, CA: Science and Behavior Books.

Satir, V., Banmen, J., Gerber, J., & Gomori, M. (1991). *The Satir model: Family therapy and beyond.* Palo Alto, CA: Science and Behavior Books.

Satir, V. M., & Bitter, J. R. (2000). The therapist and family therapy: Satir's human validation model. In A. M. Horne & J. L. Passmore (Eds.), *Family counseling and therapy* (3rd ed.). Itasca, IL: Peacock.

Scharff, D. E., & Scharff, J. S. (1991). *Object relations family therapy.* Northvale, NJ: Aronson.

Scharff, J. S., & Scharff, D. E. (1992). *Scharff notes: A primer of object relations therapy.* Northvale, NJ: Aronson.

Schiller, B. (1994). Who are the working poor? *Public Interest, 115*, 61–72.

Schore, A. (2003). *Affect regulation and the repair of the self.* New York: Norton.

Scott, W. R. 1981. *Organizations: Rational, Natural, and Open Systems.* Englewood Cliffs, NJ: Prentice-Hall.

Seeman, T. E., Dubin, L. F., & Seeman, M. (2003). Religiosity/spirituality and health: A critical review of the evidence for biological pathways. *American Psychologist, 58*(1), 53–63.

Seinfeld, J. (2012). Spirituality in social work practice. *Clinical Social Work Journal, 40*, 240–244.

Senreich, E. (2013). An inclusive definition of spirituality for social work education and practice. *Journal of Social Work Education, 49*, 548–563.

Shaw, M. (1981). *Group dynamics: the psychology of small group behavior* (3rd ed.). New York: McGraw-Hill.

Sheridan, M. J. (2009). Ethical issues in the use of spiritually based interventions in social work practice: What we are doing and why. *Journal or Religion & Spirituality in Social Work: Social Thought, 28*(1/2), 84–126.

Sheridan, M. J., & Amato-von Hemert, K. (1999). The role of religion and spirituality in social work education and practice: A survey of student views and experiences. *Journal of Social Work Education, 35*(1), 125–141.

Sherraden, M. (1993). Community studies in the baccalaureate social work curriculum. *Journal of Teaching in Social Work, 7*(1), 75–88.

Sherry, A., Adelman, A., Whilde, M. R., & Quick, D. (2010). Competing selves: Negotiating the intersection of spiritual and sexual identities. *Professional Psychology: Research & Practice, 41*, 112–119.

Siegel, L. M., Attkisson, C. C., & Carson, L. G. (2001). Need identification and program planning in the community context. In J. E. Tropman, J. L. Erlich, & J. Rothman (Eds.), *Tactics & techniques of community intervention* (4th ed., pp. 105–129). Itasca, IL: F. E. Peacock.

Silverstein, L. B., & Goodrich, T. J. (Eds.). (2003). *Feminist family therapy: Empowerment in social context*. Washington, DC: American Psychological Association.

Simon, B. L., & Akabas, S. H. (1993). Women workers in high-risk public service: Tokens under stress. In P. A. Kurzman & S. H. Akabas (Eds.), *Work and well-being: The occupational social work advantage* (pp. 297–315). Washington DC: NASW Press.

Simonic, B., Mandelj, T. R., & Novsak, R. (2013). Religious-related abuse in the family. *Journal of Family Violence, 28*, 339–349.

Skocpol, T. (1998). Don't blame big government: America's voluntary groups thrive in a national network. In E. J. Dionne (Ed.), Community works: The revival of civil society in America (pp. 37–43). Washington, DC: Brookings Institution Press.

Smart, C. (2009). Family secrets: law and understandings of openness in everyday relationships. *Journal of Social Policy, 38*(4), 551–567.

Smock, K. (1997). *Comprehensive community initiatives: A new generation of urban revitalization strategies.* [Online.] Retrieved on April 23, 2015, from http://comm-org.wisc.edu/papers97/smock/smockintro.htm.

Sonn, C. C., & Quayle, A. F. (2013). Developing praxis: Mobilising critical race theory in community cultural development. *Journal of Community & Applied Social Psychology, 23*(5), 435–448.

Sprague, D., Bogart, A., Manson, S., Buchwald, D., & Goldberg, J. (2010). The relationship between post-traumatic stress disorder, depression, and lung disorders in Northern Plains and Southwest American Indians. *Ethnicity & Health, 15*(6), 569–579.

Staub-Bernasconi, S. (1991). Social action, empowerment, and social work: An integrating theoretical framework. *Social Work with Groups, 14*(3/4), 35–52.

Sternthal, M. J., Williams, D. R., Musick, M. A., & Buck, A. C. (2012). Religious practices, beliefs, and mental health: Variations across ethnicity. *Ethnicity & Health, 17*(1–2), 171–185.

Stiffman, A. R., Brown, E., Freedenthal, S., House, L., Ostmann, E., & Yu, M. S. (2007). American Indian youth: Personal, familial, and environmental strengths. *Journal of Child and Family Studies, 16*, 331–346.

Stoecker, R. (2001). *Report to the West Bank CDC: Primer on community organizing.* [Online.} Retrieved on April 24, 2015, from http://comm-org.wisc.edu/cr/crreporta.htm#N_2_.

Stoecker, R., & Beckwith, D. (1992). Advancing Toledo's neighborhood movement through participatory action research: Integrating activist and academic approaches. *Clinical Sociology Review, 10*(1), 198–213.

Stone, L. (Ed.). (2001). *New Directions in Anthropological Kinship*. Lanham, MD: Rowman and Littlewood.

Storm, I. (2009). Halfway to Heaven: Four types of fuzzy fidelity in Europe. *Journal for the Scientific Study of Religion, 48*(4), 702–718.

Strathern, M. (1992). *After Nature: English Kinship in the Late Twentieth Century*. Cambridge, UK: Cambridge University Press.

Streng, F. J. (1985). *Understanding religious life*. Belmont, CA: Wadsworth Publishing Company.

Sue, D. W., & Sue, D. (1990). *Counseling the culturally different: Theory and practice* (2nd ed.). New York: Wiley.

Sullivan, K. T. (2001). Understanding the relationship between religiosity and marriage: An investigation of the immediate and longitudinal effect of religiosity on newlywed couples. *Journal of Family Psychology, 15*, 610–626.

Sweeney, M. M., & Phillips, J. A. (2004). Understanding racial differences in marital disruption: Recent trends and explanations. *Journal of Marriage and Family, 66,* 639–650.

Tart, C. (1983). *Transpersonaplsychoklies.* El Cerrito, CA: Psychological Processes Inc.

Taylor, R. J., Chatters, L. M., & Levin, J. S. (2004). *Religion in the lives of African Americans: Social, psychological, and health perspectives.* Thousand Oaks, CA: Sage.

The American Prospect (2014). The spirit and the law. [Online.] Retrieved on December 30, 2014, from http://prospect.org/article/little-known-force-behind-hobby-lobby-contraception-case.

Thio, A. (2000). *Sociology: A brief introduction* (4th ed.). Boston, MA: Allyn & Bacon.

Thomas, D. A., & Ely, R. J. (1996). Making differences matter: A new paradigm for managing diversity. *Harvard Business Review, Sept. – Oct.,* 79–90.

Thomas, K. M., Mack, D. A., & Montagliani, A. (2004). Challenging diversity myths: A critical analysis of backlash. In P. Stockdale, & F. Crosby (Eds.), *The psychology and management of diversity in organizations* (pp. 31–51). Malden, MA: Blackwell Publishers.

Thomas, K. M., & Plaut, V. C. (2008). The many faces of diversity resistance in the workplace. In K. M. Thomas (Ed.), *Diversity resistance in organizations* (pp. 1–22). New York: Taylor & Francis.

Thompson, K. (2012). Risks and rewards of blowing the whistle. *Phi Kappa Phi Forum, 92*(3), 24.

Thompson, S. (2012). Co-ops of all types benefit from USDA's value-added grants. *Rural Cooperatives, 79*(2), 26–28.

Thornton, A. (2010). International family change and continuity: The past and future from the developmental idealism perspective. *Demografía, 55,* 21–50.

Timm, T., Birkenmaier, J., & Tebb. S. (2011). The experiential community assessment project: Integrating social work practice skills. *Journal of Community Practice, 19,* 175–188.

Tong, R. (1989). *Feminist theory; A comprehensive introduction.* Boulder, CO: Westview Press.

Tonteri, L., Kosonen, M., Ellonen, H.-K., Tarkiainen, A. (2011). Antecendents of an experiences sense of

virtual community. *Computers in Human Behavior, 27*(6), 2215–2223.

Toseland, R. W., & Rivas, R. F. (2009). *An introduction to group work practice* (6th ed.). Boston: Allyn & Bacon.

Toseland, R. W., & Rivas, R. F. (2012). *An introduction to group work practice* (7th ed.). Boston: Allyn & Bacon.

Tudge, J. R. H., Mokrova, I., Hatfield, B. E., & Karnik, R. B. (2009). Uses and misuse of Bronfenbrenner's bioecological theory of human development. *Journal of Family Theory and Review, 1,* 198–210.

Turner, R. P., Lukoff, D., Barnhouse, R. T., & Lu, F. G. (1995). Religious or spiritual problem: A culturally sensitive diagnostic category in the DSM-IV. *Journal of Nervous and Mental Disease, 183,* 435–444.

Twelvetrees, A. C. (1996). *Organizing for neighbourhood development: A comparative study of community based development organizations* (2nd ed.). Aldershot, UK: Avebury.

United Nations. (1948). The universal declaration of human rights. [Online.] Retrieved on December 30, 2014, from http://www.un.org/en/documents/udhr/index.shtml.

United States Census Bureau. (2013). Current population survey (CPS)—definitions. [Online.] Retrieved on January 13, 2015, from http://www.census.gov/cps/about/cpsdef.html.

Vaughan, F. (1991). Spiritual issues in psychotherapy. *Journal of Transpersonal Psychology, 23,* 105–119.

Vianna, D., Claro, L. L., Mendes, A. A., Silva, A. N., Bucci, D. A., Sa, P. T., Rocha, V. S., Pincer, J. S., Barros, I. M. F., & Silva, P. R. (2013). Infusion of life: Patient perceptions of expressive therapy during chemotherapy sessions. *European Journal of Cancer Care, 22*(3), 377–388.

Von Humboldt, S., Leal, I., & Pimenta, F. (2014). Does spirituality really matter?: A study on the potential of spirituality for older adults' adjustment to aging. *The Japanese Psychological Association, 56*(2), 114–125.

Walsh, F. (1999). Opening family therapy to spirituality. In F. Walsh (Ed.), *Spiritual resources in family therapy* (pp. 28–58). New York: Guilford Press.

Walton, P. (2012). Beyond talk and text: An expressive visual arts method for social work education. *Social Work Education, 31*(6), 724–741.

Warner, H. L., Mahoney, A., & Krumrei, E. J. (2009). When parents break sacred vows: The role of spiritual appraisals, coping, and struggles for young adults' adjustment to parental divorce. *Psychology of Religion and Spirituality, 1,* 233–248.

Warren, R.L. (1978). *The community in America* (3rd ed.). Chicago: Rand McNally.

Wasko, M. M., & Faraj, S. (2000). It is what one does: Why people participate and help others in electronic communities of practice. *Journal of Strategic Information Systems, 9*(2/3), 155–173.

Watts, F., Dutton, K., & Gulliford, L. (2006). Human spiritual qualities: Integrating psychology and religion. *Mental Health, Religion, & Culture, 9*(3), 277–289.

Weaver, A. J., Pargament, K. I., Flannelly, K. J., & Oppenheimer, J. E. (2006). Trends in the scientific study of religion, spirituality, and health: 1965–2000. *Journal of Religion and Health, 45*(2), 208–214.

Weick, A., Rapp, C., Sullivan, W. P., & Kisthardt, W. (1989). A strengths perspective for social work practice. *Social Work, 34,* 350–354.

Wen, M. (2013). Parental participation in religious services and parent and child well-being: Findings from the national survey of America's families. *Journal of Religion and Health, 53,* 1539–1561.

Wexler, L., Silveira, M. L., & Bertone-Johnson, E. (2012). Factors associated with Alaska Native fatal and nonfatal suicidal behaviors 2001–2009: Trends and implications for prevention. *Archives of Suicide Research, 16,* 273–286.

Wheelan, S. A. (1999). *Creating effective teams: A guide for members and leaders.* Thousand Oaks, CA: Sage.

Whitaker, C. A. (1975). A family therapist looks at marital therapy. In A. S. Gurman & D. G. Rice (Eds.), *Couples in Conflict* (pp. 165–174). New York: Jason Aronson.

Whiting, M. (2014). Children with disability and complex health needs: The impact on family life. *Nursing Children and Young People, 26*(3), 26–30.

Wilcox, M. M. (2012). "Spiritual sluts": Uncovering gender, ethnicity, and sexuality in the post-secular. *Women's Studies, 41,* 639–659.

Wilcox, W. B., & Wolfinger, N. H. (2008). Living and loving "decent": Religion and relationship quality among urban parents. *Social Science Research, 37,* 828–848.

Williams, M., & Smolak, A. (2007). Integrating faith matters in social work education. *Journal of Religion & Spirituality in Social Work, 26*(30), 25–44.

Willits, F. K., Bealer, R. C., & Timbers, V. L. (1990). Popular images of rurality: Data from a Pennsylvania survey. *Rural Sociology, 55*(4), 559–578.

Wink, P., & Dillon, M. (2003). Religiousness, spirituality, and psychosocial functioning in late adulthood: Findings from a longitudinal study. *Psychology & Aging, 18*(4), 916–924.

Wise, G. (1998). Definitions: Community development, community-based education about the environment. [Online]. Retrieved on April 24, 2015, from http://www.uwex.edu/ces/erc/pdf/appa_communityeddefinitions.pdf.

Wooten, N. R. (2013). A bioecological model of deployment risk and resilience. *Journal of Human Behavior in the Social Environment, 23,* 699–717.

Wright, K. M., Burrell, L. M., Schroeder, E. D., & Thomas, J. L. (2006). Military spouses: Coping with the fear and the reality of service member injury and death. In C. A. Castro, A. B. Adler, & T. B. Britt (Eds.), *Minds in the military: Psychology and life in the Armed Forces, Vol. 3: Military Family* (pp. 64–90). Westport, CT: Praeger Security International.

Wright, K. M., Foran, H. M., & Wood, M. D. (2014). Community needs among service members after return from combat deployment. *Journal of Community Psychology, 42*(2), 127–142.

Zack, G. M. (2003). *Fraud and Abuse in Nonprofit Organizations: A Guide to Prevention and Detection.* Rockville, MD: Nonprofit Resource Center and Williams Young, LLC.

Zastrow, C. H. (2013). *The practice of social work: A comprehensive worktext* (10th ed.). Belmont, CA: Brooks/Cole-Cengage Learning.

Zembylas, M. (2014). The teaching of patriotism and human rights: An uneasy entanglement and the contribution of critical pedagogy. *Educational Philosophy and Theory, 46*(10): 1143–1159.

Zhang, L. (2008). Religious affiliation, religiosity, and male and female fertility. *Demographic Research, 18*, 233–261.

Zilbach, J. J. (1989). The family life cycle: A framework for understanding children in family therapy. In L. Combrinck-Graham, *Children in family contexts: Perspectives on treatment*. New York: Guilford Press.

Glossary/Index

Page numbers in *italics* refer to figures. Page numbers in **bold** refer to tables.